HOW TO OPEN AND OPERATE
A HOME-BASED
LANDSCAPING BUSINESS

HOW TO OPEN AND OPERATE A HOME-BASED LANDSCAPING BUSINESS

by Owen E. Dell

The Globe Pequot Press

OLD SAYBROOK, CONNECTICUT

This book's purpose is to provide accurate and authoritative information on the topics covered. It is sold with the understanding that neither the author nor the publisher is engaged in rendering legal, financial, accounting, or other professional services. Neither the Globe Pequot Press nor the author assumes any liability resulting from action taken based on the information included herein. Mention of a company name does not constitute endorsement.

Copyright © 1994 by Owen E. Dell

All rights reserved. No part of this book may be reproduced or transmitted in any form by any means, electronic or mechanical, including photocopying and recording, or by any information storage and retrieval system, except as may be expressly permitted by the 1976 Copyright Act or by the publisher. Requests for permission should be made in writing to The Globe Pequot Press, P.O. Box 833, Old Saybrook, CT 06475.

Library of Congress Cataloging-in-Publication Data

Dell, Owen E.
    How to open and operate a home-based landscaping business /
Owen E. Dell — 1st ed.
        p. cm.
    ISBN 1-56440-397-1
    1. Landscaping industry—Management. 2. Small business—Management. 3. New business enterprises—Management. Self-employed.
I. Title.
SB472.5.D44 1994
635.9'068—dc20   99-44131
                                            CIP

Manufactured in the United States of America
First Edition/First Printing

Contents

Acknowledgments

Behind every book is a cast of unseen characters, those patient, helpful people who offer endless advice with no trace of the annoyance they must surely feel now and then, who spend weekends critiquing sloppy, half-formed manuscripts, and who are always there with encouragement, enthusiasm, and good cheer.

It was Lili Singer, editor of Southern California Gardener magazine, who first said the right words to the right people to connect aspiring author with publisher and get this project going. Mark Wisniewski, landscape professional extraordinaire, spent untold hours on the manuscript and kept me out of a lot of trouble, I'm sure. Thanks also to my insurance agent of many years, Dart Whitmore, and to Lloyd Gibbs, intrepid CPA, who chewed up the sections on insurance and bookkeeping and spit them out in a much-improved form. Finally, to my friends, who I haven't paid much attention to while this work was in progress. I can't remember your names or exactly what you look like, but I love you and really appreciate your patience. I'm sure we'll enjoy getting to know one another again.

Introduction

In 1972 I was studying botany at the local junior college, going out into the mountains and deserts of our beautiful state of California, and looking at some of the most gorgeous natural places you or anyone has ever seen. As luck would have it, '72 was one of the great years for wildflowers, and we really got an eyeful. Having grown up in the inner city, I knew little about nature, or about gardens for that matter, and I was plenty impressed. Through that wonderful spring that I'll never forget, something grew inside me, something entirely new to me, something remarkable.

Our class would troop out into the wilderness and spend a morning, a day, or a week steeping ourselves in the incredible elegance of it all. Then we would inevitably return to civilization, which looked more and more like a bad mistake carried out on a grand scale by some very inept people. As I began to see nature, I also began to see gardens, and what I saw was how vastly different the two were. Slowly over that spring I came to understand that gardens were important and could be made better than they were. I came to love nature, but I also came to love the idea of my playing a part in nature. I came to have a passion about the dream that had unfurled inside me like the first leaves of a sprouting bean—the dream of making landscapes more like nature.

My good friend Buddy was also in the botany class. Buddy was a Louisiana boy, fun loving and easygoing. He saw this dream, too, and we talked about it a lot. That summer, broke as always, we decided that we were going to quit school and become native plant landscapers. So, suddenly there we were, our meager funds invested in a '55 Ford pickup (light blue, no major dents, ran pretty good, $100), a few hand tools (from the swap meet mostly, another $50), and a couple of straw hats (Thrifty Drug Store, $2.29 each plus tax). No, we didn't have any work, but we felt great just the same.

A cup of coffee was still a dime at Sambo's, and that was our lunch every day. We called it "Coffee Bean Soup" and drank lots of it, adding plenty of soothing "coffee whitener," the ingredients of which we avoided thinking about. We had Coffee Bean Soup and lots of laughs and not a whole lot more at first. No sensible person would have lasted a day with us.

We spent the last part of that first June and most of July driving around looking for piles of trash to haul, weeds to be cut down, anything that would get us a few dollars to pay for the next day's gas and a couple of beers in the evening. We did some pretty horrendous things. And we were having a blast.

Finally in late July we got a job building some retaining walls and a terraced garden for a kindly college professor up in the hills above Santa Barbara. I often think back on how trusting he was to let us do this, especially since our initial approach had been to ask him if we could haul away some rubbish. Still I guess we did something right, because he kept us busy right through September.

The first day we broke the gas main. August was the hottest on record. The soil was more like rock, and it never occurred to us to soften it with some water before trying to dig it. But we were doing it, that was the thing! And what a summer it was, so good to be alive. We were on our way!

Now to the main thing, the thing that has kept me going all these many years. We finished the job just as we began to feel a bit of fall in the morning air. And yes, it was beautiful; everyone agreed on that. On the last day at about 3:00 P.M., Buddy and I carried the last of our tools up to the faithful blue Ford and turned to look back down on our masterpiece. That moment with my wonderful friend and business partner and with our hard, fine work will surely always guide me through the hard times, as it has so often done in the past. We stood for I don't know how long, each thinking the same thought: If we could feel this good once a year, that would be reason enough to carry on. When we finally turned to each other we both had tears in our eyes.

Landscaping has been good to me. I'm pretty comfortable these days. I have lots of work, and if I have Coffee Bean Soup for lunch, it's because I'm trying to lose a couple of pounds. I still think about quitting now and then; we all have bad days. But when I consider the other choices I might have made, I'm glad about my life.

I believe that if you want to put your green thumb to use, and if you learn to do things really right, you will be doing something brave and noble and fine. You will have a marvelous, difficult, and rewarding life. You will meet the finest and warmest people. You will see beauty every day, often beauty of your own making. And as you grow old, you can travel beneath the shade of trees you planted with your own hands.

If this is the life you want, I'll try to help you get a good start. Remember, don't come looking for riches, easy money, or a soft life. But if you can live with your own version of Coffee Bean Soup, and if you can stick it out, I guarantee that your soul will be nourished, your heart will be moved, and your corner of the world will be much better for your having made your choice. And, yes, I do hope to save you time and trouble by keeping you from making some of the mistakes I made.

Most people who start a business of any kind know only their craft. That's not enough. You've got to run a business, too, and if you run it badly, you'll fail. Sadly, most people *do* fail because, like a garden, a business is complex and challenging. It's just too much for most who try. Let's make you the exception, the one who succeeds so that you can do what you love, earn a living at it, stay out of trouble, and have a good time.

Most of this book is about practical matters. I'm not going to tell you how to plant roses or what kind of fertilizer to use. There are plenty of books that will help you with all that. This is a book about the *business* of landscaping. You're going to learn how to set up your company, how to write a business plan, keep records, find and keep good employees, attract and retain clients, manage jobs, and a lot more. You're going to learn how to do things right the first time. Nuts and bolts? Yes, but don't be put off; you'll find it's as interesting as gardening. And remember what's behind it— a love of green things, of natural surroundings, of nurturing. It's all connected, all a part of the great adventure. Come on along.

So You Think
You Want to Be a Landscaper

Maybe you've always loved to garden and believe you could be really good at it if you had a chance to devote yourself to the craft. Then again, maybe you don't know a wisteria from a wheelbarrow, but you've been yearning to find a way to earn a living outdoors. Either way, you're motivated to get serious about gardening or landscaping and determined to go into business for yourself.

That's great. But what's it *really* like? What kinds of work can you find to do? Who will your clients be? How will you get work? What will your days be like? Does working out of your home make sense? And can you really get paid for having so much fun?

Measuring the Landscaper's Life

Landscaping is a positive thing to do—for you, for society, and for the environment—*if* you do it right. You'll be working outdoors and getting plenty of exercise, doing something that's fun and satisfying and positive, working with nice people and other living things. You'll be providing your clients with beauty, outdoor living space, increased property values, and a new appreciation of gardens and nature. You'll be improving the environment by controlling erosion, providing climate control for houses, reducing the urban heat island effect, producing oxygen, providing food, shelter, and nesting materials for wildlife, and preserving native flora. You'll always be learning something in this endlessly interesting business. And you'll be able to connect with the infinite reaches of nature in a powerful and moving way.

This is the most exciting moment in the history of horticulture. We've gone from the traditional, simple idea of exterior decorating to the complex and evolving practice of *sustainable landscaping*—the idea that landscape design can benefit both nature and people when properly done, that it can function well with a minimum of resource use and negative impacts. Today's professional landscaper deals with such important issues as water conservation, integrated pest management, fire safety, greenwaste reduction, and preservation of native ecosystems. Never before has there been such an understanding of the effects of our work. You can be a part of this. We need more thoughtful, progressive people to carry on this great work.

Then there's the day-to-day excitement of the actual physical work. Few people fail to feel the energy of a landscaping project in full swing: the tractors, the trucks arriving with plants and amendments and materials, the smell of freshly turned earth, the seemingly sudden beauty of a completed job. The physicality of the work itself can be equally energizing: stretching to prune a fruit tree, swinging a pick in the hot sun, combing through the soil with busted fingernails, drinking madly from a cool hose on a hot day, coming home tired and dirty and completely at peace.

Finally, there's the time travel—thinking ahead to the day when the flowers will be in bloom and the trees will be tall, then seeing the day that you'll walk the site with your client and share the pleasure of having done something truly wonderful. Surely it's one of the great experiences of life.

What Kinds of Work Are Available and Who Does What?

Many people think landscaping is pretty simple. Mention landscaping or any related field, and they get an image of a kind of simple person wearing old blue jeans and pulling on the starter rope of a lawn mower; some people see a suburban farmer or, worse, an outdoor janitor. Ask them what professional skills they think this person might have, and they'll likely mention weeding, fertilizing, watering, and mowing (the work of a maintenance gardener) or perhaps planting flowers and trees (the work of the landscape contractor). It's true, these jobs are all there to be done, but there's so much more to landscaping than that. The world of landscaping ranges from the small, localized work of a maintenance gardener to the bird's-eye view of a landscape architect whose tasks might include urban and regional planning, ecosystem restoration, or even global issues such as rainforest management. The landscape industry includes both the backyard grower of a few plants for the local trade and the huge wholesale nursery with hundreds of acres of landscape plants, dozens of employees, and a constant stream of trucks shipping plants all over the country and even the world. Not all landscaping is done outdoors; the interiorscape business is a profitable and fun specialty. The part you play in this amazingly diverse world depends on your interests, your energy, and your talents.

Let's have a look at who does what and how they work together. We'll work backward, from the care of the finished product to the starting point, planning and design; then we'll cover some related fields. This approach will be easier because you'll probably get your start in maintenance, as many people do. Aside from being the easiest place to begin, gardening (as it's called) is also the *best* place for most people to start. Why? Because unless you've had to care for some of the abominable landscapes designed by landscape architects (many of them school taught), you can't possibly understand why they don't work. If you make the long climb from gardener to landscape contractor and then to landscape architect, as I did, you'll have a deep understanding of what you're doing from the ground up. Everyone should be required to begin this way. So, here we go.

The Maintenance Gardener

The gardener is the base of the pyramid, the one who is called in to care for the landscaping after it is designed and installed. The Japanese say, "The gardener is a person who keeps things from growing." It's odd and very true, since the main job of the gardener is to come in on Tuesdays and make everything look the same as it did last Tuesday when he or she left. Status quo is the gardener's calling, husbanding an aura of serenity by making the landscape look as though nothing ever changes. Control is part of gardening, often made necessary by bad design; one of the gardener's main tasks is to continually cut back plants that become too big for their designated spaces. The gardener is also a nurturer, one who must look closely at the places under his or her care and make adjustments, often subtle, to keep things moving in the right direction. Because despite this illusion to which the gardener is an accomplice, the garden does change. Weather and seasons do their work, pests and their predators come and go, and plants have different needs at different seasons and at different points in their life spans. Even the soil is alive, teeming with good and bad fungi, bacteria, insects, earthworms, tunneling mammals, and dozens of other things that appear to be creatures straight from a sci-fi film. All these things and more are doing their work seven days a week, and it is the gardener who must understand them, work with them, be for or against them as the situation demands. The true gardener is a wizard, a little god.

So what exactly does the gardener do? In the real world, a gardener just starting out usually puts an ad in the classified section of the local paper, buys a cheap answering machine at Kmart, drives around middle-class neighborhoods looking for yards that look like they need a little help, and knocks on a few doors. After a while, the jobs start to add up to full-time employment. Training? Well, maybe none in a lot of cases, but I don't really recommend that. Show some class, and learn enough about your trade to give people their money's worth even if you're just mowing and cleaning up yards at first. More about that later.

Gardening is an ideal business to operate out of your home because most of your equipment can stay on the truck at night, you need little office space, and you don't need to be open to the public, since very few people bring their gardens into the shop.

A Day in the Life of a Gardener

The day starts out with a quick check of the equipment, a swipe or two at the dewy windshield with a squeegee, a cup of coffee teetering on the dash as you head to your first job of the morning.

The Parsons: retired, the old man kind of crotchety but not a bad sort, the Mrs. pretty quiet, friendly mutt dog. Corner lot (higher than average number of dog deposits on the front lawn), pine needles all over everything every week, and them so darned particular about every needle getting picked up and hauled away instead of left as a mulch as it should be. Azaleas always hungry and thirsty because of the pines. Fertilize them. Mow the lawn, edge, clean up the walks. Cut back the India hawthorn where it's trying to take over the front walk. Dump the clippings into your trash can, take them out to the truck where they get deposited in the trailer you tow around behind you all day.

The Parsons' backyard: mostly paved, a swimming pool in the middle (pool man takes care of that), some junipers along the back fence, huge oak (tree trimmer comes in every couple of years and does some pruning, you clean up after it the rest of the time), bamboo on the north (kind of a lame attempt at Japanesey from the fifties most likely, darn stuff's always trying to get into the flower beds), beautiful view of the valley this time of the morning, mockingbird on the telephone pole in the back corner. You do some pruning, chop at the bamboo runners a while, notice that the petunias are getting kind of dry and give them some water (wish these people would step outside once in a while and check on this stuff—I can't do everything!), pet the dog (who looks more like a tiny aging buffalo), hoe some weeds out of the beds, sweep.

Pretty simple place. Visit with the folks a bit, say something tactful about the petunias, make a minor fuss over the dog in their presence (never forget showmanship), then back to the truck. Lash down the mower and edger, tighten the cap on the gas can, drive to the next job.

The Constantino family: nice folks, though the kids are a bit much. (Nobody *warned* you about the weekly Big Wheels patrol?) Start with the back this time. (No reason, that's just the way you like it, and who's to say different? Aah, self-employment!) The back lawn is huge, so lots of mowing time. These folks liked your idea of composting their yard waste, so you take the clippings over to the back corner behind the hedge and mix them with leaves and a layer of soil after turning the pile. You replant the bare spots in the ground cover from the flat you bought at the nursery yesterday, water them in real well. Rotate the pots on the patio so they don't grow one-sided. Fertilize the lawn and program the sprinkler timer to come on for ten minutes to wash the fertilizer in. Move to the front, a tiny strip of shrubbery, some perennials, brick walkway. Mostly cleanup here, except in the parkway where you pull some weeds and water. The ferns have thrips again, so you spray, rinse out the sprayer, clean up the walks. Get out the pole saw and lop a couple of crossing branches out of the alder tree. Check on the sprinklers in the backyard. Go to lunch.

So it goes in the afternoon, and tomorrow and the next day. Not a bad way to go, really. You get to smell the smells, watch the birds, get a little exercise. It's pretty bucolic and sure beats an office job. Plus, when you're done, you get to admire. It feels good. If you live somewhere other than in California, the specifics will be somewhat different, but you get the general picture.

Evenings you return phone calls, do the books, make emergency repairs. Saturdays you spend working on equipment, changing the oil in the truck, maybe doing a little extra work for someone. Sundays, if you're smart, are all yours. To make a living, you need to work 50-plus hours a week, but it's a good life.

After a few years, maybe you decide you'd like to do more— get into commercial maintenance, add employees and vehicles, maybe build gardens instead of just maintaining them. These opportunities will come your way if you're good, if you take care of your clients. They'll want you to do more for them, they'll tell their friends, and you'll find yourself in demand. You'll have to make some decisions along the way about how big you want to get, which direction you want to go. But whatever you do with your career, you will have made a good start by choosing to enter at ground level. And if you stay there, there's no shame in that. Remember that in many cultures, the gardener is revered, because people understand the value of his or her work. To be an excellent gardener is a fine thing.

The Landscape Contractor

The landscape contractor is a builder who specializes in the construction of gardens and landscapes. The scope of the trade is very wide, from planting a few plants in Mrs. McGillicuty's backyard to heavy construction on a commercial site such as an office building or a public park. The landscape contractor can be a one-person operation limited to small, specialty gardens or a giant corporation with hundreds of employees. At first you will probably be more interested in a small operation, but keep in mind that the average landscape contractor will have at least two or three employees in order to be competitive.

The small landscaping business is easy to operate from your backyard. When you get bigger you may want to move the business elsewhere, but at first there's no problem with the simple, low-budget, home-based approach.

The work is hard, much more demanding than maintenance gardening; the risks are greater (and so are the potential rewards); and the amount of knowledge required to be really good is phenomenal. Most states require a contractor to be licensed. A state license is issued after a qualified applicant passes an exam and posts a license bond.

Unlike the maintenance gardener, the landscape contractor moves from job to job and is always looking for work. There are many ways to get jobs; we'll go over these in chapter 6.

Many landscape contractors specialize in what's called "design/build," which is self-explanatory I guess. Others work from plans drawn by someone else. Each approach has its merits, and it's good to do both in the beginning.

Making the move from maintenance gardener to landscape contractor is jumping in with both feet. But unless you're very Zen oriented, you'll probably become bored with mowing and weeding at some point and yearn for the crazy life of a "real" landscaper.

Related and Supporting Fields

The complexity of landscaping has resulted in the development of many specialties and subfields. Though most people begin with garden maintenance or general landscaping, you may have special interests. There are even specialties within specialties. For instance, the landscape contractor may specialize in water gardens or native plants or hardscape construction (walks, patios, retaining walls, and the like). Some people install and maintain edible landscaping. Others deal in pest problems, irrigation repair, outdoor lighting, or spas. It's endless, really. Surely you'll find your own special thing to love.

To get you oriented, here's a brief introduction to some of the general categories of related fields. (Refer to chapters 7 and 8 for information on supporting trades and services, such as electrical contractors and consulting engineers.) We won't spend a lot of time on the details of these related fields, but if you find yourself drawn to one of them, there are plenty of other sources of available information. For example, your state probably has a nurseryman's association that can help you if you want to start growing plants for a living.

The Landscape Architect

The landscape architect is a licensed designer. Unlike the landscape contractor, who can design only private gardens that he or she then builds, the landscape architect can design any type of landscaping but can't build anything. The scope of the work is broad and goes far beyond garden design.

The qualifications to become a landscape architect are stringent. If you think this is what you want to do right now rather than coming up through the ranks, look into some of the available college programs, because that's the fastest and easiest way to get the training you'll need.

There's another related profession called the landscape designer. This is usually a polite term for a "wannabe," someone who isn't really a landscape architect but wants to act like one. Some of these people are very capable, others are not. In some cases a license may not be required (to do a simple residential planting design, for example), but in others the designer is operating beyond the bounds of the law.

Many landscape architects, even some fairly renowned ones, operate out of their homes. Since design doesn't require trucks and tools, it's easy to set up a studio/office in the spare bedroom. Clients visit landscape architects fairly often to go over plans, have meetings, and so forth; thus, the office needs to be accessible and attractive. It also needs to be legal, so be sure your local zoning ordinances permit visits by clients.

The Nurseryman

What do you suppose the politically correct term for this is? Nurseryperson? Nurserier? Who knows. Nurserypersons grow and sell plants. There are two basic categories: retail and wholesale. Retail nurseries you surely know about. Like any merchant, the retailer buys plants and supplies from wholesalers and sells them to the public. The wholesale nursery, also known as the grower, produces plants from seed, cuttings, or divisions, grows them in containers or in the ground, and sells them to retail nurseries and landscape contractors. Some wholesalers grow a wide variety of plants, others specialize in one thing, such as perennials, trees, or ground covers.

Can you operate a nursery out of your home? Yes. In fact many people make quite a nice little supplementary income from plants they grow in the backyard. There are a couple of strategies that could be very successful for you. One is to grow the kinds of plants you commonly use on your jobs. You can usually produce them cheaper than buying them, even from a wholesaler. Plus, they're always on hand when you need them. If you like certain plants that are hard to find or often out of stock, growing your own makes sense. Another approach is to grow specialty plants and sell them to other people at retail or wholesale prices. Most people who become involved in horticulture soon develop fetishes about certain groups of plants. People go cuckoo over tuberous begonias or native plants or ornamental grasses or whatever. There's often a strong market for specialty plants, especially rare or choice varieties that the run-of-the-mill growers just don't handle. If zoning laws permit it, you can sell directly to the public. Alternatively, you can wholesale your plants to retail nurseries or landscapers. The profit per square foot can be high, especially if you don't have any employees. And of course you're already paying for the land. Looking out the kitchen window and seeing rows of happy, thriving plants can make you feel rich.

The Pest Control Adviser/Operator

Controlling pests and diseases is the specialty of the pest control adviser and the pest control operator, the first making recommendations for control and the second applying the herbicides, pesticides, and whatnot. Progressive pest control people also use biological methods to minimize the application of dangerous chemicals. They are highly trained and licensed and often must take continuing education courses to retain their licenses.

Now, the idea of spending your days at the business end of a spray rig squirting noxious chemicals onto rose bushes may not thrill you. But there's a whole new consciousness in pest and disease control that involves the use of beneficial insects, nontoxic and least-toxic sprays, and cultural methods to achieve the same things the chemicals attempt to achieve. This field is really opening up, and there are opportunities to do a lot of good. It's a fascinating study of the interrelationships of plants, diseases, pests, and the environment. You'll never get bored, and you may get in on the ground floor of some exciting new research.

Operating a pest control business out of your home should be fairly easy, except that you probably won't be able to store chemicals in a residential area. Check local regulations before you pursue this as a home-based business.

The Arborist / Tree Trimmer

The arborist is a licensed professional who is trained in the care of trees. An arborist can consult on and treat tree diseases and problems. Arborists are certified after taking an exam. If trees are your thing, look into this field.

Tree trimmers do just that—prune and sometimes remove trees. The work is very physical and quite dangerous. If you love trees *and* are a daredevil type, consider tree work. You can start out with a couple of chainsaws, a truck, some ladders, and safety equipment. Later, you can graduate to large trucks, chippers, and other heavy equipment. For safety reasons crew size is usually at least two, so plan on becoming an instant employer. Licensing is required in some places, not in others. A lot of knowledge is required to do a good job in this fascinating field. The small tree-care business can easily be operated from home.

The Irrigation Contractor

Nowadays most landscapes include irrigation systems, especially in arid climates. Many of these systems are very complex, and their design, installation, and maintenance is often handled by specialists. The landscape contractor frequently handles this aspect of the job, but you may choose to focus on just this specialty. For starters, consider doing irrigation repair and troubleshooting. The market is small but steady, because things are always needing repair. You can work for landscapers, gardeners, homeowners, or commercial or public clients. The best way to learn the trade is to go to work for someone else for at least a year. Licensing may or may not be required, and working out of your home is no problem. This is a nice business for the nuts-and-bolts type of person and is especially good if you don't want any employees right away, because you can do most things without help. Later you may decide to move on to design and installation, which can get you into some pretty ambitious projects.

Do You Have What It Takes?

People are always saying to me, "It must be so much *fun* to be in your business!" Well, yes, it often is. More than fun, it's deeply satisfying in a lot of ways. But there's another side to it: long hours, work that is sometimes brutally hard, emotional stress, enormous risks, and not a lot of money. Tiptoeing through the tulips it ain't. But still, it's good enough to keep me and a whole lot of other people going.

So, how do you manage the stress and strain? The best way is to be the type of person to whom this lifestyle comes naturally. There are some qualities I believe you must have if you're going to be successful and happy in this business. Take this quick quiz and see if you've got what it takes.

1. *Are you emotionally stable?* If you're depressive, excitable, or unpredictable, you'd better take up something else. You're not going to hold up under fire. Inner calm will make you more effective and happier.

2. *Do you have abundant energy?* Not just the occasional burst of steam, but the ability to forge ahead hour after hour and day after day, working steadily and quickly. It takes plenty of physical, mental, and spiritual energy.

3. *Are you a self-starter?* There's no boss to threaten you, so you can get away with goofing off for a while, but it'll catch up to you. Being self-motivated is especially important when you work out of your home, because it's so much easier to snooze away the workday.

4. *Can you handle complexity?* How many things can you keep in your mind? It had better be lots, because even if you write things down all day long (which you should), you still need a good memory. Having so many balls in the air can be thrilling or terrifying. If juggling multiple responsibilities isn't your thing, you'll be in trouble.

5. *Can you think on your feet?* All day long, people will be asking you questions, making you offers, coming to you with

problems. Many's the time your success will depend on the quick right answer.

6. *Are you a good listener?* Your business depends on your ability to meet people's needs and that means really hearing them. It also depends on the accuracy of your understanding of everything that's going on with your jobs, clients, employees, suppliers, and all the rest. You have to be able to process and store incoming information.

7. *Are you a team player?* Many misguided people approach business as though it were war. The truly successful businessperson recognizes the existence of common goals and works with the other participants (the client, the employees, the suppliers, subcontractors, architects, everyone) to achieve these goals.

8. *Are you independent?* An apparent paradox—team player and independent both? Yes. You'll be making your own way in the world with no one to tell you what to do. Much of what you need to know can only come from experience. You've got to be willing and able to think for yourself.

9. *Do you have a positive attitude?* Landscaping is a wonderful thing. It brings beauty and joy to so many people. That's easy to forget when you're having a bad day. Enthusiasm is contagious, and the ability to communicate it will be one of your most powerful tools.

10. *Do you like people?* You must genuinely like people and get a kick out of dealing with them. Grouches and misanthropes need not apply.

11. *Do you have a sense of humor?* Like insanity, it's not absolutely necessary, but it sure helps.

12. *Are you physically fit?* You've got to be able to lift heavy things, swing a pick, dig holes all day, maybe climb around in trees. This isn't a desk job. If you're not fit when you start, you could injure yourself.

Well, how'd you do? I think you need to have answered "yes" to most of these questions. If you're lacking in some department, consider whether you'll be able to improve yourself fairly quickly. Starting any business is a big challenge and is guaranteed to result in a lot of personal growth. You don't have to be 100 percent right away, but you've got to believe in your ability to rise to the occasion.

Why Do You Want to Run Your Own Business?

The conventional working world leaves a lot to be desired. Many people who have spent years in an impersonal, dog-eat-dog corporate situation or in government or any other large organization often yearn for self-employment. They're tired of feeling insignificant, like an ant or a blade of grass. They realize that no matter how good they are, most of the recognition will probably go to someone else. They're tired of being pushed around and want to follow their own star. They're willing to risk failure. They want a great adventure.

If this sounds like you, you may be ready. But don't proceed based on negative feelings—you've got to love both horticulture and business. You're not getting away from something so much as you're getting into something. Remember, you'll probably work harder, earn less, and risk more. But the personal rewards will almost certainly be greater. If you did pretty well on the quiz, and you're still reading, congratulations. You may have found your calling. So, let's look at one last aspect of your new adventure before we move on to the details of starting your business.

Making the Transition: Amateur to Professional

Puttering around in your own backyard is fun but isn't the same as being a professional. How do you go from hobby to career?

How do you learn enough to be able to really call yourself a pro? Should you begin part-time? Landscaping is a fusion of many disciplines—horticulture, engineering, the life sciences, art and design, physical work, and business management. Chances are you've got a pretty good grasp of some parts and need help with others. Fortunately, there are a number of ways for you to improve yourself to the point where you'll feel comfortable about going into business. Let's look at some.

Real World Experience

Many of the important things about landscaping can't be learned from books. Many people never go to school, yet they become very good. I think you'll find that some type of formal education (maybe just attending seminars) is necessary at some point. Still, there's no substitute for working in the field.

You may want to start your career by working for somebody else for a year or two. That way you can see how other people do things; you'll lose your innocence and get a wider perspective. You may even want to work for a few different companies, possibly even in different segments of the business—a retail nursery, a landscape contractor, a gardener, or an irrigation supply house. It's best if you work for someone who's really good, so you learn how to do things right. Remember, though, that employers won't be too interested in training you beyond their needs, because one of their biggest fears is that a sharp employee will eventually go into competition with them. Expect to learn more by observation and action than by training.

Self-Study

Begin to read voraciously. Good books abound on the subjects of horticulture, landscaping, contracting, and business management. In addition to your local bookstore or library (don't forget the library at the local college or botanic garden), check out some of the sources of professional books listed in the appendix. Read the books listed in the bibliography and more as you find them.

The other important source of written information is trade

and professional publications, many of which are listed and described in the appendix. And don't forget popular gardening magazines.

Professional Training

Attend trade shows, seminars, classes, and lectures. Join your local botanical garden or garden club. Join your trade association, and take advantage of what they have to offer. Find out what other professionals in your area do to stay informed.

Schooling

Quite a number of colleges and universities offer degrees in landscape architecture, environmental horticulture, and related fields. Many junior colleges offer two-year certificate programs in horticulture, enough to get you going. Some of these programs are even held in the evenings and on weekends for the convenience of those who can't yet give up their day jobs.

Many adult education programs offer short courses in various aspects of horticulture, taught by professionals or retirees. Botanical gardens and similar institutions also have classes. In addition to useful course content, these classes will help you get to know the other members of the professional community.

Business Education

Don't forget that you'll need to learn the business aspects, too. The basics of small business are the same no matter what your chosen field. Fortunately, there are many resources for getting up to speed. Many community colleges offer night courses in small business management with classes in financial management, computers, advertising and marketing, and other general aspects of business. Adult education programs, university extension programs, private business schools, and other institutions offer similar programs. Short courses and workshops are common in most communities. Don't forget correspondence courses and, of course, books you can study on your own. Banks, insurance companies, and large accounting firms often hold seminars and produce written material that is helpful to the small business owner. The Small Business Administration, a federal agency, produces dozens of booklets for business owners and also offers one-on-one counseling with retired businesspeople through a program called SCORE.

There are also programs and information geared specifically to the horticultural industry or to the construction industry. Check with your trade association, local builder's groups, and the local chamber of commerce for more information.

Really, there's a ton of information out there and it seems the more you look the more you find. You need to avail yourself of it. Most business failures in this country are due to bad management, not lack of business. No one is born knowing how to run a business. Arguably the biggest weakness of small business owners is that they focus exclusively on their craft or profession, because they love it first and foremost, and ignore their business. This is deadly. Don't be the next fool. Learn business and learn it well.

Does It Ever End?

You'll never really "learn" this business. It's too complex and it changes all the time. I still spend ten to twenty hours a week studying, reading journals and trade publications, and attending classes. Plan on being a student for the rest of your life. That's one of the greatest joys of horticulture. In twenty years or so, you'll start to get pretty good.

Part Time or Full Time?

Jumping in with both feet can be pretty scary. Quit your job and just . . . ?? Maybe you're thinking about starting out part time, and that's OK. Get some Saturday gardening jobs to see how you like it; if you don't, it'll be pretty easy to back out. You can keep your investment in tools and equipment to a minimum at first, perhaps borrowing some things from the family or buying used tools at garage sales. Sometimes you can use your client's tools, but I regard that as somewhat unprofessional. Besides, what if you break something?

If you do start out part time, I'd suggest you be up front with clients. Tell them you're just beginning rather than acting like an old hand. Show them you can be trusted with their valuable landscaping, but don't try to be something you're not. They'll like you that much more for your honesty.

Get two or three jobs for variety. Stick to garden maintenance at first, because the complex demands of landscaping will overwhelm you. Besides, it's pretty hard to tackle a landscaping project if you're only working Saturdays. Another strategy would be to help out a gardener with his or her route part time.

2

Getting Started

Start Up or Buy?

Compared to most businesses, getting into landscaping is a snap. There's no store to rent, no fixtures, no inventory, no fancy corporate offices, often not even any employees. Just borrow some money from the folks, buy an old truck, throw the family lawn mower into the back, and off you go. Because of this, most people choose to start their own business rather than buy a going concern.

Starting from Scratch

The advantages of starting from scratch are many. You can design everything the way you want, from the letterheads to the toolshed to the public image of your business. You don't have the sins of the previous owner to account for, or his debts. You get to do things your way. I started from scratch, and I've never regretted it.

But starting from scratch isn't for everybody. You'll make a lot of mistakes, and one or more of them could be fatal. It's a little like John Wesley Powell canoeing down the Grand Canyon for the first time, with no idea of what was ahead and only one arm to paddle with. He made it, but what a ride! Not only will you have to build a clientele from scratch, but compared to buying a business, you'll also probably spend more on advertising and work harder to convince people your new company is as good as the one they've been dealing with for years.

Buying a Going Business

If you can afford it, buying a healthy, well-respected business might be just the thing for you, especially if your horticultural and/or business experience is limited. People have many reasons for selling their businesses, and not every sale comes with the rattle of skeletons in the closet. When you buy, you step quietly into the driver's seat. You take advantage of the reputation, the client list, and the momentum of a going concern. You purchase a billing system, tools and equipment, an advertising program, the whole works. And you usually get a mentor for a while, the outgoing owner, who has years of experience to pass along to you.

However, if you fail to thoroughly investigate the background of your potential business purchase, you may be buying disaster. When you buy a business, you buy the liabilities as well as the assets, and the seller may be working overtime to conceal some of these. The worst nightmare is finding out you suddenly have a few lawsuits on your hands, but there are plenty of other things that can be wrong. Has the seller cooked the books to falsify profits? Is the equipment in good shape, or does it just look that way? Are there disgruntled employees? How many of the people on the customer list are truly happy, and how many are ready to go elsewhere? Is the owner planning to open up again down the street, taking his clients with him? Are there unpaid bills? Taxes? Well, don't buy any business without a full audit and a darn good attorney to look everything over. Remember, too, that paying for your new business is going to cost you plenty; some up front and the rest in regular payments for many years. A good business is worth it, a bad one is not.

Maintenance routes are often for sale, sometimes at bargain prices. In some cases you buy just a list of weekly mowing or gardening clients. If the price is right this can be a good deal, but consider the cost of developing the same dollar amount of business on your own. Make sure the jobs are bid at realistic prices and the clients are happy. Buying a good route can be a way to get up and running fast. Often this type of sale is advertised informally—ask around at your suppliers, nurseries, and so forth. (*Tip:* Be sure the route is being sold only to you, not to six other gardeners as well. What a shock when they all show up on the job! This happened to someone I know.)

Working Out of Your Home

I've been in business for over twenty years, and I've always worked out of my home, even when I had several crews and a secretary. I love it and hope I'll never have to have an office downtown. Now, this would sound crazy to a lot of people who, mostly for ego reasons, lust after a fancy location in a prestigious office building on Main Street. To each his or her own.

Consider all the good things about working from home. The best one is the short, usually peaceful commute to work. A close second is the opportunity to raid the fridge any time. It's easier to set your own hours and maybe spend more time with your family. And it's really cheap since your overhead is so low, an especially important factor if business slows down. You can even deduct part of your house expenses as a cost of doing business, perfectly legally (for more information on this, see page 28). The idea of journeying downtown to the office every day like most poor suckers do gives me the willies. I just stumble in to the extra bedroom (aka World Headquarters), often wearing my funkiest clothes, usually not awake enough to drive, and I get right to work. The time savings alone adds an extra hour to my day. It's the greatest.

Disadvantages? Of course there are some. The biggest potential problem is that the zoning ordinances of your community may prohibit you from running a small business from your home or limit the kinds of activities you may engage in. If you're planning to have twenty laborers show up every morning at 7:00, load tractors and mowers and equipment into a bunch of trucks, hang out in the backyard and drink coffee for half an hour before they noisily depart in a blue cloud of exhaust, you'd better think twice. That kind of activity is not only inconsiderate of the neighbors, it's probably illegal. The same is true if you're planning to open a retail nursery in the front yard.

Many communities do permit a small home office, providing you don't engage in odious behavior. (You may eventually need to rent a storage yard for your trucks and equipment and have your workers show up there, not at your house.) So before you go any further, get a copy of the regulations and be sure you can comply with them. Now's the time to find out, not later when you're kicked off your own property, maybe with the local newspaper reporter on the scene. By the way, if you're renting, check with the landlord, too.

There are some other problems with operating out of your home. One of the worst is that you can never get away from your job. Sure, go ahead and close the door; see how much good that does you. You'll still hear the phone ringing, and the stack of unfinished paperwork will cry loudly through the thin walls. You eventually grow used to this, though. If you have kids, it's not easy to make them understand that you're working. That's also true of friends who plop down in the chair next to your desk and proceed to visit. After all, you're home, right? I finally made a sign that says, "WORK IN PROGRESS. PLEASE DO NOT DISTURB." It's offensive to some, but it usually does the job. I also suggest you keep regular office hours. It'll be easier on you and everyone else.

Some types of businesses could never operate from a home, but since gardeners and landscapers do business this way more often than not, it's seen by the public as an acceptable approach and shouldn't hurt your image. Eventually, people will figure out where you live, so you'd better landscape your place pretty nicely and keep it spotlessly maintained, at least the part everyone can see. Which brings up a final point: Somewhere you've got to have a mess—trucks, equipment, soil amendments, plants that haven't made it to the job yet, leftover materials. If this mess is in your backyard, you'll have to look at it every day, even Sundays. Take a look at your yard, and make sure it will accommodate your needs.

Tools and Equipment

You'll need two basic kinds of equipment: the tools of your trade and the tools of the office. Fortunately, you can start out simply and expand as you need to.

One important rule for all purchases: Always buy the absolute best quality of everything. Not fancy, just solid good stuff that will perform well and last for a long time. I've never regretted buying a first-rate tool, but many times I've kicked myself for buying a so-called bargain. Remember that you'll be using your tools every day under severe conditions. They need to be more durable than if you were going to haul them out of the garage every few weeks for an hour's use in your backyard. Buy industrial-rated tools and equipment at places where the pros shop.

The standard array of tools and equipment will vary depending on the kind of work you do and, to a minor degree, on where you live. You'll need the following basic "starter" tools right away:

Gardener's Tools

A maintenance gardener working alone or with a helper will need the following tools:

Cutting tools: Pruning shears and holster, loppers (for big branches), a folding pruning saw, a pole pruner (for trees and tall shrubs), hedge trimmers, and a large pruning saw or small chainsaw.

Cleanup tools: Leaf rakes, bow rakes, a push broom, a utility broom, a blower.

Lawn-care tools: A rotary mower for cool-season lawns, a reel mower for warm-season lawns (where applicable), some kind of edger (most often a string trimmer, which serves many other functions), grass shears.

Digging tools: Square- and round-point shovels (avoid the short-handled kind—too hard on the back), a spade, a scoop shovel, cultivating fork, a trowel, a mattock (pick on one end, digger on the other), maybe a snow shovel in cold climates.

Hauling tools: A contractor's wheelbarrow, a garden cart, a hand truck, a couple of trash cans or burlap tarps.

Fertilizing equipment: A drop spreader, a small crank spreader.

Pest control equipment: A tank sprayer, a backpack sprayer, a dust applicator, a gopher poison injector.

Weeding tools: Various kinds of hoes including a "Hula-Hoe™" and a heavy-duty eye hoe, an asparagus knife, and whatever other weeding implements you take a fancy to.

Watering equipment: Heavy-duty ⅝-inch hoses, a pistol-type nozzle, a couple of soaker hoses, a hose-end sprinkler or two, and a watering can.

Some special things: A soil sampler tube, a gas can, oil to keep the power equipment running.

For climbing: Get an 8-foot tripod ladder; it's much steadier on uneven ground than the regular four-legged kind.

Equipment for safety and comfort: Kneepads, leather gloves, rubber gloves, rain gear, rubber boots, steel-toed boots, goggles, a face shield, ear protection, a dust mask, spray coveralls, a respirator, a first-aid kit, insect repellent, and poison oak/ivy protection.

Maintenance tools: A socket set, wrenches, screwdrivers, a grinding wheel, a sharpening stone, a couple of files.

Identify your tools with spray paint or in some other way to avoid taking home a client's favorite shovel.

Keep spare parts on hand. All it takes is the failure of some little doohinckus on your lawn mower to put you out of work and behind schedule. Carry extra doohinckuses in your truck.

A Gardener's Truck

Naturally, you have to put all this equipment in some kind of truck. Lots of gardeners are using minitrucks outfitted with flatbeds; they're a lot more versatile than a regular pickup. Still, a pickup of any size will do. You won't need anything super heavy-duty for gardening, but think ahead to the day when you'll be asked to haul a load of soil or some railroad ties or tow a trailer. Get a medium-duty truck. It doesn't have to be new. Most people expect you to show up in something a little work-worn, so a used vehicle is OK. Just keep it in good running condition, because if it breaks down, you don't work and your clients aren't happy. Whatever you buy, outfit it with high, solid sideboards for trash and soil amendment hauling and with some sort of system for storing your tools and equipment. A row of pipes strapped vertically to the backboard could accommodate the long-handled tools; you might put the smaller stuff in a couple of ready-made boxes along the sides or underneath the bed. For dump runs, you'll need a large, heavy tarp and about 100 feet of $\frac{3}{8}$-inch manila rope. It's also nice to have a pair of ramps for loading and unloading mowers; try a couple of Douglas fir 2 x 12s for starters, and graduate to the nice steel or aluminum kind later.

Whew! That's a lot of gear. Not counting the truck, all these tools and trappings should set you back around $5,000 to $6,000 if bought new. A few weekends spent snooping around garage sales and swap meets can save you a lot of money. You could also try putting the whole purchase out to bid, assuming you have the money to buy it all at one time.

Landscaper's Tools

Landscaping work requires most of the gardener's equipment (except the lawn-care and pest control things) plus some specialized equipment. Much of the landscaper's work involves heavy digging, grading, and planting. Now, don't go out and buy a tractor. I know you want to, but in twenty-two years I've never needed to own a tractor; few people really do. That's what rental yards are for. Why tie up so much capital in equipment you'll probably only rarely use? The same goes for trenchers, sod-cutting machines, and even rototillers. Until you've got a bigger business and more work, just rent what you need. Don't get in over your head.

You'll need a lot of hand tools. Here's a basic rundown:

Digging tools: A digging bar, shovels and spades, a mattock, and a posthole digger should get you through most excavating work. For larger jobs, rent the equipment you need or hire out the heavy excavating work, especially if you're not good with power equipment.

Hand grading tools: A bow rake, a wide aluminum or wood grading rake, a spring rake, a flat shovel.

For moving materials: Invest in a sturdy 5-cubic-foot capacity steel contractor's wheelbarrow. It's also great for mixing small amounts of concrete and makes a pretty comfortable easy chair at lunch.

Other earth-oriented tools: A lawn roller is used for installing sod and for compacting loose paving materials. A hand tamper is also used for compacting; rent a power tamper or a vibratory plate compactor for big jobs.

For beating on things: A sledge hammer (at least 10 pounds), a singlejack (small sledge hammer), and a stake driver for tree stakes.

Measuring: A sighting level is used to measure elevations, set grades, and level things. You'll need two tape measures—a 100-foot fiberglass one and a 30-foot-long by 1-inch-wide steel one. A measuring wheel is great for estimating and rough measuring.

For marking things: Invest in a marking paint applicator or a chalk wheel, some pin flags in different colors, and a few rolls of flagging tape.

For carpentry and other kinds of construction: You'll need (just for starters) some basic carpenter's tools—hammers, a level, a square, a plumb bob, a chalk line, a roll of mason's twine, hand saws, a worm-drive power saw with carbide blades, masonry blades, and steel-cutting blades, a ½-inch drill motor and bits.

Irrigation work: Begin with pipe shears, a hacksaw, groove-joint pliers, pipe wrenches (12-inch or 24-inch or one of each), a tubing cutter, a plumber's torch.

The inevitable miscellany: Tin snips, pry bars, vise-grip pliers, bolt and rebar cutters (24-inch minimum), and maybe a come-along.

The price of all this? About $5,000 to $6,000 new, much less if you buy it used.

A *Landscaper's Truck*

Your first truck should be a heavy-duty one (1-ton rated), preferably a flatbed with solid plywood sideboards at least 2 feet tall. Later, you can graduate to two trucks: a little pickup for errands and estimating and a big flatbed for heavy hauling. Under-the-bed toolboxes are great, but you may want at least one box mounted on the bed as well. An absolute necessity is a pipe rack, because you'll almost always have a couple sticks of pipe on board. Make it heavy enough to double as a lumber rack. A pipe vise mounted on the back is a good idea too—one clever contractor mounted his on a removable trailer hitch that could be stored out of the way when not in use. But don't get carried away with nifty truck accessories, because you'll often need the whole bed free to haul plants, soil amendments, and materials. If you can afford it, have a dumping mechanism installed; it saves you years of shoveling.

Storage Facilities

Now you know that you'll soon be the owner of a lot of cumbersome, valuable, and not very pretty (by the standards of the rest of the world) equipment. Where does it go? When I started, I had to park on the street, tools in the back of the old Ford. Sure enough, one Christmas night someone broke in and stole everything. It cost me $2,500 in 1973 prices just to go to work the next day. That was more money than I had, and it took a long time to recover. That's learning about security the hard way. If possible get a shed, or make some space in the garage, put some tool racks on the wall, find a place out back, *something*. It's not just security that's a consideration; the better organized you are, the easier and more productive your work will be.

Equipment Maintenance

For many years I spent evenings and Sundays in the shop sharpening mower blades and cleaning sprayers and doing brake jobs on trucks. You probably will too, so if you're not mechanically inclined, you'll be at a disadvantage. Taking everything to the mechanic is just too costly for the average start-up company; letting it fall apart is foolish. So, learn how to keep things clean and safe and reliable and then do it. When something's too much for you, then hire a mechanic.

Setting Up the Office

You'll be spending a lot of time out in the field, but not all of it. There's usually a good-sized heap of paperwork and phone calls awaiting you at what rightfully should be the end of the workday. You'll need a comfortable, efficient workspace; nothing fancy, just good basic furniture and equipment. Working off the dining room table is no fun.

First, locate a spot to call "The Office." The IRS wants you to put your office in a separate room or space that's used only for business. If you fail to do this, they may deny all your deductions for a home office. By the way, a 1993 ruling brings the home office deduction into question for people who spend most of their time in the field. Check with your accountant for specifics on this important issue.

Aside from tax implications, the home office needs to meet some other requirements. Not the least of these is peacefulness. Preparing bids, billing, and organizing jobs is mentally demanding. If there's a hubbub of kids and street noise and people running in and out, you'll risk disaster by inserting an extra zero somewhere. Peace and quiet also helps a lot when you're on the phone. Ever try to converse with someone who sounds like they're calling from the floor of a steel mill? How unprofessional! So pick a quiet room. It helps if there's a door leading directly outside, especially when employees or clients need to see you. I used to march everyone through the whole house to my little office, and it was often kind of embarrassing. If you don't have a perfect room, how about using a corner of the garage or a shed out back?

Now to the office contents. Get a big desk. I'd say it's humanly impossible to have a desk that's too big. Mine's a 3½-foot-wide hollow core door set on a simple wooden frame (you could also set it on two 2-drawer file cabinets). I made it in a couple of hours back in 1979 for about fifty bucks and it's still going strong. When I die, they'll probably carry my body out on it. Naturally it's always covered with stuff, except for a 2-square-foot space directly in front of me.

You'll need a phone. Simple is OK, but one with a dialer is great for making those routine calls when you're hurrying to get a bid out. An answering machine, of course, is de rigueur. One you can retrieve messages from remotely is great, and it's nice if it also tells you the time and day people called. Now if they'd only invent one that *returned* the calls for you. The best phone gadget of all is a headset. You'll feel foolish wearing it at first, but boy does it ever save your neck! Finally, you'll need a book of telephone message forms, the kind that keeps a carbon copy permanently bound in a spiral binding. Why? First, if you lose the original message, you can always look it up on the carbon copy. Second, you can look back and refresh your memory about who called if there's a question. I do this all the time. Finally, you'll have legal documentation in case of a dispute.

A desk calculator is better than a pocket one for various reasons. Speed is one, having a tape is another, ease of operation is a third. Try to get one with a mark-up/mark-down key for bidding.

My desk also holds a pencil pot, an in/out bin, my datebook, a calendar pad for scheduling jobs, a photo of my girlfriend, a stuffed monkey (don't ask), and the aforementioned heap of clutter. And a computer.

Do you really need a computer? Let's avoid the question for now and deal with it in chapter 4. You should at least allow space on your desk for one of these infernal gadgets, because sooner or later you'll be sitting there and staring at one for hours every day. You will.

If you're a computer-phobe (there's no reason to be these days, but more on that later), get a good-quality electronic typewriter, which you should be able to pick up used for very little money.

A look past the desk reveals some other office basics. One or more file cabinets hold client files, records, catalogs, and whatnot. A storage cabinet hides the office supplies. There are shelves for books. Designers need a drawing board, T-square, triangles, architect's and engineer's scales, compass, drafting pens and pencils, and colored markers. Lighting should be bright, simple, generous. And if you like sitting down, get a comfortable office chair. If you have a bad back, which you will after a couple of years in this business, you'll come to appreciate the expensive, ergonomically designed chairs available now. If you'd like visitors to sit too (a dubious approach), provide a not-too-comfortable side chair. (A clever person is said to have cut an inch off the two front legs, making guests feel vaguely uneasy and eager to leave quickly.)

You will at first think a copy machine and a fax machine are indulgent geegaws, but after you own them, you will realize they are miracles.

Some genuinely indulgent geegaws include a stereo and a cordless phone.

There's also a lot of little stuff that's necessary or handy to have around. Some things are obvious: pens and pencils, scratch paper, a ruler, a stapler, paper clips, Scotch tape, that sort of thing. If you have kids, steal these things from them. Others are more specialized. Have a rubber stamp made with the company name and address. Get some other ready-made stamps: one that says "PAID" and one that says "ORIGINAL" and one that says "CLIENT'S COPY" and one that says "THANK YOU! WE APPRECIATE YOUR BUSINESS." Those multi-purpose date stamps with a little rubber track that says "ENTERED" and "PAID" and so forth are great and cheap. Buy some postage stamps and a small postage scale (saves you hours of standing in line at the post office). Put a bulletin board on the wall next to your desk; you'll find a use for it soon enough. These are the basics.

In no time you'll clutter the place up with dozens of other things; the office supply store will love your first couple of years in business. Buy some of your office stuff from other businesses that are going bankrupt. They shouldn't be too hard to find. They're desperate, and they'll sell you great things for pennies on the dollar.

What about business forms? We'll get to those in chapter 4, but for now, know that you'll need business cards, letterheads and envelopes, invoice forms, contract forms and change orders (for landscaping work only), and a really unsettling number of other forms. Some of these are required by law, others by good sense.

Remember, these are the basics. They're enough to keep you going for a long time, though, since there's never any need to outfit your office as though you were the CEO of General Electric.

Unclassifiable Essentials

You'll need a camera for taking before-and-after photos of your jobs. If you can afford it, get a good-quality 35mm single lens reflex camera with interchangeable lenses. Get a zoom lens (I have a 28–200mm that I like a lot for its versatility) and a real wide-angle lens (I love my 20mm) that will take in a lot of landscaping and make it look great. Don't waste your money on auto-focus (plants don't move around all that much) or other doodads. Just get a good-quality manual camera.

Also get a small pocket tape recorder. Why? Remember the busy life you're about to undertake? Well, when you leave a job, you can use the driving time to the next job to record your notes from the previous job. It also traps all those other brilliant thoughts you'll be sure to have while you're driving around in your truck. Soon you won't be able to live without it.

The Bank Account

Short section. Get a separate bank account for your business. Otherwise you'll get all confused and end up with a big mess at the end of the year. Make it an interest-bearing checking account because you'll probably keep a pretty big balance on hand to cover expenses. Might as well make some money on your cash flow.

If you'll be operating your business as a sole proprietorship, you'll need to show the bank your fictitious business name statement unless your full name is used in the company name (such as Sue Wilson's Gardening Service). To get a fictitious business name statement (aka a DBA), go to the county Clerk/Recorder's Office, and they'll tell you what to do. If you're going to incorporate, you'll need to provide them with the articles of incorporation. And if your business is a partnership, they'll need to see the partnership agreement.

Insurance

I know you don't want to read about insurance. But you must, just as you must have insurance. Besides, if you think insurance is a grim topic, wait until we get to bookkeeping and taxes and lawsuits.

For a long time I said that buying tires was the least satisfying way to spend lots of money, but I now believe insurance is. The best you can hope for from insurance is that you never have to use it. Some thrill. But the law and good practice require that you carry a lot of insurance. (*Important Advice:* It's impossible to generalize about insurance, because laws and policies vary from state to state. Some of the information included here is based on what happens in my home state of California.)

Here are the basic kinds of insurance you'll need.

Business Liability Insurance

Let's say you drive a tractor into your client's bedroom; "God forbid," as the insurance agents like to say. You'll owe for the bedroom, lodging while the bedroom is being remodeled, furnishings, maybe medical costs, emotional damage, attorneys' fees, and who knows what else. No problem, because you've got $1 million of liability coverage. The settlement shouldn't run any more than that. Liability coverage also protects you against things like personal injury, advertising injury, and medical expenses. It's part of a package of business coverages that can insure against a wide range of losses, including fire damage, equipment theft, and loss of records. Work with your agent to custom-tailor a package that's right for you.

Pay close attention to the following information:

1. The insurer will defend you only up to the limits of coverage. That means if someone sues you for $1 million and you're insured for only $500,000, you have to get your own lawyer for the uninsured portion of the suit. If you lose in court, you must pay out of your pocket any amounts over the insured amount. Got half a mil laying around?

2. Generally speaking, liability insurance will protect you if you're sued for damages resulting from work you did while the policy was in effect, even if the suit is filed several years later. However, the insurance company is only required to keep your files for five years after you drop the coverage, so be sure to retain your own copies of the policies. Don't ever destroy them, because damage could result from your work many years after you did it and you'd still be responsible (at least here in California—laws may differ in your state, so check with your agent or an attorney.)

3. If you plan to quit the business or retire, have an attorney advise you whether you'll still be exposed to liability. A nasty lawsuit popping up out of nowhere can really take the fun out of your golden years.

4. If you change companies, be sure there's no lapse between coverages.

Often, you need to show proof that you have liability coverage, for example, when you apply for building permits and business licenses, and when you want to go to work as a subcontractor for another contractor. The cost of business liability insurance is based on your payroll, even if you're a one-person operation. Rates seem to vary considerably, so shop around. You also need to be aware that your homeowner's policy probably doesn't cover things like injuries to visitors to your home office. Be sure your business policy does.

Worker's Compensation Insurance

This covers employees in case they're injured on the job. If you have employees, worker's comp is required by law. Rates are set by the Worker's Compensation Rating Bureau and don't vary from one company to another. They do vary for each job classification—in your case, Landscape Gardening. The penalties for not having worker's comp are severe. In California, if an employee is injured on the job and you're caught without worker's compensation insurance, you have to pay all the employee's medical expenses out of your own pocket, plus a 50 percent surcharge, plus a possible $10,000 fine and/or up to six months in jail. (*Tip:* Some trade associations handle return-premium worker's compensation policies; these policies refund a portion of the premiums at the end of each year, based on the claims costs. This can save you big, big bucks.)

Group Health Insurance

If you have employees, you may want or be compelled to provide them with health insurance. This is a rapidly changing issue, so check with your agent.

Vehicle Insurance

Be sure your policy covers multiple drivers if you have employees. Also be certain employees are covered in their own autos if you have them run errands for you.

One of the most important exposures you'll have is vehicle-related mishaps. It's unbelievable how many employees lie to the boss about their suspended licenses, drunk driving convictions, and other offenses. Remember, these people are driving your vehicles, which are often large, heavily loaded trucks pulling trailers. You simply must check the driving records of all employees and prospective employees and keep current about the status of their driving records. The California Department of Motor Vehicles will, for a modest fee, keep an employer informed of any changes in the driving record of employees. Check to see if your state offers anything similar.

Bonds

A bond is a special type of insurance that protects third parties (in this case, your clients and the public) against damages arising from your screw-ups. If you're a landscape contractor, you'll probably need a license bond, the cost of which is minimal. The license bond pays an injured party if you, for example, leave a job unfininshed or do it improperly. In some cases it can also protect your employees in case you fail to pay benefits owed them.

If you end up bidding big jobs someday, you'll need to know about other kinds of bonds, such as completion bonds, which guarantee that the job will be completed. If you don't finish the job the bonding company brings in, at their expense, another contractor to finish. This type of bonding is a few years down the line for you, though, and you'll have plenty of opportunity to learn about it when the time comes.

The Cost of Insurance

Unfortunately, it's impossible to give you any estimate of what you'll have to spend on insurance. There are several reasons for this. First, the types of coverage and the limits of liability you choose are highly variable, therefore, so are the resulting premiums. Second, rates for all types of insurance vary by state, region, even neighborhood in some cases. Legal requirements vary, too. Rates also vary from company to company. Finally, rates are partially set by your claims record, driving records of you and your staff, kind of vehicles you own, and age and value of equipment you're covering.

Still, it's fair to say you'll spend quite a bit of money on insurance each year—at least a couple thousand dollars just to start out. The best advice? Seek out a good independent insurance agent, and plan a reasonable package for your business. Many years ago I was lucky to find a good, honest agent who spent a lot of time educating me about the ins and outs of the insurance game. If you can do the same, you'll be in good shape.

Insurance Agents

There are two kinds of insurance agents: the independent agent, who can shop around for you and seek quotes from different companies, and the company agent, who works for only one company. Select an independent agent; you'll probably get a better deal. Also be sure to choose someone who specializes in business insurance, not consumer insurance (like homeowner's coverage), which is a completely different ball game. In fact, find an agent who understands gardening or contracting, whichever you plan to go into. Why? Because there are always special quirks in any field, and landscaping is no exception. Here's a case in point: My agent discovered that a local equipment rental yard was charging for what they called a "damage waiver," which allegedly protected the renter against liability for damage to the equipment. After one of his clients had a problem with this, the agent got a copy of the waiver and discovered it offered no protection at all. He then alerted all his contractor clients. That's service only an experienced person can offer.

Insurance Tips

Check your homeowner's policy to see to what extent it covers office equipment in the home. Look into special deals offered as part of membership in a business or trade organization. Shop around a lot, since rates on all types of insurance except workers compensation can vary a lot. Also, review policies at least annually to be sure you've got the kind of coverage you feel comfortable with.

Legal Considerations

The Legal Form of Your Business

Typically, a small family-run business is operated as a sole proprietorship, at least at first. That is to say, it is not a partnership (which is where you share ownership and responsibilities with one or more people) or a corporation (where the business itself becomes a "person," protecting you to some degree from the liabilities of the business operations). The sole proprietorship is easy to set up and gives you the most control over your operation with the least hassle.

I strongly advise you not to begin your business with a partner, even though my own experience was a positive one. The partnership has been aptly described as a marriage without sex. Most partnerships don't work, and since they're often entered into by friends, the common result is the failure of both the business and the friendship. What happens? Usually one person works harder than the other and eventually gets fed up. Or one person spends all the money, enters into questionable deals without the other partner's knowledge or consent, or otherwise jeopardizes the business. You probably don't need a partner. If you do form a partnership, plan for its graceful termination when you prepare the agreement. It'll save a lot of grief later.

You probably also don't need to incorporate. Traditionally, the small corporation has been considered a way of protecting the business owner from personal liability for business problems such as lawsuits and debts. Unfortunately, you can't count on that protection as much as you used to be able to. There also may be tax advantages to incorporating, but again, they ain't what they used to be. A corporation has to have a board of directors, hold regular meetings, keep elaborate and detailed records, and jump through a million hoops set up by the government. One false move and you lose many of the advantages of the corporate structure. Talk to an accountant and an attorney about this if you're just dying to see "Inc." after your name.

Licenses

You'll need a city and/or county business license, possibly a permit for each vehicle you operate, maybe a special permit to operate out of your house. You'll need to register your company name using a Fictitious Business Name Statement that's on file with the county and is also published in a legal ad in a local newspaper. You'll have to get a "seller's permit" (also known as a resale number) from an outfit called the State Board of Equalization (or something similar) in order to collect and remit sales taxes. If you have employees, you'll need a Federal Employer Identification Number that's obtained by filing a form you can get from the IRS. If you do landscaping work (as opposed to maintenance), you'll need a contractor's license. More about that in just a minute. There's no use grousing about the burden of obtaining and maintaining all these licenses. Everyone has to have them, and you're no exception. Just grit your teeth and do it. Obtaining most of these is easy—fill out a form or two, give them some money, and off you go.

The contractor's license is different. Not just anyone can become a licensed contractor. You'll need to have several years of experience or some schooling, meet certain financial requirements, get letters of recommendation from other professionals, and take a rather detailed exam. If you pass, then you can pay more money and walk out with your license. Why bother? Because to do landscaping work (not garden maintenance in most cases) you must have a contractor's license. Yes, I know a lot of people get away without having a license, but they're risking fines, even jail time, bad publicity, and perhaps the loss of their businesses. They can't bid on big jobs or get building permits. And their clients don't have to pay them. That's right—imagine doing a $20,000 job and having the owner refuse to pay because she knows you're unlicensed. Take her to court? Forget it! You might as well call the cops because you got burned in a drug deal. You're an outlaw.

So, how hard is it to get a contractor's license? Probably a lot easier than you imagine. Requirements vary from state to state, but the California experience is typical. Work for four years for another licensed contractor, or complete an accredited college-level program to reduce the experience requirement. Have $1,000 in the bank. Don't have a felony on your record. Get a couple of friends in the business to fill out letters of recommendation. Apply for the test. Take it (about four to six hours of questions and work problems that won't be all that difficult if you have a basic level of competence). Pass (you hope), or take it again the following year. Get a contractor's license bond.

That's it. It's not all that bad, and you'll immediately feel better, get more respect, and be free to pursue the kind of quality career you dream of. No more looking over your shoulder all the time. It's a great feeling. Contact your state contractor's license board for more information. If you've never worked for a licensed landscape contractor, you may still be able to qualify to take the exam by virtue of several years of experience as a self-employed person.

There are schools that will help you study for the exam, but you'll probably do just as well on your own. You'll be tested on many things in addition to landscaping, among them safety requirements, mechanics lien laws, employer laws, business law, and building codes. The license board might be able to provide you with a reading list, which will be a big help. I used a correspondence course that was inexpensive and good. It provided copies of tests from previous years, which took away a lot of the fear of the unknown. After devouring book after book for months, I completed the test in just over two hours, out of eight allowed. Lest you think I'm some kind of genius, quite a few people had already left when I handed in my test booklet.

The contractor's license permits you to do any type of landscaping work, including grading, planting, irrigation, building decks and retaining walls, and installing low-voltage lighting systems. You can also do landscape design as long as you also install what you design. (To do *only* design work for others to install, you'd need to be a landscape architect. See page 8.) What you *can't* do is any building construction, high-voltage electrical work, house plumbing, roofing, that sort of thing. In other words, the license allows you to do landscaping, nothing more. Rules vary from state to state.

Home improvement contracting (under which landscaping falls) is one of the most regulated kinds of business. The form of your contract with the client, the terms of payment, the conduct of any sales people you hire, your relationship with your employees and subcontractors, lien law filings, and a whole lot more are rigidly controlled by state law. One misstep and you could lose your license. Still, once you get the rhythm of it, it's just like any other job, so don't suffer too much anxiety over the prospect of your responsibilities. Anyway, it's worth it.

Business Taxes

Employee Taxes

You need to deposit the taxes you deduct from employees paychecks. More on this in chapter 5.

Sales Taxes

Regulations vary, but in general, if you sell a product, either as a retail sale or by incorporating materials into your jobs, you will need to collect and pay sales tax on the value of the goods. The sales tax laws were written primarily with merchants in mind, and they apply very clumsily to contractors. The mechanics of figuring your sales taxes can be baffling, even to the bureaucrats who run the system. Check with your state Board of Equalization (may have a different name in your state) for a resale number and instructions on how to file your returns. Good luck on this one.

Defining Your Niche

What Kind of Work Will You Do?

We've discussed the diversity of opportunities in the business. Have you decided where you fit in? Here are some issues that you need to look at:

1. Do you want to do landscaping, maintenance, or both?

2. Do you want to offer specialties such as tree care, low-voltage lighting, irrigation troubleshooting, water management, organic maintenance or lawn care, yard cleanups, hauling, etc.?

3. If you'll be doing landscaping, do you want to offer design/build services or do only the installations?

4. What class of work do you want to do: high-end residential, middle-class residential, budget residential, large or small commercial, public works?

5. Do you want to eventually go after large, complex projects or stick with smaller backyard jobs?

Let me give you some advice about how to proceed. Unless you've had considerable experience working for another company, start with small residential work. It takes years to get good enough (and for your company to be substantial enough) to go after the big jobs. Give yourself time.

Include maintenance in your mix of services, even if you don't want to do it forever. That way you'll learn how things *really* work, because you'll have to care for the finished product.

If you're not sure what you'd like to end up doing, try a bit of everything. Be sure you're qualified to do the work, of course, but don't limit yourself. Be a generalist. You'll learn a lot and you won't be limiting your clients to just those who want one kind of thing.

At first, avoid complex design/build jobs unless you have training in landscape architecture. It's easy to get in over your head and design something that doesn't work. Move gradually from the simple projects to the complex ones, one step at a time.

Who Do You Want to Work For?

Each of the following potential job sources has its own personality.

The Homeowner

Most likely, this is where you'll start. Homeowners can be some of your best clients. They tend to be honest and usually won't take advantage of you the way some commercial clients often do.

A sprinkler contractor I know has a rule about clients. He will only work for homeowners improving their own homes for their own enjoyment; no landlords, spec house builders, developers, commercial jobs, or anything else where someone is trying to make a buck off his work. He's done very well by this rule, and I think he has a point. The following discussion reflects some of my own observations and prejudices about various kinds of residential clients.

Some of the best clients in the world are upper middle-class homeowners who work for a living and understand that you do, too. They're accustomed to paying their bills on time. They respect you. They're more or less your peers, so you can relate to them pretty easily. They don't look down on you. They usually want to do things right and can probably afford quality services.

Rich clients can be great, especially since they have a lot of money. A good rich client is a real find, a source of lots of top-quality work. But the rich are different and not always pleasant to do business with. They can be haughty and not a lot of fun to be around. Some people got rich by cheating other people, often in clever and devious ways; they'll eat you for a snack. Watch out for them. Others got their money the old-fashioned way: They inherited it. They've never worked and can't understand why you need to get paid on time. This trait can be exasperating and costly. To top it all off, many of them are tightwads. (You may think I'm a bigot, but what I'm telling you is true, and you might as well hear it now as learn the hard way. I've got nothing against any group, but after twenty-one years in this business, I know trouble when I see it.)

On the other end of the spectrum are homeowners who have just enough money to pay for a little bit of budget-quality land-scaping or maintenance work. Some of these folks are OK, especially when you're getting started, but be aware of the fact that such people will often persuade you to lower your quality standards. Don't do it. Doing a poor-quality job reflects badly on you. Besides, once the client sees the job you did, he or she may suddenly become a perfectionist, demanding first-rate work even though they only paid you for junk. It's a trap many beginners fall into.

There are some subsets of the homeowner trade that can be particularly rewarding to pursue. One is the two-income family. Some of these folks have plenty of discretionary income, like to spend it, and have no time to work in their yards. They need you. Another good group is affluent seniors. They have money, taste, and needs. They can be really nice. Lately I've been getting work from people in their 50s whose parents are dying and leaving them with large inheritances. This seems to be a trend. Some of these are people I started with when they were in their 30s and struggling, and now they're spending money like crazy. Another reason to stick with your established clients. (*Tip:* Never work for renters. They have no right to contract with you for improvements to the landlord's property and no obligation to pay you. Furthermore, the landlord may go after you when he finds out you've been messing around with his place.)

Landlords

Speaking of landlords, check them out thoroughly before you get involved with their projects. They tend to be cheap and often don't pay their bills. Do a credit check, and ask around about them to see how they treat other contractors. The other thing about landlords is they often don't care about quality work, so unless you like to do things badly for some reason, you'll be frustrated.

Condominium and Homeowner's Associations

More and more people are moving into condos and planned developments with common public spaces and shared landscaping. There's usually a landscape committee, made up of owners, that oversees maintenance and changes in the landscaping and deals with the gardeners and landscape contractors who work there. There's a lot of work, especially maintenance, in these places. One of these jobs can require one or more people full-time. Naturally, you have to bid against others and so your profit margins will be low, but an efficient operation can make you some money.

Warning: A huge percentage of condo and similar developments are involved in lawsuits with the builder, subcontractors, suppliers, and, yes, landscapers. People seem to go kind of crazy when they get on landscape committees, and they can be a nightmare to work with. Quite a few business people simply refuse to deal with associations. Be aware of the risks and frustrations.

New Housing Developments

There's a lot of work landscaping new housing tracts, and there are two ways to get it. One is to get in with the builder or developer and do the landscaping in common areas, front yards, and model homes. Sometimes you can do this by the back door and not have to go up against every other hungry person with a pickup in the county. That is, if the builder is your true buddy he may let you do the job without bidding against others. More often, you bid the job just like any other.

Warning: Many, many builders and developers are sharks, and when they see a fresh-faced newcomer like you, they'll count on bleeding you for all you've got. They'll give you the work all right, but not the money, and they've got a million well-tested schemes for cheating you. If you don't understand how the development game works, stay away from these situations. Not to tar everyone with the same brush, but this is often rough territory and no place for the little guy.

The other approach is to wait until homeowners move in and then go to work for them. This is a good source of jobs. They have to do something. It may be modest, since they just spent all their money on the new house, but there is work there. (*Tip:* Be careful on new tracts because the soil is often compacted and/or of poor quality and you can lose a lot of plants.)

Commercial Property Owners

Many shopping centers, office complexes, and other high-visibility properties are landscaped and maintained beautifully. The owners care a lot about their image and are willing to do things right. Usually they put everything out to bid, so you'll have to work for a slim profit margin, much less than what you can get doing residential work. Still, if you're efficient you can get lots of work this way.

Public Properties

Some of the work in the public sector is done in-house by staff workers. But this isn't true of everything, particularly new construction, which often has to be put out to bid according to law. Many municipalities and other public bodies contract out their maintenance work. Some areas also have annual lot clearing work that you can bid on.

Working for a public agency, whether it's the federal, state, or local government, involves a lot of paperwork and the ability to deal with incompetent or hostile bureaucrats, obscure regulations, and interminable delays. Many public projects also require that you pay prevailing wage. Still, it's good work, and the government virtually always pays its bills. In most cases, you'll have to work from a landscape architect's plans rather than your own. Most public jobs must go to the lowest qualified bidder. Bidding is often cutthroat, and profit margins are low. Don't get into public work until you've had plenty of experience in the private sector.

Conclusion

Congratulations on making it this far. I know this chapter has been a little heavy and you may feel as though going into business is a lot more trouble than it's worth. Remember, you have to do some of these things only once. Anyway, you'll adjust to all this in time, learn to make peace with the situation, and even enjoy the process. If you're careful and honest, you'll probably never have a serious problem. I haven't, and I've been at this for a long time. Despite the burdens, it's still fun to go to work every day, the most fun I've ever had.

3

Writing a Business Plan

Chances are, you've never had to write a business plan before. Maybe you've never even heard of such a thing. So let's begin at the beginning: What is a business plan? What kind of information does it include? What's it for?

A business plan is a detailed description of your proposed business: What kind of business will it be? Who will own it? Where will it be located? Who will your clients be? What geographical areas will your business serve? What kinds of products or services will it offer? Who's the competition? How will your business be better than or different from the competition? How will your services be advertised to the potential clients? What kinds of equipment will you need to start up? What are your other start-up costs? What will the total costs be to start the business? What will the overhead be? When will your business begin to show a profit? What are the seasonal variations in sales? Will there be employees? How many? What kind—laborers, supervisors, office help? What will the cash flow be for the first few years? How much money do you need in order to make a living and put something away for your retirement? These are some of the important issues the business plan addresses.

Though you can find plenty of books that provide ready-made business plan formats, there's no universally accepted way to prepare a business plan. In fact, the way your business plan is organized will depend to some extent on what you'll be using it for. First, decide if you'll be using the plan to attract capital—a bank loan, money from Uncle Harry, Small Business Administration financing, or whatever. You'll tailor the business plan to the source of funds. For example, a bank is interested in how you're going to pay off the loan. They'll be justifiably cautious in loaning money to something as risky as a landscaping business. They'll want to see lots of financial projections: five years' *pro forma* (projected) income statements and balance sheets and other evidence of your good financial planning. On the other hand, Uncle Harry might be more interested in the personal or philosophical aspects of his nephew's proposed business.

If you won't need start-up capital, then the plan is mostly for you and possibly for key employees when you expand some day. It'll be a road map to guide you as you develop your business. Though you still have to do the financial projections (trust me— you do), you can format the plan more to your own liking.

Either way, there are some essential elements the business plan must contain, and there's a systematic approach to preparing it that will make it pretty easy for you to get the job done well. I'm going to give you my version of what a business plan for a small gardening or landscaping business should look like and how to go about writing it. That's what we'll spend most of this chapter on, but first, let's deal with the obvious question.

Why Do a Business Plan, Anyway?

Thinking about actually preparing a business plan may give you a bad case of anxiety. "Hey," you may ask, "isn't this all a waste of time? After all, I'm not starting General Motors! Why not just get some jobs and start making money?"

The answer is, this is not just a job, it's a business. It has to function smoothly over the long haul. It's complex and your success depends on your understanding, in depth, what you'll be doing and why—understanding it now, before you begin. You wouldn't build a garden by going out and buying any old plants and throwing them into the ground any old way. That would lead to a mess, not a garden. You plan first, then plant. Similarly, your business needs guidance and form right from the beginning and that's what a business plan is all about. It's a plan for success.

Hopefully you'll do really well and attract a lot of business. That's good, but if you don't have management systems in place first, you'll soon be overwhelmed. Your business plan forces you to develop, in nitty-gritty detail, a strategy for exactly how you'll do things—marketing, hiring, financing, and a lot more. That way, you can create a business that really works. As your business grows, your business plan will continue to guide your development and help you prosper.

Speaking of financing, you may very well need some money for your start-up business. Remember how costly those tools and equipment are? Well, if you go to the bank and tell them you want to start a landscaping business and you'd like, say, $20,000, what's the first thing they're going to do? That's right! They're going to say, "Let's see your business plan." You don't want to be caught short at this important moment. Even good old Uncle Harry, if he's got anything on the ball, will ask for a business plan before he empties part of his bank account into yours.

Putting together a business plan, while certainly not as much fun as going to the beach, isn't all that bad. Parts of the job are even enjoyable. It'll give you a lot of clarity about your new business. When you're done, you'll have new confidence and enthusiasm, knowing you're well prepared for your adventure.

Finally, a business plan doesn't have to be fancy. There are certain tasks you want your business plan to accomplish. Accomplish them and stop. No glossy printing, no vast acreage of numbers, no frills. A business plan is like a shovel; it's a tool, nothing more.

When Do You Prepare a Business Plan?

Easy: before you commit any significant time or money to the business. Don't put this off as you would cleaning behind the fridge. Get it done. Remember: business plan first, business second.

Preparing the Business Plan, Step by Step

Step One: *A Statement of Purpose*

Can you describe in thirty-five words or less what your new business is all about? If not, maybe you're not too sure yourself. Hammering out a statement of purpose, though it may seem silly, is a terrific way to focus your mind on what you're doing and boil it down to one pithy definition that you can use to remind yourself (and everyone else) what your business is about. Try it. To help you get the idea, here's a statement a friend of mine developed (with the help of his employees) for his landscaping business:

> Boulder Creek Landscaping Company is a quality-oriented organization specializing in ecological enhancement of the environment for the benefit of the entire community.

So, will you just be doing landscaping? Not really. You'll also be serving the needs of the clients, your employees, your suppliers, the community, and the environment. You'll be a business manager, an employer, a public relations person, and so on. Each task and each role you play takes a place in the ecology of your little business. Which ones are the most important to you? Use your statement of purpose to define the basic character of your business. Then frame it and hang it right in the middle of your bulletin board, or put it on your desk where you'll see it every day.

Step Two: *General Information about Your Business*

This is the place for some very basic facts about your proposed business. What general classes of service will you offer (maintenance, new landscaping, etc.)? Where will your business be located (your spare bedroom)? Who will own it (just you, you and your spouse, two or more partners)? What will the form of the business be (sole proprietorship, partnership, corporation)? When do you plan to start doing business? What will the name of your business be?

Choosing a company name can be difficult. After all, your company name will be with you for a long time. Select something that sounds solid, not frivolous. Make sure it'll appeal to a wide range of people, but especially to the well-to-do, who tend to be pretty straight-laced. Avoid trendy names that'll sound dated in a few years (imagine if your company name was Frieda's Far-Out Garden Service). Make sure the name conveys what you do. Finally, be sure you choose something that makes sense. There was a company here in town a few years ago called Inner-Plant-A-Terrarium. Honest. I never did figure out why they chose such a goofy moniker, but it didn't matter because they weren't around for very long.

Step Three: *Your Background*

One of the goals of the business plan is to try to convince potential investors of your management and technical skills. Here's where you sell yourself.

Write a couple of paragraphs telling how you came to be interested in landscaping and why you've decided to go into business. Describe any applicable training or degrees you have, employment experience, volunteer work, and anything that demonstrates your dedication to your profession. If you don't have any professional experience but have always had a beautiful backyard, put that down; it counts, too. The bank will need to see this information, just as a prospective employer needs to see a resume. It'll be good for you, too—a clear perspective on where you've come from and why you're qualified to follow this dream of business ownership. Remember, keep it brief and to the point.

Naturally, the above applies to partners and any other key employees you propose to have on board when you start up.

Finally, mention any licenses you will need for the services you offer and indicate whether you have them yet.

Step Four: *Services Offered*

In detail, tell what you plan to offer. Do you want to specialize in water gardens or organic lawn care or commercial landscaping? Do you want to do design/build? Irrigation troubleshooting? Pest control? Are you interested in selling any products in addition to services? What are they? The chart on page 53 lists some of the services typically offered by small gardening and landscaping companies.

Consider, too, what you'll do in the off-season. Many companies offer snow removal service, for example, to keep crews busy and produce income.

Your decisions should be based in part on what you like to do, of course, but also on what services the community needs and will purchase from you. You may want to do water gardens, but if nobody's interested you'll have a hard time making a go of it. It might be easier to mow lawns or do irrigation work or whatever else is in demand.

Remember, too, that most successful businesses offer a range of services. I've always done well because I tried to do whatever people wanted, as long as I had the necessary skills and it made sense in other ways. There are limits, of course, but the point is to try to serve people's needs. Try to never say no. If you're not capable of doing a job, find someone who is and use them as a subcontractor (then learn by watching them). So, prepare your business plan with a wide spectrum of services in mind. After due

Gardening Jobs vs. Landscaping Jobs

GARDENING	LANDSCAPING
Lawn care (mowing and edging, fertilizing, pest control, weeding, aerating, renovating, overseeding)	Lawn installation (sod and seeded lawns)
Plant care (pruning and hedge trimming, fertilizing, pest control, weeding, replanting, mulching)	Plant installation
Tree care (pruning, fertilizing, pest control, cabling and bracing, usually for smaller trees only)	Tree planting and transplanting, guying and staking
General cleanup and refuse management (sweeping, washing down walks, trash hauling, composting)	Hardscape construction (walks, retaining walls, fences, patios, planters, decks, arbors, etc.) and lighting installation (low-voltage walkway and landscape lights)
Irrigation maintenance (replacing sprinkler heads, repairing valves, etc.)	Irrigation installation (sprinkler and drip systems, water mains, backflow devices, automatic controllers, etc.)
Water management (watering, programming automatic controllers)	Drainage system installation (grading, drain pipes, catch-basins, etc.)

consideration you may want to narrow your focus somewhat (some people are successful because they pursue a small niche), but start with the broad view.

Is there something different about your business? Will you offer all-organic lawn care, landscaping with native plants, or construction using recycled materials? Do you plan to include a year's free monthly inspections with each landscape? Tell it. Investors often equate innovation with potential for success. If your ideas are good, they'll make a favorable impression.

Step Five: *Markets*

Who will you do business with? Homeowners? General contractors? Property managers? Developers? Architects? Landscape architects? Realtors? Apartment house owners? Owners of commercial property? Federal, state, or local governments? Will you focus on young families, middle-aged homeowners, or retired people? What income level will they be in? (Do you see how a business plan forces you to answer all kinds of pointed questions? Isn't it great?)

Now, how many of these people are out there? Ten? Ten thousand? Ten million? How many will you need to attract? How do you find this stuff out? For some categories, it's easy. For instance, if you're interested in working with realtors, get a head count from the Yellow Pages. Others are more difficult, such as apartment house owners, because they don't advertise anywhere. But I bet there's an association of apartment house managers or something similar in your community. Ask around. Your local library probably has a reference desk that's staffed with nice people who can help you research the most obscure things. Give them a call or stop by.

Next, where are these potential clients located? That is, how far afield are you willing to go to look for business? (For starters you'll probably want to stick to your local community. It's too much to try and become Statewide Landscaping Company right away.) How many people move into your community each year?

What percentage of these people do you intend to grab away from the competition in the first year, two years, five years? The marketing people call this "market penetration." It's an important question because you need to know not only what the potential for your company is but also how much business you'll need to do to be successful. This also relates to the financial projections we'll be getting to soon.

Finally, take a look at overall industry growth trends to see whether your strategy is really viable. In other words, is the work actually out there? For example, if you choose to only landscape new homes, working for builders and developers, make sure there's going to be a sufficient volume of new construction in your area over the next couple of decades. If not, you're kidding yourself about your potential success.

Step Six: *Competition*

You won't be the only one out there. The Yellow Pages is the best place to size up the competition. You'll quickly see who's in the business, what kind of services they offer, whether they give free initial consultations, whether they run large or small ads, give discounts to seniors, offer services you may not have thought of.

Go down to the phone company and compare the current phone book with one a couple of years old. This will give you an idea of the turnover of companies; that is, how many of them don't make it. In my community there's a pretty consistent 50 percent turnover every year. Half the ads from last year are gone, half are new. Scary? You bet, but don't be discouraged. Most of those people didn't take an orderly approach to business management like you're doing. They crippled themselves with ignorance and lack of professionalism right from the get-go. You'll do better. (By the way, somebody needs to service the clients of these failures. Why not you?)

Because most gardening and landscaping companies are privately owned, it's pretty much impossible to find out what their sales volume is, how many employees they have, or how profitable they are. Even if you've seen a company's shiny new trucks running around town, it doesn't mean they're profitable. It also doesn't mean their clients are satisfied with the services they offer. Remember, to be successful you need to be better than the competition, not necessarily flashier or bigger.

One good way to learn about competing companies is to ask a few questions at their suppliers. Who's busy? What kinds of work are available, and who's doing what? Who's hiring? You might even find out who's behind in their bills.

Another approach is to apply for work with a few companies, even though you're not looking for a job. During an interview, you can probe for information about the company and get a good inside look at their operation. You can even bring up the subject of other companies and get some interesting dirt. Remember, of course, that not everything you hear will be true. You'll need to read between the lines.

Once you've gathered information, you need to write a short summary and evaluation of the results. How many companies are there? How many are large, how many small? What's the sales volume? How many people are employed locally? What are the major services being offered? To whom? Who's booming and who's just hanging on?

Finally, how will you fit in? Which competitors are the most important to you and why? How will you draw business away from them? (*Tip:* Maybe you could offer your competitors some kind of service.) Why will your business be better? Be brief, but be specific.

Step Seven: *Marketing*

How, exactly, are you planning to attract business? Read chapter 6 to understand marketing, then choose strategies that are right for the type of business you're going after, the clients you're interested in, and the economic conditions in your area.

Pricing

Describe your price strategy in detail. Are you planning to appeal to small clients by offering low prices and discounts for seniors, or will you be trying to attract top-end work where prices are high? Will you offer specials or coupons to get new clients? An hour's free consultation? Special prices on the first month's garden service?

Warning: One of the most annoying and potentially deadly problems in this business is "low-balling competitors"—super cut-rate operators who somehow get by charging less than the actual cost of the job for their work. There are a number of variations on the basic theme (see chapter 7), but for now be aware that low-ballers exist. They drive prices below the profit level for everyone, and they may affect you, especially if you plan to enter into the cutthroat world of competitively bid maintenance or landscaping jobs such as commercial work or bidding for landscape architects.

Low-ballers never go away (a new crop sprouts every year like crabgrass), but they really come out of the woodwork during difficult economic times or when there's little work around. So, before you get too far, check out the situation in your area. You can still do fine even with a heavy population of low-ballers, but you'll need to avoid going head-to-head with them. Stick to custom work, provide top-quality service, and retain your clients. Don't waste your time getting into bidding wars.

Advertising

How will people find out about you? Will you go door to door? Send out direct mail pieces? Join the Chamber of Commerce and network with influential business people? Advertise on radio or in the local paper? Stand on the corner in a gorilla suit? What? Tell it.

Show it, too. Do a mock-up of your proposed Yellow Pages ad and any other advertising you plan. Lay out any brochures and handouts you plan to use. You'll force yourself to see whether you actually like your ideas once they're on paper.

If you plan on working with an advertising agency or a graphics company, describe the work they'll be doing for you.

Next, describe the results you expect to get from your marketing program. That is, X dollars invested in marketing should produce Y dollars in sales. Be realistic. For example, direct mail campaigns usually produce a 2 or 3 percent response. Believe it or not, that's considered a success. If you project a 50 percent response, you'll look like a rube to investors. Plus, you'll be in for a shock when you put your plan into action.

Remember to think about both short-term and long-term strategies. That is, you'll probably do one set of things to get started and then switch to a different set once you're rolling. What's different about them? Why? Justify your choices.

Step Eight: *Company Organization*

In years one through five, how many employees will you have and what are their duties? Who answers to whom?

Let's have a quick look at big versus small. The first year, your organizational chart may look like the one below. Pretty silly, but still, there's no shame in being a one-person operation. By year five, it may look like the flowchart on page 59.

```
+---------------------------------------+
|          Marsha Wong                  |
|        Owner/Head Gardener            |
|    Sales Director/Office Manager      |
|         Mechanic/Janitor              |
+---------------------------------------+
```

Now you've got twenty mouths to feed (plus their families), plus casual labor brought in as conditions warrant, subcontractors, consultants, and who knows what else. You've got a big, consumptive company on your hands, and you'd better know how to run it because you're not in Kansas anymore, as Dorothy once said. Here's where the lack of management skills can do you in quickly.

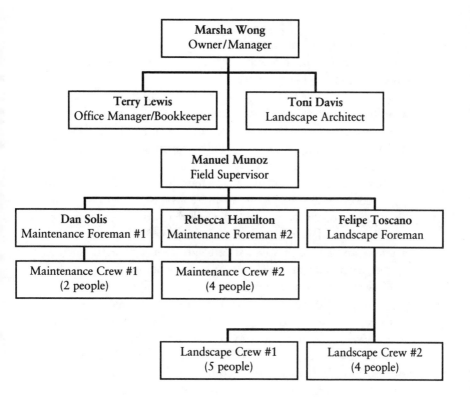

Big Versus Small

Though "big" looks a lot like "successful" to most people who haven't been there, "big" is actually a whole lot riskier, more stressful, and more unstable than "small." Here's why: If you're little Joe Gardener working out of the spare bedroom, your overhead is practically nonexistent, the volume of work you need to do in order to get by is minimal, your exposure to risk is small, and you can easily keep a lot of things in your head without losing control. (Does working out of your home start to make sense now?)

Get big, and you've got a lot of potential problems. First, you have people (including yourself) who are part of the overhead of the business—in the example above, the office manager, the field supervisor, and possibly the landscape architect. You can't bill for their time like you can for the laborers, but they cost you lots of money nonetheless. (Maybe more than the laborers whose work pays *all* the bills, including overhead.) They're probably on salary, which means you have to pay them even if business is slow. That can drain you dry in no time.

Similarly, you've suddenly got an office, a storage yard, equipment loans, upkeep on everything, lots more insurance. All this is overhead, it's all expensive, and it can't be shut off. So the rules of the game change. Suddenly, you've got to sell jobs like crazy because you need so much more cash every month. Your daily overhead has gone from literally a few dollars in the good old spare bedroom days to $1,000 or more (yes, that's per day!) with the big fancy outfit. Naturally, doing all that work exposes you to more liability—defects, accidents, lawsuits. And, of course, sooner or later those employees will start to give you problems, such as injuries, theft, substance abuse, and personality conflict.

How do you control this huge organism? When do you find time to stop by all your many jobs that may be scattered over two or three counties? How do you know if you're making any money? When do you have any time for yourself?

The point is, now is a good time to think hard about whether your goals include eventually getting big. Hopefully, you understand that there's a world of difference between the small home-based business with maybe one or two employees and the big company downtown. What about that fifth year? Maybe you'll be a lot happier if you're still working out of your spare bedroom.

You might have guessed that I favor staying small. I got bigger for a while, but soon decided that even though I could probably learn to handle it as well as the next person, I didn't want to. I like running a really small business because it's safer, more fun, and just as profitable if you play your cards right. Most people think getting big is an inevitable aspect of business success, but that's folly. Always run your business with your head, not your ego. If you decide to get big, be sure that it makes business sense, that you can handle it, and that you want that kind of life.

Now, all this drives your sales and staffing projections. Once you've decided how big to be, it's easy to figure how many people you'll need. Refer to chapter 5 for a rundown on the wonderful world of employees, and use the information to calculate your staffing needs year by year for the first five years.

Briefly describe what each person will do, whether they'll be full or part time, permanent or temporary, and whether they'll be part of overhead or of cost of sales. Tell how much you'll pay them. Indicate what the labor burden (worker's compensation insurance, social security taxes, fringe benefits, and so forth) will be. Describe vacation and sick-leave policies, paid holidays, and so forth.

Also describe how you'll use subcontractors and outside services. Justify all staffing that's not part of the cost of sales—do you really need a secretary, for example?

Step Nine: *Facilities and Equipment*

Based on the amount of sales for each year, describe the kinds of equipment you'll need to own, lease, or rent (tools, vehicles, heavy equipment, office furnishings, etc.) and the kind, location, and size of facilities you'll need (office space, storage yard, employee facilities, etc.).

For instance, if you plan to have two gardening crews in year three, that means you'll need two trucks (plus one for yourself unless you're part of one crew), two sets of tools and equipment, and a place to store it all. You may or may not need a bigger office; this is still a reasonable-sized company to run from home, provided the employees don't create a nuisance for the neighbors.

Add up what all this will cost, item by item and year by year. Don't forget to allow for inflation in the cost of future purchases.

Step Ten: *Financial Projections*

OK, we've put this off long enough. Now that you know what you're planning to do for the next five years, you need to get down to the details of how much money this is going to cost and how much you're going to make. Here are some questions your number crunching is going to answer:

1. What are my start-up costs?

2. How do I plan to meet those costs?

3. What's my cost of doing business (years 1–5)?

4. What are my projected sales (years 1–5)?

5. What are my projected profits (years 1–5)?

6. What's my equity (years 1–5)?

7. What's my cash flow (years 1–5)?

8. What accounting and control systems will I have?

How will you answer all these questions in an orderly way that others will understand? Well, there are several standard formats for presenting this information that are universally accepted and are required in any business plan. These include:

1. The Balance Sheet

2. The Income Statement (also called Profit and Loss Statement)

3. The Cash Flow Statement

Add a form for start-up costs and a description of your accounting system, and you've got it. Yes, this is going to hurt, but not that much. You may even find it interesting. But just in case you're tempted to skip this part, here's a *BIG WARNING: If you're not the numbers type, then get a job.* You haven't got what it takes to run a business. Nobody cares whether you make money or go broke.

The only way you'll make money is to keep track of everything via the income statement and the balance sheet. Do this now, and do it regularly after you're actually in business. Skip it, and you'll probably go broke. It's that simple and that cruel. The successful business owner manages money well, no matter what type of business he or she is in. Now let's get to work.

Start-up Costs

Make a list of all the things you'll need on your first day in business. It should look something like this:

Fixtures and Equipment (tools, trucks, etc.)	$_____
Materials and Supplies (parts, etc.)	$_____
Office Supplies	$_____
Decorating and Remodeling	$_____
Legal and Professional Fees	$_____
Licenses and Permits	$_____
Initial Advertising	$_____
Operating Cash	$_____
Owner's Draw Prior to Start-Up	$_____
Contingency	$_____
TOTAL	$_____

The total is the amount of money you'll need to set up your business. Most of these are pretty easy to figure out. Be realistic about the cost of things, and allow enough to cover actual costs. For example, don't figure you'll spend $500 for a truck, because you know you can't get a reliable one for that price. It'll soon break down, and the repairs will probably be more than the purchase price. Some costs, such as advertising, you simply carry forward from your work in previous sections of the business plan. Others require a little homework.

A couple of items need to be explained. Operating Cash is the money you'll need to run the business until it becomes profitable. (*Warning:* The chief cause of failure for start-up businesses is insufficient capital.) Ever optimistic, new business owners assume all they have to do is hang their sign out and in no time they'll be driving around in a fancy European sedan, talking for hours on their car phone, and having lunch in Paris. No way. If you have debts, you'll have to service them. That's a fancy banker's way of saying pay off your loans. Also, you may not have a lot of business at first. Finally, it'll take you a while to figure out how to make a profit, especially if you just quit your job at the burger stand. The bottom line? You have to have funds to cover yourself while you're getting started. (You'll get an exact amount for this item after you've done your cash flow projections in a little while. For now, leave it blank.)

Owner's Draw Prior to Start-Up is grocery money, shoes for the kids, and that sort of thing. Allow for it.

Finally, something you'll soon be familiar with: Contingency—the money you've allowed to cover your very human tendency to underestimate the cost of nearly everything and your understandable tendency to assume everything will go just the way you planned it.

Now, when you go to the bank, you can say, "Here's what I need, so how 'bout it?" But, hold on. Did you think they'd finance you 100 percent? Sorry, but investors (banks or anybody else with half a brain) are going to expect you to risk your own money first, up to reasonable limits. That's called owner's equity. If you were to work entirely off of other people's money, you could just walk away if things started going bad, couldn't you? Investors know that. They want *your* neck on the block along with theirs, otherwise they won't play. So that means you'll have to put up at least some of this money. You don't need to sell the house, but you may be asked if you'd be willing to take out a second mortgage on it. Or pull some money out of savings.

So now you need to look at your own financial picture and ask yourself how much you can come up with on your own. Maybe you don't need investors after all. If you do, how much money are you going to ask them for? That's the bottom line.

If you're buying a business, you need to look at the price of the business plus the carrying costs and contingency. Other than that, the same rules apply.

Sales Projections

Let's think a minute about your sales projections in general terms. Are you going to remain a one-person operation forever? That's fine. Are you planning to employ several people after the first year? That's fine, too. To achieve your goals, you have to know how much you'll need in sales. In other words, it takes a lot more business to keep ten people working than just one.

What's the dollar volume of your sales expectations over the first five years? For the one-person maintenance operation you might be satisfied with $20,000 in sales the first year, operating part-time, and $60,000 every year thereafter. This would be a modest goal, and your expectation would be to make a basic living for yourself. These sales figures are the total amount you take in. They include the big four: labor, materials, overhead, and profit. You don't get to keep the whole $60,000. Too bad.

On the other hand, you might need $300,000 per year to keep a three-person landscaping outfit in business. (*Note:* Sales per person in landscaping are higher partly because there are a lot more materials used.) Can you realistically expect to achieve that in the first year? Or should you make that your third-year goal? In the financial section, you'll fully justify these projections; for now you need to simply state them.

One more thing about sales: They'll vary seasonally. In cold climates, winter is the slow season. In hot climates, it may be the opposite. For me, fall is busier than spring because people procrastinate, then panic at the last minute. Summer's slow because everyone's on vacation. Ask around and find out what the seasonal sales curve is for your area. You won't be able to get straight answers from your local competition unless you resort to some very sneaky spy tactics. But guess what? People a couple of counties distant from you might tell you a lot because you're not a potential competitor. Try going to a state gathering of your trade association and buying drinks for a few successful people.

Profit-and-Loss Projections

Also known as an Income Statement, a P&L is a list of all your income and expenses for a given period, usually a month or a year. When you're actually in business, you'll do these at the end of every month. For now, you're going to project the same information, on a monthly basis, for the first five years. Simplified just a bit for now, a typical landscaper's P&L looks like the one on pages 66–67.

Let's look first at the general structure of the P&L. Income is pretty self-explanatory: Whatever checks you get from clients for

Sample Profit-and-Loss Projection Sheet

INCOME

Sales, Landscaping $ _____
Sales, Maintenance $ _____
Sales, Other $ _____
TOTAL INCOME $ _____

COST OF SALES

Dump Fees $ _____
Equipment Rental $ _____
Labor $ _____
Materials & Supplies $ _____
Miscellaneous $ _____
Outside Services $ _____
TOTAL COST OF SALES $ _____

GROSS PROFIT (income minus cost of sales) $ _____

GENERAL OVERHEAD

Accounting $ _____
Advertising $ _____
Bank Charges $ _____
Car & Truck Expense $ _____
Depreciation $ _____

Dues & Subscriptions $ _____
Entertainment & Meals $ _____
Insurance $ _____
Interest Expense $ _____
Legal Expense $ _____
Licenses & Permits $ _____
Meetings & Seminars $ _____
Miscellaneous $ _____
Postage $ _____
Professional Fees $ _____
Rent/Real Estate $ _____
Repairs & Maintenance $ _____
Supplies, Office $ _____
Taxes, Sales $ _____
Taxes, Other $ _____
Telephone $ _____
Tools $ _____
Travel & Lodging $ _____
Uniforms $ _____
Utilities $ _____
Wages $ _____

TOTAL GENERAL OVERHEAD $ _____

NET PROFIT (LOSS) (gross profit minus overhead) $ _____

work you did for them go here, sorted out by whatever categories you choose. In this case, we're segregating Income into Landscaping, Maintenance, and Other. Cost of Sales is sometimes called Variable or Controllable Expense. It's the stuff that goes into the actual work you do for your clients, as opposed to overhead. The more work you have, the higher your Cost of Sales. Buy a bag of fertilizer, it gets entered into Cost of Sales under Materials & Supplies. Buy a box of pencils for the office, it gets entered into General Overhead (aka Fixed Expenses) under Supplies, Office. Simple, right?

Now look what happens. In July, you take in $1 million (let's dream). Your Cost of Sales is $750,000, due to the unpleasant fact that you have to pay your employees, vendors, and a bunch of other people. The quarter-mil you have left over is your Gross Profit. "Gross, indeed," you might say, "I had a lot of money there for a little while. Could've gone to Brazil and lived like a king." Now you're getting the idea. Still, you're an honorable person, so you pay everybody.

Next, there's the General Overhead. All the costs of operating your business, the ones that continue even if there's no work, go here. Let's say they add up to $200,000. Deduct that from your Gross Profit, and you're left with a Net Profit of $50,000. Not bad for a month's work. But wait—that's only a 5 percent profit. You can do better than that at the bank! Fifty grand is *lousy* for this sales volume. You should feel rotten! To justify your existence you need to make at least 10 percent. Next month, you'll just have to try harder.

Besides, what if your General Overhead was $270,000? You would have *lost* $20,000! Yikes! Time to start looking for a job!

Well, naturally this is a bit fanciful, because you'll probably never take in a million bucks in one month, even your best month. Still, I hope you get the idea of how profit and loss works, because understanding this concept thoroughly is important to your success.

Now, let's suppose you do these projected P&Ls for the first five years. Things look good to you on paper, but any banker can see you're nuts to put in such optimistic figures. For example, if you project that Cost of Sales will run 10 percent of Total Income and General Overhead another 10 percent, leaving 80 percent for you, you'll look stupid or conniving or both. There goes your credibility and your loan. So, how do you know what to put in all those little blank spaces? Let's take it step by step. (See chapter 4 for a discussion about cash versus accrual accounting, another important aspect of financial control. The following examples use a cash basis for the accounting.)

Income. How much work can you realistically do each month and each year? That depends on a lot of factors. Among them are crew size (think of each person as a profit center, capable of generating a certain amount of work per day), productivity, quantity of work available, and selling prices in your area at any given time.

First, consider exactly what kind of work you'll be doing. Mowing lawns? Great. What's the going rate in your area? (*Hint:* Call a couple of competitors and ask them what they charge.) Maybe it's priced by the square foot. Now, given a certain mower type and allowing for travel time and nonproductive time like loading up in the morning, how many square feet can you mow in a week? A little arithmetic, and there's your income.

Some kinds of work are a little harder to figure. For example, let's suppose you'll be doing custom landscape carpentry—fences and arbors and decks. Let's say you and your helper are working a forty-hour week. You figure you'll bill yourself out at $22 per hour and the helper at $15. Your total labor billings would be $1,480 per week or about $6,170 per month, assuming you could work every week ($1,480 times 50 weeks divided by 12 months. No, there aren't exactly four weeks in a month.)

Now, let's say you'll sell your materials for an amount equal to your labor. Conveniently, labor and materials often equal each other on many kinds of work. For projections like these, it might be safe to go with this assumption. Better yet, call the lumberyard, get some prices, figure out how much lumber you can use up in a week.

Remember that you should be marking up most materials at least a little bit, 10 percent minimum. You should make money on materials as well as labor. That's normal. Some items, such as plants, are quite profitable—you can usually increase the wholesale price (the price you pay the supplier) by 50 to 100 percent and still remain competitive. Others, such as the lumber in this example, are sold to you at maybe a 10 to 20 percent discount off retail, so there's not as much profit. How you express these prices depends on whether you're working on a time-and-materials basis or a lump-sum bid, but either way the markup is still there. Often, the markup on materials is what makes the difference between profit and loss on the job. Read about bidding in chapter 7 for more information on this important subject.

You'll have some other expenses, too, such as equipment rental and maybe subcontractor costs. You'll need to at least recover these costs, and you should make a 20 percent profit on them. So, after figuring out what those costs will be (do some test bids, call subs, etc.), you might decide to add another $2,200 a month to cover them. Your Total Income would then be $14,540.

Of course, in winter your income will probably drop. That's why you do P&Ls for each month, then add them up to get the year's income.

Remember, projecting this stuff is a fine art. Do all your homework, figure things as best you can. Project, don't just guess. Spend time, examine your assumptions, take it to your accountant, run your numbers by that landscaper you met at the state convention. It's important that you do this right, because if your assumptions are wrong, you'll be in for a shock after a year in business.

Cost of Sales. Next, you deduct your anticipated variable costs one-by-one to arrive at a total cost of sales. Remember that these expenses vary directly with the amount and kinds of work you do.

Here's where you put the actual amounts you pay for labor, materials, and incidental expenses. For instance, the *cost* of your lumber goes into the Materials & Supplies category. Money you pay employees goes into Labor. Money you pay to subcontractors gets entered into Outside Services.

General Overhead. Under normal business conditions, these figures don't change with the ups and downs of sales. You enter them month-by-month, remembering that some of them will only occur at certain times of the year or will vary throughout the year. For example, your accounting costs will increase markedly at tax time. It's important that you enter expenses in months when they actually get paid, because they'll affect your cash flow then. Figure your Advertising budget based on the marketing strategy you developed earlier in the business plan. Depreciation is based on the cost and age of your equipment; ask your accountant for help on this one. Continue the process, entering an amount in each category, for each month. Add it all up, and there's your General Overhead.

Net Profit (Loss). Hopefully, you'll show a 10 or 20 percent net profit. Why? Well, recently someone asked me why businesses should show a profit, as if it was some kind of crime against the people. First of all, without a profit, you're just making wages, and if you're going to settle for that, well, why not get a job and save yourself all this hassle? Second, without profit, there's no reserve to pay for problems, replacement of expensive equipment as it wears out, research and development, or improvements in service. Finally, profit is the earnings you hope to make on the money you and your investors put up to start and carry the business. So, don't be afraid of honest profit. You're taking the risk, making the investment, doing the hard work. You've got a right to that profit.

By the way, if you're sharp, you're wondering where *your* salary comes from. Good question. The answer is, that depends. When you start, your income will come out of Cost of Sales ("above the line," business people sometimes say), because you'll be helping to do the jobs and should be paying yourself an hourly wage just as if you were an employee. Later, you may abandon the fieldwork and become a full-time manager. Now, you've moved "below the line" and become a part of overhead. Now your income must come out of owner's draw or out of profits. Many, many people get to this point and don't understand that they've just added $30,000 or more to their overhead. Fail to account for that money in your bids, and you'll go broke. Remember to check on this in a few years when you think things are going just swell.

The easiest way to grind through five years of monthly P&Ls

is with a computer. Any spreadsheet program can make this task much easier. Can you borrow one? If not, go ahead and do it manually, but just do it.

Don't forget to increase sales by a realistic amount each year to account for anticipated improvements in your business and, incidentally, to take care of inflation. Naturally, when sales go up, so do expenses. Overhead probably goes up, too, especially if you're planning to grow. Every time you add a new element to your business, such as a secretary, more insurance, or a storage lot, your overhead takes a sudden large jump. This may cause you to lose money for a few months until the increase in business begins to pay for the added expenses. On the other hand, if you continue to work out of your home and keep your crew size small, maybe your overhead won't increase much at all.

Play around with the figures, make test assumptions, see what happens. When you're satisfied that everything is as accurate as possible and believable and you're comfortable with the scenario, put it all together in a neat form. Include a brief written explanation for your projections—what your reasoning was behind the major assumptions you've made.

The Cash Forecast

The Cash Forecast (aka the Cash Flow Projection) is a tool for predicting how much actual cash you'll have at any given time in the future. It's a simple way to tally up cash on hand, anticipated income, and anticipated expenses.

Why bother? Because you might be making a great profit on paper but have no money on hand, leading to what business people call a Cash Flow Crisis. How does this happen? Well, there are many possible scenarios, but often it's a simple matter of having too much month left over at the end of the money. If you get a big job and have to pay cash up front for materials, and maybe the progress payments weren't structured right, you'll suddenly be paying out more than you're taking in. The Cash Forecast is a way to avoid this unpleasant surprise. It's a tool you'll use to operate your business in the black, but you'll also include it in your business plan. Look at the example on page 73.

Cash Forecast Sheet

	JAN	FEB	MAR	APR	MAY	JUN	JUL	AUG	SEP	OCT	NOV	DEC
1. Cash in Bank (start of month)												
2. Petty Cash (start of month)												
3. Total Cash (add 1 and 2)												
4. Anticipated Cash Sales												
5. Anticipated Collections												
6. Other Anticipated Income												
7. Total Receipts (add 4, 5, and 6)												
8. Total Cash and Receipts (add 3 and 7)												
9. All Disbursements												
10. Cash Balance (subtract 9 from 8)												

You can see this isn't too complicated, but there are a couple of tips that will help you do it right. Where do you get the Cash in Bank figure? The first month, it's whatever you put into the account. For subsequent months, you simply carry forward the Cash Balance from the previous month. Petty Cash is incidental money set aside in the desk drawer or your pocket for incidental purchases. Anticipated Cash Sales are any amounts you may receive in cash or checks from clients. Anticipated Collections is money received for bills you sent to clients. All Disbursements refers to your total monthly cash outlay—payroll, materials purchased for cash, amounts paid on your charge accounts, office supplies, everything you expect to spend that month.

What if your Cash Balance is a negative number at the end of a month? Well, that means you're going to run out of money. It's a signal that you had better make some arrangements for a cash infusion from some source during that time period. As a part of the business plan, those negative numbers prove that you'll need start-up money and tell you approximately how much. Naturally, your forecast is based on educated guesswork, but attention to detail can get you pretty close. You should know by now what your overhead will be, so that's easy to include in Disbursements. Cost of Sales is, of course, a little trickier, as is income, but if you remember that your figures represent goals, and if you're willing to work hard to achieve those goals, you should be fairly accurate.

The Balance Sheet

The Balance Sheet shows your Assets, your Liabilities, and the difference between the two, called Net Worth. There's nothing mysterious about it. Unlike the Profit-and-Loss Statement, the Balance Sheet looks at the big picture: What's the final judgment on how you're doing? The example on pages 76–77 shows what it looks like.

As you can see, a balance sheet is simply a list. Fill in the blanks, and you're done. "Current Assets" are your liquid assets, ones you'll normally use within a year. If you have any doubtful Accounts Receivable (ones you think you'll never get paid for), use "Less allowance for bad debts" to exclude them. Use "Prepaid Expenses" for things like insurance that you've paid in advance. "Inventory" for a service business is usually small—maybe just a few bags of fertilizer in the toolshed, but they're still assets. "Fixed Assets" are ones you normally don't liquidate within the year. "Improvements" would include any office remodeling, sheds you've built, things like that. Liabilities are similarly separated into Current and Long-term. Now, the reason this is called a Balance Sheet is that the "Total Assets" have to equal "Liabilities & Net Worth." The difference between Assets and Liabilities is Net Worth. Well, that's all there is to a balance sheet.

These few simple forms have answered all the questions you or an investor might have about your financial projections for the first five years of your operations. True, the actual numbers will be different once you're in business, but if you're careful you won't be in for any rude surprises.

Description of Accounting Systems

The final step in preparing your financial information is to describe your proposed accounting and bookkeeping systems. Study chapter 4, then write a simple description of how you'll handle record keeping.

Some Tips on Raising Money

What if your projections show a net loss for the first year or two? That's not improbable, since you'll be paying for your start-up costs and maybe not having such great sales. That's when you know you've got to find some money to carry you through.

Conveniently, you now have an impressive document. Potential investors can see what your goals are, how much capital you'll need, and when and how you plan to pay it back.

Alternative Sources of Financing

The bank will probably be happy to lend you money for a piece of new major equipment, because they can repossess it pretty eas-

Balance Sheet

ASSETS

CURRENT ASSETS

Cash:

Cash in Bank	$ ____
Cash on Hand	$ ____
Petty Cash	$ ____
Accounts Receivable	$ ____
Less allowance for bad debts	$ ____
Adjusted Accounts Receivable	$ ____
Prepaid Expenses	$ ____
Inventory	$ ____
TOTAL CURRENT ASSETS	$ ____

FIXED ASSETS

Land	$ ____
Buildings	$ ____
Equipment & Fixtures	$ ____
Less allowance for depreciation	$ ____
Adjusted Equipment & Fixtures	$ ____

Improvements $_____
TOTAL FIXED ASSETS $_____

TOTAL ASSETS $_____

LIABILITIES

CURRENT LIABILITIES
  Accounts Payable $_____
  Notes Payable (due w/in one year) $_____
  Payroll Taxes, Current $_____
  Sales Taxes, Current $_____
TOTAL CURRENT LIABILITIES $_____

LONG-TERM LIABILITIES
  Notes Payable (due after one year) $_____

TOTAL LIABILITIES $_____

NET WORTH (Owner's Equity) $_____
LIABILITIES & NET WORTH $_____

ily if you get behind in your payments. They'll be less likely to give you a loan for general operating expenses. If you can't get a bank loan for general funds, what do you do to cover your needs?

Well, there are two basic classes of financing: debt and equity. A loan is an example of debt financing: You borrow money and then pay off principal and interest over a period of time. Remember that you have to pay loans back in full and on time. Failing to do so will ruin your credit rating, a major mistake when you're in business. Guard your good credit with your life, just like your dad told you to.

Equity financing is different: In exchange for money, you give up part of the ownership of your company. Since you'll be starting out small, you'll probably want to use debt financing, but you should know about both. Here are the commonly used alternatives.

Vendor Credit and Progress Payments (Debt). Fortunately, there are a couple of important methods of financing built right into standard business procedure. One is vendor credit; another is progress payments. They're linked in an important way. (See chapter 8 to learn more about these topics.) These are the everyday sources of money for your business. Here's the idea: You buy on credit, collect money your clients owe you, and use it to pay your bills. There's no interest charge if you pay on time. (Related to this is accounts receivable financing, which is sometimes used as a short-term solution to a cash crunch. A bank or other lender advances you a percentage of the value of your good receivables. It'll cost you, so don't use this unless you get into trouble.)

Vehicle Loans (Debt). If you choose to buy a new truck, you'll have no problem financing it as long as your personal credit is OK. Using a loan to purchase the vehicle is the commonest and least costly way to do this, but you can also lease a vehicle. A lease costs more than a loan and has some other disadvantages, but unlike a purchase you can usually take possession with very little money out of pocket. Buy if you can, lease if you must.

Turning Fixed Assets into Cash (Debt). Take out a second mortgage on your house if you need to. If you have an old high-interest loan, you might consider refinancing, which could lower your monthly payments, freeing up cash you can put into the business. You may even be able to pull some cash out of your equity. Talk to a reputable mortgage broker to find out what your options are.

Personal Loan (Debt). If you have good credit and a good relationship with your bank, maybe you can get an unsecured personal loan. Then there's the loan (gift?) from mom and dad or good old Uncle Harry. As for loans from your boyfriend, girlfriend, best friend, or whatever, do what you want, but you might want to ask a few people who've been there whether that's such a good idea. It can be a great way to end a relationship. Be careful.

Partnerships (Equity). Partners share ownership, investment, and risks. Not all partnerships are 50/50; they can be structured any way you want. Read the section on partnerships, and decide whether you really need a partner.

Nonprofessional Investors (Equity). Mom and dad, Uncle Harry, a co-worker, a friend, possibly a supplier or even a client—all could potentially be equity investors in your company. Do you want to share ownership with them? Remember, they'll be looking over your shoulder all the time. Maybe this is a good idea, maybe not. Before you do this, talk to an accountant, an attorney, and yourself.

SBICs and Similar Investors (Equity). The government operates or sponsors numerous kinds of small business investment organizations. Call the Small Business Administration for current information.

Selling Assets. Do you have idle personal assets that you could liquidate, either now or if you need them in the future? Look at your entire financial picture, not just your proposed new business.

4

Learning to Live with Record Keeping

If I have you figured right, you're probably not a records type of person. You love the outdoors, physical work, action. You hate bean counting, writing little things in little boxes on little pieces of paper, keeping track of numbers. "My momma didn't raise me to be no clerk!" is your motto. OK. Fine. But listen carefully to some of the best advice in this book:

Records, believe it or not, make life easier. Just ask anybody who's been audited by the IRS. Or who's been sued. Or anybody who ended up losing a million-dollar job because they lost track of an important piece of information. *Records are your friends. They are life itself.*

Here's something your momma may have told you. I know mine did, over and over, and she was right. "You'll just have to learn to like certain things. That's life." If you hate record keeping, learn to like it. I can help.

Let's get you set up with a good basic record-keeping system so you avoid all the stupid and unnecessary hassles other beginning business owners go through. It's another step in doing things right the first time, in being a true professional. It's not hard. It's a lot easier than the alternative. It is. Let's go.

Bookkeeping

Bookkeeping is the recording and management of financial information relating to your business as a whole. This includes the checking account, income ledger, expense ledger, income and expense statements, balance sheets, and cash flow projections.

For some reason, bookkeeping terrifies most people. In reality, the worst thing that can be said about bookkeeping is that it's tedious. There's nothing mysterious or all that complicated about it, and it can be mastered easily by anyone. But, of course, there are things you want to know.

Why do I need to keep books? First, the Internal Revenue Service requires that you keep records of where the money went. They have certain well-defined minimum standards, and if you don't adhere to them, they take your house. A pizza box stuffed with a mish-mosh of receipts and invoices and cancelled checks doesn't meet minimum standards.

Next, *you* need to know where the money went, too, because it may be going down the toilet and taking your business with it. That's where bookkeeping comes in; it's a record of income and expenses, money owed to you, money you owe others, and money in the bank account. Period.

Is this going to get real complicated? No. You're going to learn how to set up a simple set of books that will serve you well in the early years of your business. Later, you can get real complicated if you need to. But even if you do, the basics are still the same.

How much time will I have to spend doing bookkeeping? For now, probably under half an hour a day, every working day, to keep everything current, then three or four hours every month to reconcile everything. Less if you use a computer.

What if I just hire somebody else to do it? No. Not at first. Hire someone, and you'll never pay any attention to the matter again until you're in bankruptcy court. The bookkeeper will hand you things, and you won't have the slightest idea what you're looking at. And if the bookkeeper is a larcenous type, he or she will soon figure out how to rip you off. Keep your books yourself.

But what about an accountant? An accountant is another matter. First, let's talk about the difference between a bookkeeper and an accountant. The bookkeeper enters the day's activities—income and expenses—into the books. The accountant periodically takes that information and uses it to generate profit-and-loss statements, balance sheets, and (perhaps most important) tax returns. An accountant also advises you on the direction your business is going and can keep you out of financial trouble. Yes, you probably do need an accountant. Good ones, though expensive, will pay for themselves in tax savings alone. Tax laws, always complex, have become truly Byzantine, impossible for the layperson to understand. Understanding them is the accountant's job. Budget $200 to $300 per year to pay for the accountant.

Can a computer help me? Yes and no. No computer program can replace an accountant. That's like letting a robot do brain surgery. But a good accounting software package can help you with routine bookkeeping chores and will produce an impressive and useful set of financial records at the click of a mouse button—income-and-expense statements, balance sheets, and others. A computer can make bookkeeping easier to do, and it can save you lots of time. Many systems will even write checks for you.

Finally, accounting software for the small business is cheap. You still need to understand the principles, though, so we're going to look at bookkeeping in more traditional terms. If you decide to computerize, it'll be easier because you learned the old-fashioned way. (*Tip:* When you do get a computer, one possibility is using a spreadsheet program to replicate the forms used here. The advantage of this approach is that you'll be adapting something you're already familiar with. You'll have the benefits of perfect accuracy, automatic calculation, "what if" analysis, and more, without a lot of new learning to do.)

Forms of Bookkeeping

Single-Entry Versus Double-Entry

With a single-entry system, you record each transaction only once. For example, when you write a check to the nursery, you record it in the expense ledger as check number so-and-so, Wilsonville Nursery, May 8, $416.50. You do the same with income, in the income ledger. At the end of the month, you total them up, subtract expenses from income, and hopefully end up with a positive number. It's a simple system that's adequate for many small businesses. The drawback is that there's no way to know if you made a mistake. Since it's easy to transpose numbers or add wrong when doing the entries, this is a significant risk.

In a double-entry system, each transaction is recorded twice—once as a "debit" and once as a "credit." The check to Wilsonville Nursery would be entered in two categories: once in Merchandise & Materials as a debit (increasing the amount) and once in Cash in Bank as a credit (decreasing the amount). The debits and credits must balance, which is how you check for errors. The drawback here is that it takes more time. It's also harder to understand.

I suggest you begin with either a manual single-entry system or a computerized double-entry system. Either is easy to learn and adequate for your needs. I began with a ready-made single-entry system from the office supply store. I learned to use the system in about an hour, and it served me well for many years until I finally got a computer. Then I went to a computerized double-entry system that I'm still using.

Cash Versus Accrual

Using the cash method, you enter income when it's received and expenses when they're paid. Even though it's called a "cash" system, checks and money orders are treated the same as cash. If you deposit a check from Mrs. Jones, you enter it into the income ledger as of that date. Likewise, you enter the check you wrote to Wilsonville Nursery as of the date you wrote it.

Using the accrual method, you record income as of the date the transaction occurs. For instance, when you send Mrs. Jones a bill for last month's gardening work, you enter the amount as a sale in your income ledger even though you haven't received the money yet. When you charge something at the nursery, you enter that as an expense, even though you haven't paid the bill. Accrual accounting, like double-entry bookkeeping, is more complex and requires more work. Either cash or accrual bookkeeping can be a single- or double-entry system.

So, why would anyone want to use the accrual method? Because it gives a more accurate picture of your financial condition. Do you *need* to use the accrual method? No. In fact, because yours is a service business with no inventory, the cash method is preferred. (*Tip:* The IRS needs to know which method you're using. You can change from cash to accrual without asking permission, as long as you do it at the beginning of a fiscal year and tell them about it. Ask your accountant for more information.)

The key to using a cash system successfully is collecting from your clients as soon as the jobs are finished and paying your bills as soon as they're due.

Fiscal Year Versus Calendar Year Accounting Period

Large businesses often use a "fiscal year" as the basis for their bookkeeping: a twelve-month period beginning at some time other than January 1. If you'll be operating as a sole proprietor or a partnership, you're required to use a standard "calendar year"—January 1 through December 31.

A Simple Bookkeeping System, Step-by-Step

Here's a basic set of books and instructions for how to use them. It's a single-entry, cash-basis system that operates on a regular calendar year. You can set them up in under a hour using a couple dollars worth of ledger paper and a box of file folders.

The Chart of Accounts

The heart of the system is a list of all your income and expense categories called a Chart of Accounts. Accountants will include other items in the Chart of Accounts, such as asset and liability categories that are used to produce the balance sheet, but for now all you need is the income and expense portions. Every transaction—income and expenditures—is then entered into one of these categories, using the income and expense ledgers. Each category is given a four-digit account number. To conform with standard accounting practice, numbers for income accounts are in the 4000 range and expense accounts in the 5000 range. Numbering is done in steps of 10, which allows you to enter new categories later without disrupting the system; you just insert the category as 5055, in between 5050 and 5060. A typical landscaper's chart of accounts looks like the one on page 87.

Naturally, many of these categories require a little explanation. First of all, notice the layout: first income, then expenses, with the expenses divided into variable and fixed expenses so that you can separate the job-related costs (variable) from general overhead (fixed). Notice, too, that the numbering jumps from the 5000s in variable expenses to the 5500s in the fixed expenses. That keeps them both in the 5000 range but gives them a little breathing room from each other. Now let's look at specifics.

Income

You could divide your income up any which way. You might want to put each crew into its own income category, or subdivide maintenance into commercial and residential, or add categories for other kinds of work you specialize in, such as sprinkler repair or tree work. All the IRS will want to see on your profit-and-loss statement is income, period. The special categories are for you, so set them up however you want.

Expenses, Variable

Remember, these are all your job-related costs. I've shown some of the common ones, but again, you may wish to add or delete.

Labor is payroll and its related labor burden (taxes, worker's compensation insurance, etc.), but you might wish to divvy this up to show labor burden as one or more separate categories. Up to you. Don't put the office help or other employees that aren't

CHART OF ACCOUNTS
JOE'S LANDSCAPING & GARDENING CO.

INCOME

4000	Sales, Landscaping
4010	Sales, Maintenance
4020	Sales, Other

EXPENSES, VARIABLE (COST OF SALES)

5000	Dump Fees
5010	Equipment Rental
5020	Labor
5030	Materials & Supplies
5040	Miscellaneous
5050	Outside Services

EXPENSES, FIXED (GENERAL OVERHEAD)

5500	Accounting
5510	Advertising
5520	Bank Charges
5530	Car & Truck Expense
5540	Depreciation
5550	Dues & Subscriptions
5560	Entertainment & Meals
5570	Insurance
5580	Interest Expense
5590	Legal Expense
5600	Licenses & Permits
5610	Meetings & Seminars
5620	Miscellaneous
5630	Postage
5640	Rent/Real Estate
5650	Repairs & Maintenance
5660	Supplies, Office
5670	Taxes, Sales
5680	Taxes, Other
5690	Telephone
5700	Tools
5710	Travel & Lodging
5720	Uniforms
5730	Utilities
5740	Wages

doing the actual landscaping work here. They'll have their own category that you'll learn about in a minute.

Use Materials & Supplies only for things that actually get incorporated into your jobs, not for mower parts or building materials for your shed—those go into fixed expenses since they're not job related. But suppose you bought a tool and wore it out on one job. Should you call it a material for that job and therefore a variable expense? You could argue this either way, but I would think its cost should be included in the cost of the job, therefore it's a job related expense.

Miscellaneous is a good friend—it'll accept stuff you can't figure out where to put. But if you keep putting the same kind of stuff into this category, set up a new category for it.

Outside Services is for subcontractors you bring onto your jobs, such as the electrician who puts in an outlet for your sprinkler controller or the arborist who diagnoses and treats a diseased tree.

Expenses, Fixed

Advertising could include a number of things other than ad space you buy in the local paper. For instance, the cost of business cards could be put here (or in Supplies, Office if you prefer.) Photos you take of your jobs to show to prospective clients could be posted to Advertising. So could "Joe's Landscaping & Gardening Co." T-shirts.

Bank Charges are monthly charges for your checking account, overdraft charges (shame!), and the like. However, interest on your credit card purchases (shame again!) might preferably be put into the Interest category. (Do you see that there aren't such rigid rules here? Figure out how you want things, ask your accountant if it's OK, then do it.) Those bank charges are an exception to the rule that every expense must be represented by a check, since they're simply deducted from your account balance by the bank. So remember to post (that's accountant language for writing something into a ledger) them here even though you didn't write a check for them.

Car & Truck Expense is any money you spend on maintaining your vehicles: oil changes, repairs, etc. You can put your vehicle insurance here or in the Insurance category. *Warning:* These categories (all of them) are for *expenses*, not Capital Expenditures such as the purchase of a truck or major improvements to assets (like remodeling your office). These major purchases are called Fixed Assets and are depreciated in the next category, Depreciation.

Any asset (truck, mower, office remodel) that you expect to last longer than one year must be depreciated, that is, written off over the anticipated life of the asset. Let's say you buy a mower for $800.00. The IRS has rules about how fast you can depreciate various things and maybe they say you have to depreciate your new machine over a four-year period. That means you can write off only $200.00 this year, $200.00 next year, and so on. (That's real oversimplified; you need to get the IRS booklet on depreciation or talk to your accountant. Please do it.) So if you want, you can enter $1/12$ of $200.00, or $16.67, into this category each month. If you prefer, you can just wait until the end of the year and enter the whole thing, but posting it every month will give you a more accurate picture of your financial condition. (Like Bank Expenses, this isn't going to be represented by a check, of course.) Remember that depreciation is a big expense, even when you're small, so whatever you do, don't forget to account for it.

Dues & Subscriptions can be used for trade association dues, membership in the botanic garden, business magazine subscriptions.

Entertainment & Meals might puzzle you. "Who am I going to be entertaining?" you may ask. Well, maybe you'll take a prospective client to lunch, or a general contractor you're trying to impress. You also use this category to account for any meals you have while out of town on business, at a trade show or a seminar.

Insurance can cover all your insurance, or you could break this up into several categories like liability insurance, vehicle insurance, bonds, and so forth.

Interest Expense is a catch-all category for any kind of interest you pay, such as interest on vehicle loans, business loans, credit card purchases, or mortgage interest. *Warning:* If you work out of a home you own, you can deduct a percentage of the mortgage *interest*, but not the entire mortgage payment. The IRS won't let you get away with having the business pay for the principal on your house; they consider that going too far. So, if you use, for example, 20 percent of the total square footage of your house and land for business purposes (office, storage yard, sheds, etc.) then you deduct 20 percent of the interest you pay to the mortgage company each month.

Legal Expense is for attorney fees. You'd better hope this category stays real empty, except for an annual legal checkup with your friendly attorney.

Licenses & Permits covers fees for business licenses, contractor's license, and related expenses.

Meetings & Seminars is for fees you pay to attend professional educational events. (No, not that Saturday golf clinic. Sorry.)

Then there's Miscellaneous again for whatever didn't fit elsewhere. These Miscellaneous categories had better not get too full of questionable expenses. The IRS will raise an official eyebrow.

Postage is for stamps, overnight package services, courier services, and similar items.

Rent/Real Estate: If you rent your house rather than owning it, or if you rent a storage yard, use this category to account for these costs.

Repairs & Maintenance is for repairs to anything, though you may want to use it only for tools of the trade, not office equipment.

Supplies, Office is used for letterheads, copier paper, pens and pencils, books, etc.

Taxes, Sales is used when and if you pay sales taxes (see Tax Planning, chapter 9).

Taxes, Other is for business property tax, real property tax (a percentage of your home's property taxes goes here), and any other business taxes. (*Tip:* You can't enter your personal income taxes here as an expense. They're not an expense, and the IRS knows that just as well as you do. People who pull that one get a little room at Leavenworth. Nice try.)

Telephone ought to be simple, because you'll have a separate business phone line not used for personal purposes (won't you??). Sometimes the phone company bills you for Yellow Pages advertising, and that really should be separated out of the total amount of the payment and posted to Advertising.

Tools is for small tools like rakes, pruning shears, gas cans, and whatnot. Remember, any big items that last over a year have to be depreciated, not posted here. *Exception:* You can "expense" (write off in one year) a certain dollar amount of tools and equipment if you choose to. A reasonable maximum is $200 per purchase; there's also a limit to the annual total. Ask your accountant first, because there are rules and are also important tax consequences.

Travel & Lodging is for hotel, airfares, taxis, anything related to a business trip. A business trip? That's travel for business purposes like meeting with a client, attending a seminar or convention, researching new developments in your field. Not golf, even if you *are* a turf expert. By the way, you can take a trip that's only part business and still write off that portion. There are, of course, rules, so ask first.

Uniforms: Naturally, you'll want to look professional, so you'll have a category for the cost of purchasing, maintaining, and replacing uniforms.

Utilities: You'll write off a percentage of your gas, water, and electric bills and post them here.

Wages: Payroll for any non-job-related employees goes here. This could be a part-time office helper, a salaried estimator, a salesperson, or a mechanic. Admittedly you may not use this category at first, but it's a good idea to have it in there, if only to remind you of the bright future ahead of you as a landscaping big shot.

The Bank Account

For cash-basis accounting, the bank account is the beginning of all transactions. First, get a separate checking account for the business. (See chapter 2 for information on how to do this.) You'll deposit all business income into this checking account and pay all your business bills from it. No exceptions. That way, things are simple and orderly. If you somehow end up paying for something any other way, such as out of your personal checking account (a pox on you!), pay yourself back by writing a check from the business account. If you pay for something in cash (sometimes necessary), reimburse yourself by check. (See Petty Cash on page 98.) If you want to pay yourself, write a check to yourself and label it "Owner's Drawings."

Just as you don't pay business expenses from your personal checking account, never pay personal expenses from your business account. It's just too difficult to separate things later.

Finally, when you write a check, always record the payee (the person or company you're writing the check to). Never write a check to "cash," because you won't be able to post it to a specific expense account later. Regarding deposits, need I warn you to deposit all business income into this same checking account? No cashing client's checks to get beer money; they all have to go through the account first. (*Tip*: When you open your account, request "end-of-the-month cutoff" so that your statement will only be issued at the end of each month. This makes reconciling your bank statement easier.)

Be sure to identify each transaction completely. For payments, write the payee, the job name (if appropriate), the date, and the payee's invoice number in the check register. (Some checks cover multiple transactions, such as paying off your credit card statement. Remember that for such checks, you'll be posting them to several expense categories.) For income, enter the details into the income ledger, which we'll get to in a minute, and the total amount into the check register, using a date or a deposit number to cross-reference the two.

Checking Account Tips

Balance the account every month, as soon as you get the statement in the mail. It's easy and quick and keeps you from running out of money without knowing about it in advance. Balance just to the end of the month even if you've written checks into the next month. File all canceled checks and statements, and retain them for at least three years just in case you're audited. Use business-style checks, not small personal-style checks. If possible, don't carry your checkbook around with you, and *never* leave it unattended in your truck while you're in the donut shop. Theft is just too common nowadays, and having your checkbook stolen can cause you unimaginable disruption and agony. I know this from grim personal experience.

An Option: The One-Write System

With this special system, each time you make a deposit or write a check, you're automatically posting the information to the ledger. For a small business, this can be a great way to go. It's cheaper than a computerized system and easier than a manual system.

Accounts Receivable and the Income Ledger

Accounts receivable are simply the amounts owed you from clients. You need to keep track of what's coming to you.

The Invoice

Recording sales requires two steps. First, you prepare a written invoice for each sale. This could be a simple handwritten form from a preprinted invoice book you got at the office supply store. Use a rubber stamp with your company name and address to identify your business. Alternatively, you could have invoices printed with your company name or use a computer to generate invoices.

Sequentially numbered invoices provide you with a way to track each invoice thorough your system. If you make a mistake on an invoice, mark it "VOID" and keep it in your book. When you prepare an invoice, be sure to write in the date, the amount of the sale, a description, and whether it's paid for or not. If you're doing a time-and-materials job, be sure to enter the sales tax as a separate line item, because you'll need this later to do your sales tax return. Your client gets the original; you keep the carbon copy. Consider keeping a third copy in the client's file, so you'll have a record of all their transactions over the years. That way, if a question comes up, you can go directly to their file rather than having to search through your master invoice file.

Accounts Receivable

Until the client pays you, the invoice is part of your Accounts Receivable—the amounts owed you.

Here's a simple, reliable way to keep track of your receivables: Put a copy of each invoice into a file folder titled "Accounts Receivable," and keep it there until it's paid. Then move it to another file titled "Accounts Paid." That's it. Periodically, add up the totals on the invoices in the A/R file—that's how much money people owe you. If an invoice sits in the A/R file for more than 30 days, send the client a reminder. If it's still there after another 30 days, give them a call and ask when you can pick up the payment. (See chapter 8 for more information on getting paid.)

Keeping Track of the Accounts Receivable Balance

One of the things you need to do every week or two is reconcile the total value of your unpaid invoices with the reality of how much money people owe you; in other words, the two should be equal. Here's how you do it: First, you'll need to keep a running total of your receivables called an Accounts Receivable Balance. It's the sum of the previous A/R Balance plus the invoices you've written since then, minus the money you've been paid. Once you get that total, it becomes the new A/R Balance. Compare it to the total value of all the invoices in your A/R file; they should equal. If they don't, you know there's a mistake somewhere—a lost invoice, an incorrect amount entered somewhere, an arithmetic error. Here's how this looks on paper:

Previous A/R Balance	$ 1,756.49
New Invoices	914.16
Subtotal	$ 2,670.65
Bank Deposits	<- 1,122.03>
Checks on Hand, not deposited	0.00
New A/R Balance	$ 1,548.62
Total, Current Invoices Due	$ 1,548.62
Difference	$ 0.00

Income Ledger

When a check comes in, you'll deposit it into your checking account. But first, you need to enter it into the income ledger, a record of all your deposits. Look at the example on page 96. Although somewhat simplified, this format will probably work fine for quite a while. (*Tip:* You might consider adding a column for Sales Tax Collected, where you separate out the amount of sales tax on time-and-materials jobs. This makes doing your sales tax return easier and also reminds you that you owe this money to the government.) Let's look at some of the features of the income ledger.

The Date column will reflect the date of your deposit—the day you put the checks into your bank account. You'll notice that each deposit includes several checks and that each check has its own separate row of information. Description tells what portion of the job this payment is for. Code helps you remember whether this was a deposit (D), a progress payment (PP), a final payment (FP), or a payment on account (A/C).

(*Note:* A payment on account differs from a progress payment in an important way. Any payment made during the time you're doing the work is usually a progress payment. Any payment made after you've finished the work, but not a final payment, is called a payment on account. This doesn't come up too often, since you'll try to get a final payment as soon as you're done and not let people pay you off in stages. Still, now and then you have to make deals with people, so the indication A/C helps you.)

Cash and Check are partners: They're for entering the total amount of the payment. The next three columns separate that payment out into the different income categories. Notice the Gillon deposit on 3/12: Part of the check they wrote was for maintenance ($675.00) and that was payment in full; the rest ($1,000.00) was a deposit for the landscaping work that's going to start soon.

The Totals column on the right adds up the total amount that each client paid you. Note that if someone paid you part cash and part check, this Totals column would reflect the sum of both of these. Finally, there are totals for each column at the end of each

Sample Income Ledger

DATE	JOB NAME/DESCRIPTION	CODE	CASH	CHECK	4010 SALES, LANDSCAPING	4020 SALES, MAIN-TENANCE	4030 SALES, OTHER	TOTALS
3/4	Koenig/Front Slope Planting	FP		1,430.00	1,430.00			1,430.00
	Bowman/Maintenance Feb.	FP		240.00		240.00		240.00
	Northside Plaza/Consultation	FP		350.00			350.00	350.00
	TOTAL DEPOSIT			2,020.00	1,430.00	240.00	350.00	2,020.00
3/12	Gillon/ Landscape & Maint.	D/FP		1,675.00	1,000.00	675.00		1,675.00
	SWX Corp./Soil Test	A/C		100.00			100.00	100.00
	TOTAL DEPOSIT			1,775.00	1,000.00	675.00	100.00	1,775.00
3/27	Mullins/Maintenance Feb.	FP	165.00			165.00		165.00
	Lee/Back Yard	PP		10,000.00	10,000.00			10,000.00
	TOTAL DEPOSIT		165.00	10,000.00	10,000.00	165.00		10,165.00
	TOTAL FOR MONTH		165.00	13,795.00	12,430.00	1,080.00	450.00	13,960.00

deposit and grand totals for the month. With this simple system, you can easily see who paid you what, how much income you have in the different sales categories, and your total sales. Whenever you make a bank deposit, spend a couple of minutes recording this information into the income ledger (which you keep with your checkbook) and you'll always be current. There's no end-of-the-month bookkeeping nightmare. (*Warning:* Post the information to the ledger first, then fill out your deposit slip and enter the deposit total into the check register. That way you won't forget. It's a pain to have to reconstruct the information from invoices.)

Accounts Payable and the Expense Ledger

If your business was all income and no expenses, that'd be nice. Unfortunately you do have to pay people and companies for the things they provide you. To keep things simple, you make all these payments by check, all from the same business checking account. Then, to keep track of where the money went, you maintain an expense ledger, which is simply a list of expenses, segregated into categories and totaled up. Here's my simple system that's served me well for many years.

Accounts Payable

The job of your Accounts Payable system is to keep track of what you haven't yet paid. Like Accounts Receivable, there's a simple system I've used since time immemorial.

First of all, you need to understand that there are two kinds of purchases. One is *cash purchases*. An example is when you go to the mower shop and write check number 1416 for mower blades. The other is *charge purchases*, of which there are several kinds. The commonest is when you buy plants at the nursery and sign an invoice but don't write a check. The invoice goes into your file at the nursery and at the end of the month they bill you for all the invoices you've signed for that month. When you get the bill (known as a statement), you write a check and send it to the nursery. Another kind of charge purchase is a credit card purchase. For instance, you use your MasterCard to charge a repair for your truck. At the end of the month, you receive a statement, which you pay.

There are also recurring expenses such as rent and utilities. These are paid every month, usually at the same time of the month.

First, you need a file folder in which you stick all the invoices you get from your charge purchases. You call this folder "Invoices Unpaid." Second, you need a folder to keep your current Accounts Payable. In it you put statements from suppliers (note that these statements are related to the unpaid invoices in the previous folder), credit card statements, utility bills, phone bills, anything that you'll need to pay soon. To make this even better, I use three folders marked "Accounts Payable 1," "Accounts Payable 8," and "Accounts Payable 20." I pay my bills three times a month—on the 1st, 8th and 20th—and it's a snap to just pull out the appropriate folder and pay whatever's in it. That way, I don't have to sort through a messy stack of bills and figure out which ones are due and which ones aren't. It helps me be a lot more prompt, which is important in keeping the goodwill of my creditors.

Why those dates, you ask? Well, the mortgage payment is due on the 1st. Many suppliers offer a 2 percent discount if you pay your bills by the 10th of the month, so I pay on the 8th to take advantage of that. Finally, I pay the rest of the suppliers on the 20th; they can wait since they don't offer me any incentive to pay earlier, and I get interest on the money I keep in my checking account.

You should also create a temporary resting place (another set of folders) for all your paid bills, all sorted out by expense category. They'll sit there until you post them to the Expense Ledger, after which they'll get stamped PAID. You'll write the date and check number on them, and then they go into an identical set of folders called the "Posted Expense" files. That's the final resting place, at least until the end of the year when you pull them out and put them in the archives to make room for the next year's bills.

Petty Cash

What about items you paid for by cash, not check? The receipts for these go into yet another folder marked "Petty Cash." At the end of each month (or week if you prefer), you sort them out into the standard expense categories and make a simple ledger sheet listing them by category, with subtotals for each category and a grand total. You write yourself a check for the total, make as many copies of the petty cash ledger as there are expense categories, staple the invoices for each category onto a copy of the ledger and put it into the "Unposted Expense" files in their appropriate categories. Then later when you post the expense ledger, they show up along with other related expenses. See the example of a Petty Cash Ledger below.

Sample Petty Cash Ledger

PETTY CASH, 3/94	CHECK NO. 3452, 4/8/94	
DATE	ITEM	AMOUNT
ENTERTAINMENT & MEALS		
3/4	Doug's Deli (Ashville Job)	6.33
3/15	Harborview Restaurant (Boland Job)	26.55
3/22	Taste of Thailand (Optimist Club Meeting)	9.14
	SUBTOTAL	42.02
POSTAGE		
3/7	Postmaster (stamps)	2.90
3/19	Postmaster (Mail bid to Wallace)	2.16
	SUBTOTAL	5.06
SUPPLIES, OFFICE		
3/12	Office World (pencils)	3.45
3/27	Northside Bookshop (Marketing book)	10.59
	SUBTOTAL	14.04
	GRAND TOTAL	61.12

Expense Ledger

There are a couple of ways to do the Expense Ledger. However it's arranged, the information you need to include is the same: check number, date paid, to whom paid, amount, and expense category.

If you had just a few expense categories, it would be a simple matter to line them up across the page as in the example on page 101.

Unfortunately, you've got so many categories your spreadsheet would spread all the way across your desk and onto the floor. So, what to do? The cleanest approach I've seen uses two separate sheets, one for all the checks and one for the categories. It looks like the example on page 102.

Of course, a real system would include all the categories in the chart of accounts, but this shortened version will give you the idea. As you can see, it provides a running total of your expenses to date, which makes it easy to prepare a profit-and-loss statement.

Profit-and-Loss Statement

Go back to pages 66–67, and look at the sample profit-and-loss statement. You'll see that it's an easy matter to transfer the numbers from your income and expense ledgers to the appropriate categories and get yourself an instant P&L. You should do this at the end of each month so you stay informed on the condition of your business. Remember that with a cash bookkeeping system you won't get an exact picture of what's going on, because there may be outstanding income or expenses not shown in the current entries. To avoid the problems this may cause, adjust your figures to account for these anticipated changes.

Fixed Assets

You need to track the depreciation of your fixed assets. Either discuss depreciation with your accountant or get the current rules from the IRS or from a tax book. The rules change all the time, so stay current.

Sample Single-Sheet Expense Ledger

CK. NO.	DATE	TO WHOM PAID	AMOUNT	5020 LABOR	5030 MATLS & SUPPLIES	5510 ADVER-TISING	5530 CAR & TRUCK EXP.	5560 SUPPLIES OFFICE	5690 TELEPHONE
217	5/14	Coast Nursery	314.22		314.22				
218	5/16	Mary Cook	280.12	280.12					
219	5/16	Shell Oil Co.	56.10				56.10		
220	5/20	Bell South	221.50			195.00			26.50
221	5/20	Office Depot	12.70					12.70	
222	5/20	Farm Supply	201.88		201.88				
223	5/20	Auto World	83.14				83.14		
		TOTALS	1169.66	280.12	516.10	195.00	139.24	12.70	26.50

Sample Double-Sheet Expense Ledger

PAYMENTS

CHECK NO.	DATE	TO WHOM PAID	AMOUNT	ACCT. NO.
217	5/14	Coast Nursery	314.22	5030
218	5/16	Mary Cook	280.12	5020
219	5/16	Shell Oil Co.	56.10	5530
220	5/20	Bell South	195.00	5510
220	5/20	Bell South	26.50	5690
221	5/20	Office Depot	12.70	5660
222	5/20	Farm Supply	201.88	5030
223	5/20	Auto World	83.14	5530
		TOTAL	1,169.66	

EXPENSE LEDGER

ACCT. NO.	ACCOUNT	TOTAL THIS WEEK	TOTAL TO LAST WEEK	TOTAL, YEAR TO DATE
5020	Labor	280.12	6,715.22	6,995.34
5030	Materials & Supplies	516.10	7,783.65	8,299.75
5510	Advertising	195.00	817.14	1,012.14
5530	Car & Truck Expense	139.24	2,502.67	2,641.91
5660	Supplies, Office	12.70	224.60	237.30
5690	Telephone	26.50	107.13	133.63
	TOTALS	1,169.66	18,150.41	19,320.07

Balance Sheet

Reread the section on the balance sheet on pages 74–77 to refresh your memory about how this works. Note the connection between the profit-and-loss statement and the balance sheet: Your net worth will change in relation to the profit (or loss) you make. Therefore, you should do a balance sheet every month along with your P&L.

Tax Returns

At the end of the year, you or (preferably) your accountant uses the year-end Profit-and-Loss Statement and Balance Sheet to prepare your taxes. See the section on tax planning in chapter 9 for tips on avoiding nasty surprises at tax time.

General Business Records

You need to keep more records than just those required for taxes. Records accomplish several important tasks that just aren't possible any other way. There are two purposes to communications: to provide information to others ("Here's the price of the work." "Please be ready to pour the walkways on Friday." "You're fired.") and to get information back ("How much will the lighting system cost?" "Can you supply the roses by early next week?" "If I do this job, will you be able to pay me?"). Good communication achieves one or more of several important goals: It informs ("We'll be there Tuesday."), it clarifies ("Although the drawing doesn't specify, please use ³/₈-inch bolts on the gate."), it verifies ("Your price for the elm trees is OK."), it documents ("The lawn was sprayed on February 19."), and it protects ("You are hereby given a third and final warning about showing up late for work."). The best way to accomplish these goals is to put everything in writing and provide copies to all interested parties.

Remember that it's your job as a businessperson to make sure all parties (employees, suppliers, clients, etc.) are informed of what the others are doing. It will be one of your most constant and demanding tasks. If something goes wrong, it will automatically be assumed to be your fault, because you are at the center of the action, the hub on which all activities turn. You will answer for everything everybody else does, both good and bad. Without your active management of the communications process, people will make incorrect and potentially damaging assumptions ("He's going to do the additional work for free."). Bad communication is the stuff of which lawsuits are made.

The following information will provide you with some effective ways to keep yourself and your projects organized and to keep you out of trouble. Some are pretty standard, others I've developed over the years. They work for me, so they'll probably help you, too.

Client Files

Before you start developing a lot of forms, you'll need a place to put them and a system for their organization. The heart of the business record system is the client files. The simplest way to keep things orderly is to have a separate file folder for each client. Stapled to the inside is a sheet of paper with basic information about the client and the job. The sample printout on page 105 is from my computer database. If you start with a manual system, that's OK, just use the same information in any format you choose.

Filing Blueprints and Plans

Whether you design or bid from other people's plans, you'll accumulate a lot of blueprints. They're a nuisance. First, always fold up one copy and put it in the client's file. That's where you'll need to find it, after all, not in some dusty pile of rolls out in the garage. For originals (always keep the originals of any plans you draw) and additional copies, there are two ways to go. Rolled-up plans are space wasters, but easy to throw together in a box and call it a system. The problem is, how do you tell one from the other? Use special labels you can order from drafting places or tie hang-tags onto rubber bands and loop them around the end of the roll. The other approach is to use a flat file, but they cost a lot

Sample Client File

Owner's Name Petersen, Mr. & Mrs. Tim		Home Phone 453–2212		Type RES
Owner's Address 2389 East Madison Parkway				
Owner's City/St/Zip Gullville, CA 00456			Business Phone 883–2212 (Mr.)	
Company Name	Referred By Yellow Pages			Code/Misc.
Attention Mr. & Mrs. Tim Petersen	Creation Dt. 05/23/94		Salutation Mr. & Mrs. Peterson	
Job Name Petersen Residence			Job Phone 453–2212	
Job Address 2389 East Madison Parkway	Job City/State Gullville, CA		Job Zip 00456	
Agent's Name	Rating A		Can use as reference? Y N	

of money. Whatever you do, keep forever all plans for all jobs you've ever done. You may need them again.

Should You Computerize?

Computers are great at repetitive chores; they never forget anything, and they can do certain jobs you could never accomplish any other way. For example, suppose you were preparing a special mailer and wanted to find all your clients living in a certain zip code who did more than $2,000 in business with you last year and always paid their bills on time and have lawns larger than 5,000 square feet. If you were to rely on a manual search of your records, you'd be at it for hours. With a computer, it's a simple matter of telling it what you want and waiting a few seconds for the results.

On the other hand, computers are a pain. You'll spend many hours learning to use even the most user-friendly computer and software. Then you have to enter all that data, which takes more hours, and maintain the system, which will demand at least a couple of hours a month. And of course if it crashes, you lose everything.

Still, you'll gain more than you lose, and besides, computers are more fun than paper. Here are some of the things a computer can do for you:

Database. A database of your clients, coupled with a system of forms, can automate your entire flow of paperwork from the first contact with the client to the final bill. Your ability to respond (and therefore please) your clients will increase markedly once you computerize.

Bidding. Computerized bidding is faster, easier, and more accurate. You can plug your numbers into a spreadsheet and play "what-if" until you get the bid just right. Computer bidding can improve your competitiveness, responsiveness, and profitability.

Promotion and Presentation. Documents produced on the computer look worlds better than typed ones. Since you don't have much to impress potential clients with (no fancy store or zippy corporate image), your bids, promotional literature, and other handouts are your best chance at convincing them you're an OK person. Put something together on the computer, print it on your laser printer on some really classy paper, hand it to them in a nice folder, and wow! You're miles above your competition.

Bookkeeping and Taxes. Use a spreadsheet to automate your single-entry system or buy off-the-shelf software that will do your ledgers, accounts payable and receivable, profit-and-loss statements, and a lot more. It'll write the checks, post them, and spit out reports all day long.

Some Frequently Asked Questions About Computers

What kind of computer is best? The computer world has settled down to two kinds of systems: the IBM (or IBM compatible) and the Macintosh. Each has its fans and foes. Either approach is OK. The IBM has a couple of advantages: They're still somewhat cheaper, and there's more vertical market software available.

What's vertical market software? Any software package that's specially tailored for a particular industry or application, such as a package just for landscape contractors, is called vertical market software. The idea is that everything is all set up (computer guys call it "turn-key") and you can do everything you need to without much training. Theoretically it's written by people who understand your business and know what you need. Vertical market software is usually incredibly expensive.

Do you need it? Probably not. First, you're starting small, with relatively simple needs that can easily be met by a good off-the-shelf integrated package and a few hours of tinkering. You can set it up the way you want, not the way somebody thought you wanted. In fact, the way people do things in this business is so varied that I've never seen a vertical package that truly pleased very many people. Finally, how do you know if this fancy vertical market hot rod actually works? Or for that matter, if the little company (they all are) that produced it will even be around in a year to answer your questions?

Still, if you were to get started with a vertical market package, you wouldn't have to retool your entire operation later should you decide to change over. If you do go this route, find something that's been around for a while, preferably something a few other people use and like. Insist on a demonstration disk so you can try it out at your own speed without some salesman breathing down your neck.

What's an "Off-the-Shelf Integrated Package"? A readily available, single, relatively inexpensive package that includes a database, a word processor, a spreadsheet, and a graphics program. At the moment, this beats the knickers off any other approach for the small businessperson. Have a look at a few integrated programs, try them out if possible, and see what you think. This may be the way to go for you.

How much should I plan to spend on a computer system? Advice on the cost of computers is usually obsolete before it's written down. The great news is, prices drop constantly. The longer you wait, the cheaper and better computers get. Also, you can buy a good used system for practically nothing.

How much equipment do I need? A good basic computer, either IBM compatible or Macintosh. A good printer, preferably a laser printer, but an ink-jet is OK. A hard-drive, preferably 50 megabytes or greater. Good basic software that meets your needs.

A Basic Set of Forms

As your business grows and becomes more complex, you'll develop many kinds of forms. There are infinite ways to design forms. In upcoming chapters you'll find many examples of forms, both ready-made ones you can buy from a catalog and specialized forms that other people in the business have developed.

Some forms are required by law, others by good sense. For really small jobs, you may not need or want to use all these forms. Check your state law for minimum legal requirements and then decide how far beyond these you want to go. Remember, legal requirements vary from state to state, so don't just copy these forms without knowing if they'll be OK for you. Unless noted, these forms are useful for either maintenance or landscaping work.

Here are a few helpful general forms and other ideas for management of your records that you'll want to know about.

Speed Letters. You won't have time to type a nice pretty letter every time you need to communicate with someone. Sure, there's a place for that, but these multipart forms are an accepted alternative. They'll save you a lot of time.

Appointment Book. You cannot live without some kind of calendar or appointment book. I use two. One is a big calendar pad that sits on my desk; it's for scheduling jobs. The other is my appointment book. The pioneers carried guns wherever they went; the modern businessperson carries a Day-Timer. Write down every appointment, reminder, note, and scheduled event. Every one. Two reasons: (1) You can't remember it all, and how could you dare forget? (2) You might need to prove you were somewhere or did something at a certain time. I refer back to past entries every day for some reason or another; you will, too.

Meeting Notes. I've been using this form for years. It contains spaces for all kinds of salient information and is versatile enough to be used in many situations.

Things-to-Do Lists. I keep a list with the names, addresses, and other vital statistics of all my current clients; below the listing for each client, I note all the unfinished things that need to be done for them. Nothing leaves the list until it's done. Since one of the biggest complaints about service people is how they forget about little details on every job, leaving clients unhappy, this is a great way to be better than the competition. Put the form on the computer and you won't have to retype it each time; just eliminate completed items and add new ones.

Contact List. You'll be in the field most of the time. You'll need to call subs, suppliers, and others. You'll need their phone numbers and other information. Carry a list around in your truck. This is especially important if you have a mobile phone.

Window Envelopes. If you set up your forms so they all fit in standard window envelopes, you won't have so much addressing to do. It'll be pretty easy to do if you're creating custom forms. Many ready-made forms already come this way.

5

Employees: A Joy and a Nuisance

If you're planning to do only maintenance, you can do quite well working by yourself. Forty hours of fieldwork, plus another ten in the office, can make you quite a nice little living if you're efficient, energetic, and price your services right. Eventually you may want to get a helper or two.

Landscaping requires much more labor. Unless you plan to do very small jobs, you'll soon need someone to help you. So, even if you're going to go it alone for the first year, read this chapter carefully, because you'll soon be an employer.

As you add employees, you gradually move from being a worker to being a manager of workers and then finally to being a manager of managers. There comes a time pretty early in this progression when it just doesn't make sense for you to be out there digging holes, because it means you're neglecting your other duties.

How Many People Will You Need?

Workloads vary so much that determining your manpower needs is a continuous process. A good manager looks ahead to the coming few weeks to determine how many people she or he will need each day. Routine residential maintenance is best done by two people in most cases (more just get in the way), but installing 10,000 square feet of sod lawn requires a crew of five to six because the work has to get done promptly or the sod will die.

Key Employees

Your key employees, the ones you plan to keep for a long time, should be full-time. They should be paid well, given good benefits, and kept happy. They're the heart of your business; without them you're in big trouble. One of your main jobs is to get enough work to keep these people busy. Laying off key employees and then starting over is a disaster.

Your Second-String Employees

These employees come and go as the workload changes. Sometimes you'll need people for only a day or two, sometimes for a few months. Second-string employees are full-time or part-time, depending on the workload. Seasonal layoffs are common. Clearly, it's better for everyone if you can keep people busy with off-season tasks, but there are limits.

The reality is that *most* employees in this business are temporary, and you should make that explicit when you hire people. Don't feel that this is cruel or unfair—it's a commonly accepted reality of the construction industry. The people you hire will understand it if they have any previous experience.

The disadvantage of this high turnover of employees is that you're always dealing with new people—hiring them, getting to know them, training them, and weeding out the bad ones. The advantage is that you have a flexible workforce that can vary with your needs. The other advantage is that you don't have to keep giving people raises that will eventually make them unprofitable to you.

Subcontractors

In addition to your regular employees, you may use the services of other contractors to do portions of the work. In this relationship, they're subcontractors working for you (not the client), and you are acting as the prime contractor. Over time, you'll build up a team of subs you can count on and with whom you enjoy working. You'll move them on and off jobs as you need them, with no obligation to keep them employed full-time. Using subs is a great way to expand the services you offer without having to learn new skills and invest in new equipment.

Like employees, subcontractors are a source of profit for your business. Normally, you'll ask a sub for a bid and then mark it up (you customarily take 10 to 20 percent of the bid price). When you submit your bid to the client, it includes the subcontractor costs and your markup; you can show this as an itemized part of the work (the *total* price, not your markup!) or as part of a lump-sum bid. When the work is done, the sub bills you, and you bill the client.

(*Tip:* Subcontractors have to carry their own liability and worker's compensation insurance, with limits of coverage at least equal to your own. You must get certificates of insurance from all your subs and keep them current and in your files. If your insurance company audits you—which they often do annually—and you can't produce certificates, they'll charge you for subs as if they were your employees. This can get expensive. *Never* do business with a subcontractor unless you have current certificates.)

Finding Good Subs

A good subcontractor can be a valuable asset; a bad one can drag your business down into the hole he's in. Remember, you're responsible for the work of your subs, and if it's not right, you'll have to fix it. That means you have to be able to evaluate and control the quality of the sub's work. If you're working from plans drawn by a landscape architect, the specifications included with the plans will dictate the details of how the job is to be done. If you're working from your own design, you supply the specifications. Problems can occur if you don't give enough detail or don't say the right thing. For help with this critical item, study the specifications of landscape architects or get a book on the subject.

It's vital that your subs be the best you can find. Approach the job of finding subs just as you would if you were looking for someone to work on your own house. Ask suppliers and others who they'd recommend. If you see a beautifully done job, ask the owner who did it. Keep an eye out for jobs in progress, and see who's doing them. Notice the bad jobs as well as the good ones. Get to know the ins and outs of everyone in all the trades you might need.

Have the prospective sub show you some of his work. Check with the contractor's license board to make sure his license is current, and ask if there are any complaints against him. Talk to people the sub has worked for. (See chapter 8 for more information on working with subcontractors.)

Employee or Independent Contractor?

Often, employers treat employees as if they were independent contractors, paying them without taking any payroll deductions, offering no benefits or job security and not paying worker's compensation or liability insurance for them. The advantages are obvious: more profit, less hassle.

The catch is that if the IRS decides your subs are actually employees, you'll be stuck with back taxes, interest, and stiff penalties that could bankrupt you. Since this kind of abuse is so common, especially in the construction industry, they'll be watching you. Fortunately there are pretty clear differences between employees and independent contractors, and if you're careful, you'll stay out of trouble. The chart on pages 116–117 shows some of these differences.

There's no simple test of whether someone's an employee or an independent contractor; it's a matter of how many of the conditions they've met and that's pretty much up to the IRS, who can be as arbitrary as they want. The burden of proof is on you. (*Warning:* You cannot make someone an independent contractor simply by getting a signed agreement saying she is. The requirements still have to be met. Sorry.)

Temps

Some employers solve their employee problems by hiring people through temporary help agencies. The employee works for the agency, not you, and the agency handles all the paperwork and taxes and takes responsibility for the performance of the employee. Although this costs more per hour, it can be cheaper if you factor in the time you'd normally spend on employee bookkeeping. It's a good way to get a few people quickly for that big sod job.

Job Categories (Field)

The Laborer

The laborer is the base of the pyramid. It is these least-paid, first-laid-off, and generally underappreciated people who will make you most of your money. They'll earn you far more than markups on materials ever will and more than their supervisors, whose contribution to profit is often indirect, based on their ability to increase the efficiency of the laborers. Ultimately, your financial success will be borne on the backs of your laborers.

The laborer is a follower of instructions. Laborers dig and move earth, plant, install irrigation, construct hardscape features, and do whatever other semiskilled tasks are needed to complete the project. Some laborers will have specialized skills, others may come to you ignorant of which end of the shovel is which. Some will have the potential for advancement; others are satisfied (or doomed) to dig and dig forever.

Employee or Independent Contractor?

FACTOR	EMPLOYEE	INDEPENDENT CONTRACTOR
Control over methods	Methods of doing the work and sequence in which it is done are controlled by the employer.	Responsible only for results.
Availability for work	Work is done only for employer.	Services are offered to the general public.
Training	Training is done by the employer.	No training is necessary to do the job.
Tools and materials	Supplied by the employer.	Furnishes own tools and materials.
Profit or loss	No risk of loss.	Risks profit or loss.
Contractor's license	No license required.	Has own license.
Insurance	No insurance required.	Has own insurance.
Relation to business	Part of employer's regular business.	Not part of regular business.
Personal rendition of service	Must do the work personally.	May hire others to do the work.

Hours of work	Working hours set by the employer.	Can set own hours.
Full or part time	Full time.	Free to choose.
Investment	No investment.	Significant investment.
Right to discharge	Employer has right to discharge. Employee has right to quit.	Cannot be discharged. Must complete work or face liability.
Hiring, supervising, and payment	Done by the employer.	Hires, supervises, and pays workers.
Works under boss	Works under supervision of a boss.	Works under own supervision.
Title or position	Has a specific title or position.	Operates an independent business.
Premises	Works on employer's premises.	Right to choose location of work.
Reports required	Employer may require reports.	Reports not required.
Expense account	Expenses paid by employer.	Pays own expenses.
Payment	Paid salary or by the hour.	Paid by the job.

A good laborer is physically fit and strong enough to do heavy work, aware of good safety practices, reliable, and cooperative, a good team player.

Some employers and their foremen treat laborers like dirt. Laborers are often considered disposable—get rid of one and there'll be six to take his place. This is a mighty poor approach. First of all, it's just morally wrong. Laborers have the same needs as you do, and the same rights, too. They respond to attention, warmth, and encouragement. Many of them, though they might be uneducated, are intelligent and willing to learn. Treat them like winners, and a certain percentage of them will rise to the occasion and may become your most loyal and valuable employees.

The Foreman

The foreman has multiple responsibilities. He leads the laborers, instructing them in what to do, and he watches them to be sure they do it right. He maintains quality standards and safe conditions on the job. He keeps track of tools, equipment, and materials. He often handles picking up materials and supplies for the job. He keeps track of paperwork: purchase orders and invoices, employee time cards, daily job reports, and equipment logs. He talks with the property owner, general contractor, landscape architect, their agents, delivery people, subcontractors, and others who show up on the job. He makes sure tools and equipment are in good condition. He starts up the job in the morning and shuts it down at night. He handles employees' problems and reports to management on their performance. Sometimes he even pitches in and helps with the physical work.

The foreman has to have at least a few years of broad experience in landscaping. Preferably he has some formal education. He must understand construction techniques and standards and know how to read blueprints and specifications. He must know how to run equipment and be able to teach others. He must be aware of safety practices and know first aid. His driving record must be excellent. He has to be able to direct manpower efficiently and get the best out of his people. His communication skills, both verbal and written, have to be excellent and are preferably in Spanish as well as English. People have to like him.

The first people you hire will be laborers, and you'll be the foreman. Later, you'll probably promote your most promising laborer to foreman. Be sure you train that person in the skills needed to become a really good foreman. (See the section on training later in this chapter.) Don't ever just put someone in charge without teaching them what to do—it's been the downfall of more than one promising company.

Finding Good Employees

It's easy these days to whine about the poor quality of the work-force, yet there are lots of good, enthusiastic people out there. You just have to find them. You're lucky because you don't need highly trained workers. Most of the people you hire will be young, relatively uneducated and malleable. Spend some time with them, and you can turn them into real pros, people who don't know any way to do things but yours—the right way. If you wind up with poor-quality employees, you'll have to ask yourself who hired and trained them.

Here are some places to look for employees, presented in order of importance.

Promote Your Company to Impressive People. Now and then we all encounter a clerk or a gas station attendant who's doing an exceptional job, someone whose spirit really shines. Take the opportunity to sell them on the benefits of working for your company.

Promote from Within. Move your good people up. You already know their strengths and weaknesses. An opportunity for advancement is the best thing you can offer them. They already know how the company operates, which means you'll have to do less training.

Referrals from Your Present Employees. This is one of the best sources of new people. Spread the word, then reward anyone who produces a good new employee: Give them a bonus, a paid day off, tickets to the ball game.

Rehire Former Employees. Sometimes a good person leaves for one reason or another. If you'd like them back, give them a call. Maybe their circumstances have changed.

Trade Associations. The landscape contractors association in California operates a very progressive testing and certification program for field personnel. See if something similar is offered in your state. They may also have a placement service.

Schools. Contact schools with landscape or horticulture departments. Keep in touch with instructors; sometimes they'll point out an exceptional student. Also check with high-school counselors; they may also have exceptional people they can recommend. Sometimes a student you take on for the summer will become your best employee.

Advertise in the Paper. A lot of people, many of them unsuitable, will call. Don't sign up for a week-long ad—you'll get *way* too many calls. You can show the company name or not, depending on whether you want your current employees to know you're hiring. Describe job requirements. Make it easy for people to respond. Watch for discriminatory language that mentions sex, age, race, etc. Omit salary figures.

Off the Wall. In my town there's a stone wall next to the unemployment office where day laborers congregate in the morning, hoping to be picked up by a contractor or other employer. If you hire in this casual fashion, remember that you have no idea who these people are and whether they're right for your needs. Some are OK, most are not. Remember, too, that you have to go through the whole routine of paperwork, deductions, and so forth, whether you hire someone for an hour or a decade. (Anyone who tells you it's OK to pay cash to "casual labor" is misinformed.)

Chance Applicants. If you advertise in the Yellow Pages, job seekers will call you constantly. Sometimes these aggressive people are good candidates.

The Spanish-Speaking Employee

Immigrants, legal and otherwise, from Mexico and Central America are becoming an ever-larger portion of the workforce, especially if you live in the Southwest. The language barrier is becoming an important factor in managing employees. Everyone has a story about some minor misunderstanding that led to a big problem. You and your key people need to be bilingual, at least enough to train and instruct people and to listen to their problems. You also need to keep one English-speaking person on the job at all times, since clients resent not being able to talk to someone during the course of the work. Finally, you need to explain to your Hispanic employees that their chances for advancement will be limited until they learn English. Support them by letting them know about classes in English as a Second Language and by paying for tuition and books if they show interest. This helps them and you.

Legal Requirements of Employers

Employee Rights

Some of the following laws apply to everyone, others kick in when a company reaches a certain size. Remember that part-time employees have the same rights as full-time ones. (*Warning:* Check with your state labor board for the latest requirements. Don't count on the information included here to cover all the bases. Do your homework.)

Firing (applies to all employers)

Wrongful Discharge: The Employment at Will Doctrine states that nonunion workers have no automatic legal right to their jobs; the employer may fire them at will, for any reason or no reason. Conversely, no employer can force an employee to remain on the job. In recent years, this doctrine has been modified by various court cases that protect employees from wrongful discharge under certain circumstances. To protect yourself against a wrongful discharge lawsuit, develop a system of written warnings for misconduct. Have the employee sign them, and state clearly what will happen if the misconduct continues. That way, if you have to fire someone, you can document the fact that they were given plenty of opportunity to clean up their act.

Wage and Hour Laws *(applies to most employers)*

Minimum Wage: Establishes federal minimum wage; state laws may set higher standards.

Overtime: Employers must pay time and half for any work over 40 hours per week. For salaried employees, compensatory time must be granted at time and a half, and the employee must take compensatory time within the same week as the overtime.

On-the-Job Time: Workers must be paid for any time that is controlled by and benefits the employer. Exceptions are mealtimes and changing clothes and washing before or after work. Travel time must be paid if employees have checked into the office first.

Calculating Hours Worked: You may round off to the nearest five-minute period, but you must not pay for any less time than was actually worked.

Pay Interval: Employees must be paid at least once a month.

Final Paycheck: State laws regulate how soon you have to give an employee his final paycheck after he quits or is terminated.

Child Labor: You can't employ anyone younger than age 14, and there are restrictions on the employment of 14- and 15-year-olds.

Free Labor: You can't (believe it or not) have anyone work for free, even if they want to. Too bad.

Breakages and Shortages: If you charge employees for things they break or lose, such charges can't reduce pay below minimum wage.

Loans to Employees: If you loan money to an employee, you're allowed to withhold a portion from the paycheck, but you can't reduce pay below minimum wage.

Garnishments: The IRS can require you to garnish (withhold money from) employee wages to pay back taxes. You can also be required to withhold money for child support payments. You're prohibited from discriminating against these employees.

Withholding: You have to withhold taxes and deposit them in the bank.

Blacklisting: You can't set up a deal with other employers to never hire a person.

Giving Notice: Surprisingly, there's no legal requirement for either employers or employees to give notice of termination. It's just a tradition.

Discrimination (applies to all employers in most cases)

Federal laws prohibit you from discriminating against people on the basis of race, color, gender, religious beliefs, national origin, physical handicaps (unless they prevent the person from doing the job), smoking habits, or age. You may also be prevented from discriminating based on HIV+ status, pregnancy, marital status, weight problems, or sexual orientation. These laws are changing all the time, so check for current requirements if you're planning to discriminate against someone. Also, you may be subject to additional state and local laws.

Sexual Harassment (applies to all employers)

Sexual harassment is defined as the creation of an abusive or hostile working environment as a result of unwanted sexually oriented behavior. This can include demanding sexual favors or using offensive words or actions. It can be direct or indirect (such as a Makita Girl calendar in the break room). If someone is offended, it can lead to a big lawsuit.

Other Rights

Drug Testing: Legal as long as the employee is properly informed.

Lie Detectors: Except for security-related jobs, the use of polygraphs is against the law.

Workplace Searches: Except for private storage areas, it's OK to search through employees' belongings. It's also OK to monitor phone calls. But secret, intrusive monitoring is not OK, nor is any intrusion into the employee's private life.

Credit Checks: It's legal to do a credit check on a prospective or current employee.

Dress Codes: Legal unless you're using them to discriminate against a group.

Workplace Safety

According to the Occupational Safety and Health Administration (better known as OSHA), all employers are required to maintain a workplace as free of safety hazards as is reasonably possible. A workplace is any place people work, including Mrs. Wilson's backyard. A safety hazard could be anything that might injure or harm an employee, either through an accident or long-term injury, such as exposure to toxic chemicals. The law covers such things as hazardous substances, tools and equipment, safety gear, etc. Check with your state's labor board or industrial relations department for specific information.

Injury and Accident Reports

If there's a workplace accident that results in the death of a worker or the hospitalization of four or more workers, you have to report to OSHA within forty-eight hours. If you have ten or more employees, you have to keep a record of work-related illnesses and injuries and post a report on them for at least thirty days per year.

Discrimination

You can't fire or discriminate against an employee for filing a workplace safety complaint or for taking part in an investigation.

Pesticide Safety

Pesticides are considered one of the greatest threats to worker safety. Because the landscaping industry uses so many chemicals, many of them highly toxic, we're closely watched and heavily regulated. The Environmental Protection Agency oversees pesticide regulations, but state and local laws vary greatly. You have to check (now, not later) with local authorities for a complete set of the regulations that apply to you. Restrictions involve purchasing, storage, handling, disposal, and training. In many states, you need a license to apply pesticides. A permit is required to purchase or apply certain pesticides. Some communities require you to post properties that you spray.

La Migra—Dealing with the INS

The Immigration Reform and Control Act of 1986 places burdens on the employer that can be devastating to anyone who hires illegal aliens. The employer has to have an I–9 Employment Eligibility Verification Form on file for all employees, along with a proof of identity and proof of the person's eligibility to work in the U.S. The employee has to produce these documents within three business days of filling out the I–9. The employer is responsible for verifying the authenticity of all documents (no small task, since the U.S. is crawling with counterfeit ones) and will be fined if caught without documents or with falsified ones.

To top it all off, it's illegal to discriminate against anyone on the basis of their country of birth or their status as a naturalized citizen. You can't refuse to hire Hispanics. It's also illegal to require that English be used in the workplace. ¿Comprende?

Unions

In many places, unions are no problem for the small business. In others, you have to hire an electrician to plug in your circular saw. No kidding. Unions can be a pain in the rear.

Shop Categories. If your company is involved with a union, it will fall into one of three categories. An *open shop* is one where workers aren't required to join the union or pay union dues. (Right-to-work laws in some states require all unionized workplaces to be open shops.) An *agency shop* is one where workers aren't required to join the union, but have to pay dues. In a *union shop* all workers must join the union as soon as they are hired. (The legality of this arrangement is in question.) A fourth, illegal, category called the *closed shop* is one where workers must already be union members in order to go to work.

Employee's Rights. Employees have the right to discuss union membership on nonwork time in nonwork areas. They can read and distribute literature and display prounion sentiments. They can ask the employer to recognize the union.

Employer's Limitations. Employers can't grant favors to employees who oppose efforts to unionize. They can't fire, harass, demote, or punish union supporters. They can't close a work site, transfer work, or deny benefits because of organizing efforts.

Union Limitations. Unions can't pressure or coerce employees. They can't encourage the employer to discriminate against employees involved in deunionization activities. They can't interfere with the employee's freedom to express opinions unfavorable to the union. They can't prevent employees from going to work. They have to bargain in good faith with the employer.

Union Dues. A Check-Off Clause may require you to deduct union dues from paychecks and send them to the union.

Prevailing Wage Jobs. Many jobs that are put out to bid by the government require that employees be paid "prevailing wages," usually union-scale wages including benefits, even if the employees (or the company) aren't unionized. If you bid one of these jobs, you suddenly have to figure the cost of your labor at many times the normal rate (unless you're already unionized, of course). If you get the job, you have to actually pay people at those rates. This tends to spoil them for everyday backyard-variety work. Before getting into a situation like this, consider the effect on employee morale.

Hiring

The Job Application

There are many limitations to what you can ask prospective employees, and job applications must conform to strict standards. Go to the office supply store and get a pad of the latest version. (*Tip:* Be sure to get the applicant's driver's license number and classification so you can check his or her driving record.)

In addition to the standard application, have the applicant fill out a form indicating whether they can operate the equipment you use. Ask them to rate their proficiency on a scale of one to ten. Provide space for them to list any special skills, abilities, or interests. Remember that job applications are full of information beyond what's actually written down. Naturally, you'll be interested in the applicant's work experience and education, but reading between the lines will tell you more. Look for periods of unemployment or long periods with no advancement. Watch out for job-hoppers with a lot of short-term jobs. Look at handwriting, grammar, punctuation, and spelling.

Even if you're desperate for help, don't ever take anything at face value, because a lot of people will lie like crazy to get a job. Before you ever agree to an interview, check references thoroughly. Make sure that college degree is real, not invented. Call the applicant's previous two or three employers, not just the last one, who may be so anxious to get rid of this person (or get her off the unemployment rolls) that he'll overstate the person's qualities. When you talk to former employers, verify the information on the job application, then ask about the person's duties, promotions or demotions, the quality of their work, how well they got along with others, whether there were any problems, if they were a team player, and whether the employer would rehire this person. Be sure to let them know that all information will remain confidential.

Interviewing That Works

The only thing worse than being interviewed for a job is being the interviewer. I've always felt uncomfortable with this, and you probably will, too. It helps to understand the purpose of the interview and to have specific goals in mind. It also helps to create a welcoming atmosphere right from the start: Get up to greet the applicant, offer a chair, and sit nearby, not behind your desk. Make a little appropriate small talk to put the person at ease. Remember, it's to your advantage to see them at their best. You'll learn a lot about their social skills and self-confidence even at this early stage. Even a handshake will tell you a lot—soft hands mean that person hasn't done any physical work for a while.

So, what do you ask them? Here are some key questions:

Previous/Current Job(s): What are/were your specific duties? How many people did you supervise? What equipment did you operate? What did/do you like/dislike most about your job(s)? What did you find most challenging? Why are you thinking about leaving? Why did you leave your previous job(s)?

Education and Training: Why did you decide to go into this line of work? What classes did you enjoy most/do best at in school?

"How Would You . . . " Questions: Pose some real-world problems, technical or managerial as appropriate. For instance, "We've had a problem with sod webworm that we just can't seem to solve. Do you have any ideas?" or "What do you think of those new Toro riding mowers?" or "We have a lot of Monday absenteeism among the laborers. How would you handle it?" A good applicant will really come on strong with this treatment, a poor one won't be humiliated.

(*Tip:* Tell something about your company—how long you've been in business, the kinds of work you do, the opportunities for advancement, even something personal about yourself. Remember, the interviewing process is a two-way street. The applicant needs to decide whether he or she wants to work for you.)

At the end of the interview, ask the person if they have any questions. If you're especially impressed, let them know that. Thank them for coming and give them an idea of when you'll choose someone. *Important:* Be sure to contact everyone, by phone or mail, to let them know you've made a decision. Remember, they took the time to go through this difficult process, and they're anxious to know the results.

Testing

You might want to test your top applicants. A simple multiple-choice and true/false skills test is a good start. The skills test on pages 130–131 contains questions I've used. It's not too complex, but it lets you know whether the applicant has basic skills.

Probationary Periods

Always hire people on a provisional basis—one to three month's trial period. Make it clear that you can let them go at the end of the period if they're not up to snuff. For this to be effective and fair, you need to tell the employee what's expected of her, then you need to sit down with her and do an evaluation halfway through the period so she can correct any problems before the final evaluation. That's a lot better than just waiting three months and canning her.

Developing an Employee Manual

In a personnel management seminar a few years back, one of my competitors described in great detail his employee manual. The seminar leader, impressed, asked him how many employees he had, and he replied, "Oh, well, I don't have any employees yet!" It sounds funny, but just a couple of years later he had one of the biggest outfits in the area, with over forty employees. Maybe he succeeded because he was prepared for success.

No off-the-shelf employee manual will be right for your company. You need to develop your own policies and procedures, ones that are right for your situation. However, putting them into a standard format makes sense. There are some excellent books and even computer programs that will help you with this job (see the appendix). Find out what your trade association has to offer. Check your library or bookstore for help. (*Tip:* Many of your employees will be only marginally literate. Keep language simple and clear and keep everything brief.)

Sample Skills Test

Irrigation

- Above-ground pressure lines may be PVC or galvanized. (T/F)
- Modern drip emitters don't require filtration. (T/F)
- Most digital controllers have a battery backup. (T/F)
- The distance of throw of a Toro 570 is (a) 10–15 feet, (b) 30–40 feet, (c) 18 inches.
- The flow rate of a drip emitter might be (a) 600 gpm, (b) 1 gph, (c) 21.2 PVC.
- Describe the flushing procedure on a new sprinkler system.

Plants and Planting

- Roundup is effective against common Bermuda grass. (T/F)
- Malathion is a popular flowering shrub. (T/F)
- Ground covers should be watered (a) one week after planting, (b) after they have died back to the ground, (c) immediately after planting.
- List the steps in planting a one-gallon plant.

Hardscape

- Nails used in outdoor construction must be galvanized. (T/F)
- A joist is the same thing as a pier block. (T/F)
- Dry-laid brick is usually installed on a sand base. (T/F)
- Which of these is a brick pattern: (a) double runner, (b) basket-weave, (c) salt-finish.
- A swale is (a) a rock-moving tool, (b) a type of cinder block, (c) a shallow gully for draining water.

Equipment Use and Care

- A trenching machine may be operated for up to one hour without any attention. (T/F)
- Chainsaws run best on straight gasoline. (T/F)
- Rototilling compacted soil should be done at slow speed. (T/F)
- A mattock is similar to (a) a pick, (b) a pushbroom, (c) a tree stake.
- Oil levels in gasoline-powered equipment should be checked (a) monthly, (b) hourly, (c) before each use.

Safety

- Power equipment should be adjusted while it is operating. (T/F)
- Valve solenoids may be tested by applying 110 volts to the coil. (T/F)
- Lifting and carrying railroad ties requires two people. (T/F)
- Injuries should be reported (a) at the end of the week, (b) immediately, (c) only if doctor's care is required.
- Heavy lifting should be done by (a) bending at the knees, (b) bending at the back, (c) both.

Job Management and Cost Control

- On a crew of three or more, one person is for standby. (T/F)
- A crew leader is responsible for directing the work of his subordinates. (T/F)
- Actual hours spent on the job are not important to job cost. (T/F)
- A change order is (a) a refund slip for overpayments, (b) used to add or delete work, (c) just like a purchase order.
- List some of the major responsibilities of a foreman or crew leader.

Make sure every employee gets a copy of your manual. Have them sign a receipt, and keep it in the employee's file. Leave copies of the manual in the toolshed; put a copy on the bulletin board. Update it every year, and distribute new copies to everyone. Consider printing a Spanish-language version.

Training Employees

One of the commonest complaints I've heard from former clients of my competitors is, "He just dropped off some untrained people and left. Nobody seemed to know what they were doing." *You* are a pro; what about your employees? They won't automatically know what to do—you have to *teach* them!

There are four stages to a good training program. First, decide what training is needed. Next, set goals so you and your trainees can measure their progress. Then develop methods of training. Finally, go back and evaluate the results.

What Training Is Needed?

First of all, do you have written job descriptions for your employees? No? Better get to work. It's no big deal—just write down the purpose of the job, what tasks you expect the person to do, what skills they'll need to do them. Then make a list of specific things the employee needs to learn.

Set Goals

No employee can learn everything at once. Break up the training into manageable chunks and set specific goals for learning each chunk.

Develop Training Methods

The best methods are those that teach by example. Remember, your employees won't be the academic type, so lots of lecturing and book work just won't help them. Remember the rule, "Show, don't tell." Here's a good approach:

1. Explain the task—what's to be done, how it's to be done, and what the results should be. (Explain how to plant a tree.)
2. Show how it's done. (Plant a tree.)
3. Have the employee do it. (Have him plant a tree.)
4. Evaluate the employee's performance and make constructive suggestions.
5. Have the employee do it again.
6. Evaluate again.

Be sure to offer plenty of encouragement; don't just tell him what he did wrong. Encourage the trainee to ask questions. Remember that everyone learns at their own speed. Be an ally, not a punisher.

Evaluate the Results

Check up on employees regularly to be sure they're doing things right. Give them encouragement when you can and correct problems when you need to.

Training Tips: Good training is the basis of quality control. Training never ends; we all have a lot to learn. Encourage a team spirit in your entire staff; be sure everyone is thinking "improvement" at all times. Share your excitement with your people. Provide resources—books, videos, classes, and seminars—for all employees. Don't forget about your trade association; most provide an array of training materials. If your association has a certification program, encourage key employees to take the test, and reward them if they pass.

Safety Training

This is a special category of training that's required by law. In California employers are required to conduct "tailgate" safety meetings for all employees at least every ten days. These can be brief and informal, but you have to do them. (Regulations in your state may vary.) Keep a record of all meetings: who attended, instructor, time and date, subject(s) discussed, new ideas from employees.

Many employers don't have safety meetings because they don't know what to talk about. You'll find a few suggested topics in the sidebar below; surely you can think of others.

Topics for Safety Meetings

Equipment
- Safe Mower Operation
- Using a Trenching Machine Safely
- Chainsaw Safety
- Reporting Equipment Malfunctions

Safe Practices
- Dig Carefully!
- Ways to Prevent Back Injuries
- Refueling Equipment Safely
- Defensive Driving
- Tie Down Your Load!
- Watching Out for Others
- Keeping the Jobsite Safe for Everyone

Chemical Safety
- Using the Respirator
- Proper Mixing of Chemicals
- How to Handle a Chemical Spill
- Avoiding Spray Drift

First Aid
- What to Do if Someone Is Injured
- Stopping Bleeding
- How to Call for Help

Managing Employees

There are a million management books out there. Most of them say the same things. Boiled down, it comes to this: Care about your people. Put yourself in their shoes. Listen. Provide them a satisfying job with fair pay. Train them well. Recognize their accomplishments. Treat them as you want to be treated. Be honest with them. Be on their side. If you do all this, your employees will be eager to come to work every day because there's an adventure awaiting them.

Of course, your role as employer often requires you to help people deal with personal problems that affect their work. How do you do it? After all, you're a landscaper, not a shrink! Well, it's not always easy and there's certainly a point at which you should recognize your limitations and stop trying. But, within those limitations, there's a lot you can do. (*Tip:* Don't assume that an employee with a problem is necessarily a problem employee.)

You can only solve an employee problem by working on it with the employee. Set up a meeting with him. Create a non-threatening atmosphere—no sitting behind the desk. Ask him how things are going. Listen to him. Ask what *he* thinks could be done to make things better; some of it may make a lot of sense. Explain why you can't do certain things. Agree on the course of action, summarizing who'll do what. Send him out to give it a try, letting him know your door is open. Now you've both got something to work on, a goal. Check back after an agreed-upon period of time. Readjust and try again.

Performance Evaluations

Periodic performance reviews keep people tuned up. Reward good behavior and achievements; shine a light on things that could be improved. Don't wait to do a performance evaluation until you're so darned mad at the employee that you could pitch him out the window. Evaluations aren't meant for beating people up.

Firing People

Giving somebody the axe is just about the hardest thing you'll ever do as an employer. No matter how much the person has driven you, your clients, and your other employees nuts, it still hurts to fire them. Not only that, it's scary these days: Will they sue you? Shoot you?

First, review the section on employee rights to be sure you're not firing the person unjustly or exposing yourself to liability. Fire for just causes like dishonesty, repeated absenteeism, substance abuse, insubordination, or inability to do the work. Be sure you've given adequate *written* warning and that the firing is within your company's guidelines.

Fire the person privately, quickly, and without recourse. Have their paycheck waiting for them. Be kind even if you can't wait to never see this person again. Allow them to save face. Tell them you're sorry things didn't work out, and wish them luck.

Keeping Good Employees

Sometimes your key employee, the one you taught everything he knows, will up and quit on you. It hurts. It may not be the first time it's ever happened, but knowing that doesn't really help. Your first reaction will be, "What good is it to train somebody if *this* always happens?" How could this situation have been avoided? How can you retain good employees? *People leave because some other situation meets more of their needs than the one you offered them.* Sometimes this is unavoidable, but other times you lost an employee because you were asleep at the wheel.

So, what do people want? Money. Do you pay them enough? Recognition. Do you praise them enough? Satisfaction. Do you offer meaningful work? Advancement. Could your people get promoted? Answer these questions often with each employee, optimize your offerings to them, and you'll have the answer to a stable, faithful workforce. Ignore them, and you'll have a constant turnover.

Raises

Raises should be given for improved performance and value to the company. A cost-of-living adjustment isn't a raise. Employees always feel they deserve a raise. When you can't give them one, explain why and suggest (if you can do so honestly) that a raise would be possible if certain *specific* things were improved. Explain what they are, and set a date for a review of the situation. Offer encouragement so the employee doesn't feel totally rejected. People often base their self-worth on their earnings, so it's a touchy subject.

Don't equate a raise with length of service. A person's pay should be based on merit, not on ability to stick around. Also, be aware that a long-term employee can eventually reach a pay scale where it's no longer profitable to have them working for you.

Bonuses

Bonuses should also be tied to performance. If the employees do something exceptional and you have an unexpected profit because of it, share it with them. They'll love you for it.

Promotions

Promote from within whenever you can. It's good for morale and easier on you. Be clear about what you expect from someone before you promote them—new skills and improved performance. Promotions aren't based on seniority; be sure people know that. Sadly, you've also got to make it clear that few people can be promoted in such a small company.

Benefits

The trend is for employers to offer fewer benefits to employees. It's especially difficult for a teeny company to pay for health insurance, pension plans, vacations, sick leave, profit sharing, bonuses, tickets to the amusement park, and all the rest. Fact is, you just can't compete with a big corporation when it comes to benefits. Provide what you can, but realize that the real benefits you offer are a personal atmosphere, job satisfaction, and a sense of purpose. Those don't cost you anything, and they'll keep people around just as well as the fancy stuff.

Record Keeping

If you have employees, payroll will be one of your biggest expenses and also one of your biggest sources of paperwork. Federal and state laws require certain record keeping procedures, and additional records are necessary for reasons of good management. Here's a summary of the records you must keep:

1. Time cards for each hourly employee

2. Payroll checks

3. Detailed earnings records for each employee

4. Payroll ledger

5. Labor cost information, broken down by types of work (for cost analysis and future bidding)

6. Payroll tax tracking forms

7. Federal and state payroll forms

Most of your field employees (laborers and foremen) will be paid an hourly wage. If you expand to the point where you need office staff, estimators, and supervisors, you'll probably pay them a salary—the same amount each week regardless of the amount of time they put in. For starters, you only need to worry about the hourly workers.

Time Cards

For each hourly worker, you need to keep a weekly time card that shows how many hours were worked each day. Break those hours down by job or by category of work, since this will help you bill your clients for time-and-materials jobs and will also give you the information you'll need to analyze your labor costs for future bids.

Many states require that you hold on to time cards as part of your payroll records. Time cards are also needed if you get into a dispute with a former employee over unemployment benefits or the correct payment for overtime.

Employees should be required to fill out time cards themselves. Most employees just hate doing this, and you really have to ride them. Don't count on them to do it right; check each time card yourself for accuracy, or have their foreman help. Make it clear that guesswork isn't acceptable. And you know, it *is* hard to remember what you did all day. (*Tip:* Require employees to turn in their time cards every day, so you can be sure they don't put off filling them out until the end of the week when it's humanly impossible to reconstruct what happened.)

Time cards like the sample shown below can be purchased at an office supply store. They're fine for your needs.

DAILY TIME CARD					
EMPLOYEE'S NAME				DATE	
JOB NAME	DESCRIPTION OF WORK		IN	OUT	HOURS
		TOTAL REGULAR HOURS			
		TOTAL OVERTIME			
FOREMAN					

Payroll Checks and Earnings Records

When you do payroll, you add up the number of hours worked, multiply by the hourly wage to get the Gross Pay, then itemize the various deductions and subtract them to get Net Pay. You then write a check to the employee for the net pay. Later you deposit the withheld taxes plus employer-paid taxes into a special account at the bank so they can be forwarded to the government. (Yes, that's right. You're not just a landscaper, you're a tax collector, too.) Detailed records of withheld amounts are required by law. Naturally, you also need to file tax returns of various kinds. Dealing with all this can be confusing and burdensome.

Back in the old days, employers did their own payroll and kept track of when tax deposits were due. Thanks to computers, smart employers now hire a payroll service to handle this job for them. These services do nothing but handle payrolls; most communities have at least one. All you do is provide initial information on each new employee and then just phone in the regular and overtime hours each week. The company handles the rest, including paychecks, tax deposits, tax returns, and a payroll report for you. The cost is amazingly low, especially when you consider that most employers do payroll wrong and end up paying hundreds of dollars in fines. Rather than try to learn all the ins and outs of payroll, I recommend you use this method.

Form 1099

If you hire subcontractors or outside help and pay any one of them over $600 per year, you need to report this to the IRS using Form 1099, Miscellaneous Income.

Change of Status Form

Use this to document promotions, demotions, warnings, changes in pay, and dismissals. Nowadays you have to prove everything sooner or later, and if you don't have this stuff in writing, the labor commission or whoever's after you will assume you're guilty. They'll probably do so anyway, but these records might help.

6

Getting Work

Remember Buddy, my partner in the early days of my business? When we were struggling to get started, we made a lot of mistakes. Looking back, I just can't believe some of the things we did. Take marketing, for instance.

One day, while we were out knocking on doors, a lady asked us for a business card. I hate to even tell you this, but of course Buddy and I looked at each other, excused ourselves, and made a beeline for Buddy's '62 Mercury Comet to have a conference. No, we didn't have a business card. We had *thought* about getting some, sure, but well, let's just say it wasn't time. So we rummaged around on the disgusting floor of this old heap and finally found one of those little raisin boxes from somebody's lunch years ago and a filthy stub of a No. 2 pencil. Tearing off one side of the box, we wrote at the top LANDSCAPERS, then our names and a phone number. What excuse we gave to this bewildered woman for our shabby marketing efforts I can't recall anymore, but I remember well how quickly and decisively she shut her front door. Naturally we didn't get that job.

Well, I've learned a lot since then. You don't have to present the same image as a big corporation; in fact it wouldn't be appropriate. But you do have to look professional. Remember, you're asking people to trust you with what is probably the biggest investment they have: their homes. You're asking them to spend anywhere from a few hundred dollars to tens of thousands. If they don't believe in you, you're not going to get anywhere. So how do you do it? That's what this chapter is all about.

Serving the Client Well

The most important thing about marketing has to do with getting your head screwed on right. Let's look at the one basic premise that guides all successful businesses.

Rule Number One: *You are in business to serve the needs of your clients.* If you do that well and keep them happy, they'll stay with you for years, refer you to other people, and make you successful. If you make them unhappy, they'll go elsewhere and (this is the worst part) tell everyone else in town what a jerk you are. Make enough people unhappy, and you're finished. There are no other rules worth discussing.

Why is this so hard for people to understand? Most people are well intentioned, but they have a hard time figuring out how to make this principle work on a day-to-day basis. And yes, keeping everybody happy all the time is a big challenge, especially when you're putting in fourteen-hour days and still leaving a lot of stuff unfinished. But if you always think about things from the *client's* point of view in addition to your own, you'll soon learn a lot about priorities. Let's look at a few of the common complaints about home-improvement businesses and how to eliminate them.

"I left three messages but no one called me back." This is a great way to end a relationship before it even starts. Why would anyone fail to return a call from a prospective client? Too busy? Sorry, but that just doesn't cut it. The phone call is the heart of your business. Naturally, you can't sit by the phone all day, but do take an hour at the end of each day to answer your calls. Start

with the oldest ones, leave detailed messages on people's answering machines, and keep trying until you reach someone. Remember: No calls = no appointments = no sales = no work. Too tired? Just do it. I believe you'll find the process energizing. Think of it: All those nice people want to do business with *you*! Call them back promptly and you'll stand out from the crowd.

By the way, there are so many neat ways to communicate now that there's practically no excuse anymore for being out of touch. Get a remote-retrieval answering machine, a pager, a mobile phone, or a fax machine. Use call forwarding. Make it easy for people to communicate with you. Your phone is your store; keep the doors open.

"We made an appointment, but he was late/never showed up." First of all, always ask the client, "What's a good time for me to come by?" not "I could come out Tuesday at one." Then be there. I try to be at the door at exactly the time I said I would. It impresses the heck out of people. Five minutes early is sometimes just as bad as five minutes late, since your premature presence may be intrusive. Five minutes late is never OK, but is sometimes unavoidable. Remember to apologize on the rare occasions when you are late. Use your mobile phone to call and tell them you're on your way; they'll be pleased. If you're chronically late, change your habits.

"He said he'd get back to me within a few days, but I never heard anything from him." People will not call you to find out how you're coming with their bid or design or whatever you promised them. They'll just wait a week, get sore, and give the job to someone else. For crying out loud, if you don't want the job, just *tell* them. This is common courtesy. Still, we all drop the ball now and then and, as the days wear on, find it ever harder to call the person back. My experience is that when I finally do screw up my courage and call them, they're perfectly delighted to hear from me, and we proceed as if nothing had happened. Try it. It'll set you apart from the rest. But more important, develop the "do-it-now" attitude so you don't have a festering backlog of stale bids and forgotten appointments. It's better for your client and for you, too.

Look, I could go on and on about how attitude affects your success, but I think you must have the idea by now. If you find ways to please your clients (and potential clients) and overcome the very human but very bad habit of making excuses for why you've displeased them, you'll do well. Your every action should convey the idea that you care, that you're responsible, and that you can do the job. Don't tell people what you *can't* do, tell them what you *can* do. There are plenty of flaky competitors out there, and with a little effort at professionalism, you'll rise above them.

Marketing Basics

Marketing and Advertising are Not the Same Thing

Marketing is the total of all your efforts and strategies for developing your business. Figuring out what services people in your area need is marketing. Designing a business card is marketing. Wearing attractive clothes to a meeting is marketing. Asking a satisfied client to tell their friends about your services is marketing. *Doing a good job is marketing.*

Advertising, on the other hand, is one of the many tools you might use in marketing. Placing an ad in the classified section or the Yellow Pages, posting flyers on local bulletin boards, or giving out pens with the company name on them are all advertising methods.

Marketing Is the Art of Making Friends

Sometimes people think there's a secret to marketing or that it involves some nefarious techniques of psychological manipulation. True, highly sophisticated marketing methods are used by major corporations, but they don't have much to do with you and your little business.

Marketing is simple: Meet as many people as you can (either personally or through your ads, handouts, or other ways of communicating), get their attention, make them like you, tell them what you can do for them, tell them why they should do business with you instead of with somebody else, make them want to hire you, close the sale, then keep them happy so they tell others. (Don't skip any steps or you're not marketing, you're wasting your time and money.)

At bottom, what you're doing is making friends. There's nothing mysterious or nefarious about it.

Advertising May Not Do You Much Good

There's a lot of evidence that conventional advertising methods don't work very well for small businesses. Even the Yellow Pages, trusted (and expensive) friend of businesspeople, isn't very helpful in building a loyal group of quality clients for a service business. Advertising is often not cost effective (many kinds of advertising are a total waste of money), the public is suspicious of advertising, and clients you get through ads are often cheap, difficult, and disloyal. Finally, most small businesses don't advertise professionally enough or consistently enough to make it work.

Word of Mouth Is Your Best Advertising

If you're good, most of your business, and certainly most of your best business, will come from referrals. A referral client is already sold on you—they've heard great things about you (from more than one person, if you're really lucky), and they've probably seen your work. Unlike someone who responds to your Yellow Pages ad, they're probably not shopping the job around to a dozen people or looking for the lowest bid. They feel they can trust you, since your performance has spoken for you. There's no better client than a referral client. Nor is there one who will come to you at less cost.

It Costs Less to Keep an Existing Client Than to Get a New One

I lied. There is one better client—the one you already have. You've already gone through all the rigmarole of getting to know each other, explaining the details of how you do business, and making sure you get along with each other. Work harder to hang on to your existing clients than you do to get new ones. Make sure they're thrilled with everything you do for them. Make sure they understand that you're giving them more value for the money than any of the competition could. See to it that their every need is taken care of, one hundred percent and on time.

There's Always More Work Than You Could Possibly Handle

Even when things are slow, there's a ton of work out there. Your competition may not realize it. Your clients and potential clients probably won't realize it. But if *you* realize it, you'll always be busy. Here are some examples:

1. *Find more work on existing jobs.* Make a habit of constantly looking around your jobs. What else could you do to make them better? Maybe that flower bed by the front door is getting a bit tacky; why not suggest replanting it? Come up with some ideas and a price and mention it to the client. Chances are they'll appreciate the fact that you care so much, that you're watching out for them. If you make them see how much better a new planting will be, they'll probably agree to have you do it. (Remember that landscaping is always changing and so are the people who own it.)

    Make a habit of stopping by your jobs. If no one's home, leave a business card and a note in the door: "Mrs. Petersen, I stopped by today and noticed that your mulch is getting a little thin. It would be a good idea to add some more. Give me a call if you need help with this or anything else. Thanks. Jill. P.S. You've got some aphids on your camellias; try washing them off with water." People will be amazed, since no one else ever did this for them. They'll be faithful to you forever.

2. *Talk to the neighbors.* You do a nice front yard. People on the block are watching you, you can be sure of that. Come back in a few months and you may find that neighbors have followed your lead and fixed up their front yards. Kick yourself for not going after that business. Next time, knock on a couple of doors at lunchtime each day, introduce yourself, explain the benefits of the work you're doing across the street, leave a business card and a brochure, offer to provide an estimate. What has this cost you? Virtually nothing. What are the odds of your getting a job from it? A lot better than the odds of your getting a good job out of a newspaper ad.

3. *Find ways to improve the landscaping of total strangers.* Let's say you pull into a shopping center one morning to get a cup of coffee. Naturally you look around at the landscaping, which is probably not as good as it could be. Find out who owns the place (go to the county hall of records or ask the owner of the coffee shop), then write them a letter suggesting a few things you could do to improve their property. Offer to meet with them at no charge or obligation. Tell them to call you, or tell them you'll call *them* in a week. Nine letters will probably get ignored. The tenth may land you your best job ever. Your cost? Pennies per letter plus a little of your time. Think of yourself as someone with a cause—improving the landscaping in your community. Then pursue it. You'll leave the competition in the dust.

The moral to the story? Find a need and fill it, as the old saying goes. Find out where the gaps are—gaps in the way properties are being managed and also gaps in the services offered in your community. Maybe there's no one in your community doing sprinkler repair; there's an opportunity for you. Maybe your church has been paying high water bills because their landscaping uses too much water; there's another opportunity. *Solve people's problems.* Business is everywhere; you've just got to develop a nose for it.

Your Competition Isn't Who You Think It Is

You probably think other gardeners and landscapers are your competition. You're wrong. Sure, you may bid against them for work, but they're actually one of your least important forms of competition. Why? First of all, you're better than they are, in a different league altogether. Let them compete against each other if they want to; you go after your *own* jobs. Second, most of them are so lame that it's easy to outshine them just by showing up on time, being honest with people, and doing a good job. It doesn't take much, just the basics. Third, the other things you're competing against are far more powerful. See the sidebar on the next page for a rundown of what they are.

You've Got Some Selling Problems

Compared to most businesspeople, you're at a disadvantage. You don't have a store or a showroom, you can't carry your product into someone's living room, no one can test drive it, you can't leave samples. Furthermore, what you offer is complex and hard to explain. You may walk onto a piece of property and instantly have a vision of how you'd landscape it, but how do you convey that vision to the owner?

Marketing Is a Contact Sport

Many people in the trades are passive about marketing. When the phone doesn't ring, they just sit around and wait. That doesn't work. Sometimes you've got to get out and mingle with people, seek out possibilities, tell your story to any qualified listener, be aggressive.

If You Want to Sell It, You've Got to Tell It

Do your clients know about everything you offer? Do your mowing clients know that you also trim trees? Does the family you built the deck for know that you also do irrigation systems? How *would* they know unless you told them? Heck, most people aren't

The Real Competition

Your client's other interests. Often, a prospective client is trying to decide whether to do the landscaping or get a new car, take a trip or put some money into the stock market. The dilemma of discretionary spending can take people in many directions. Your job is to convince them that landscaping is their best investment.

More powerful marketing forces. The car manufacturers, the travel industry, and all the other mega-industries have huge advertising budgets and sophisticated marketing people whose only job is to get people to buy their products. The benefits and advantages of spending money on these items are well known. Who helps *you* explain the benefits and advantages of landscaping?

The economy. When things are slow and money is tight, landscaping is one of the first things to go. When people are feeling anxious about the future, it's pretty hard to convince them to pour their life savings into their yards. For example, when interest rates are low, it can be easy to sell work—people refinance, they move (which gives you two potential jobs: one for the seller and one for the buyer), they have more money to spend. But when interest rates are high, there's less discretionary spending.

The public image of gardening and landscaping. In many cultures people hold the gardener in high regard. In this country the gardener is thought of as an outdoor janitor. The landscaper isn't considered much better. Who's helping you educate people about your level of professionalism?

The reputation of home improvement business. Because there are so many incompetents, fly-by-nights, and crooks constantly preying on people, many of your potential clients have understandably negative reactions to anyone trying to sell them services. You often have to prove yourself to a suspicious public.

really sure what a landscaper does, much less do they have a list of your services in their minds! *You've got to tell them!*

Print out a simple list of the services you offer. Make sure everyone you meet has a copy of it. Go over it with people. Or print your business card on double-sized stock, with a short list on the inside, then fold it over so it becomes a little brochure.

Marketing Doesn't Just Happen

Like creating a landscape, marketing requires a plan. You need to decide who your potential clients are, what you have to offer them, why your services are better than those of the competition, what's unique about your services, how you're going to get people's attention, how you're going to tell them about what you're offering, how you're going to motivate them to do business with you.

Each of those questions is important, so list them right now, each on a separate sheet of paper, and then brainstorm. For example, under "What's Unique About My Services?" you might list, "Offer organic lawn care" or "Only company in town that designs and builds water features." Under "How to Tell Them?" you might list "print and hand out flyer at malls, canvassing in new housing developments, seminar at home show in May, Yellow Pages ad, classified ad for maintenance jobs."

Getting in through the Back Door

One time I needed a place to dump excess soil that we'd removed from jobs. I put a classified ad in the paper. All it said was FILL SITE WANTED and a phone number. It cost me around $5. I got about fifteen calls and learned something astonishing. Seven of those calls turned into landscaping jobs, a couple of them quite nice ones. Why? Well, I hadn't thought of it, but why were these people filling in land? They were going to *landscape* it afterward! I thought I was advertising for a fill site, but I was also advertising for jobs. That's when I learned about the Backdoor Approach.

Sometimes it's hard to go in through the front door. Sometimes it's just plain locked up tight. For instance, consider the difference between "Give me $40,000, and I'll landscape your yard," and "For a hundred dollars, I'll design a planting for the front flower bed, then I'll sell you the plants at a discount so you can put them in yourself." Very few people will respond positively to the first offer; it's just too alarming. But a lot of folks who need help with the flower bed actually need $40,000 worth of landscaping but don't know it. If you can help with their little project, maybe you can get the big one.

That was the strategy behind an idea of mine that worked beautifully for many years, the "Do-It-Yourself Landscaping Kit," subtitled "We Provide the Design and the Materials, You Provide the Labor." I advertised in the Yellow Pages for years and got a lot of work. Sometimes things would go just the way the ad said, but often (and here's where the Backdoor Approach comes in) the client would get part way into the project and realize that for lack of time, energy, or skills, he needed help. I'd step in and finish the project at full price.

One more example. I used to sell sod to homeowners for their own installation. During the course of the sale, we'd discuss sprinklers, weed control, all the aspects of doing the job. Often, they'd want to have part of the work done. Snap—I had a new client. Then I'd give them some of my famous excellent service, and they'd never go anywhere else for their landscaping.

The back door gets you in, same as the front door. Don't be afraid to use it. Offer a lot of small services and even products if you wish. Then develop a relationship with the client. Become his landscaper, the only source he'd turn to.

Related to this is the principle that you should never turn down small jobs, especially when you're just starting out. You might do some half-pint little thing for an old lady, and six months later you get a call from her son and daughter-in-law who did real well in commodities and need somebody to landscape the new house they're building. Naturally, they'll be happy to talk to the nice young landscaper that mom liked so much.

Getting the Work

As the old saying goes, it's not what you know, it's who you know. So, who can get you work, and how do you contact them? That's the heart of the marketing question.

Who Controls the Work?

Homeowners

Homeowners take a couple of routes to having landscaping done. The commonest is to work directly with a design/build landscape contractor. This means you can approach homeowners directly and expect good results. Naturally this is also true of maintenance work. There are a number of ways to get the homeowners' attention, including referrals, door-to-door canvassing, flyers, direct mail, telephone solicitation, Yellow Pages ads, newspaper ads, radio spots, home shows, classes and seminars, public demonstrations, sponsoring events, and advertising specialties like T-shirts and advertising pens. We'll get into the details of this when we talk about kinds of advertising.

Some homeowners hire a landscape architect to draw plans, then put them out to bid. Often, they take the recommendation of the landscape architect about who to invite to bid, so to get this kind of work it really helps to be on the landscape architect's bidders' list.

Landscape Architects

Since the landscape architect only does design, he or she is always recommending landscape contractors and gardeners. Every landscape architect has a bidders' list—people with good reputations who the landscape architect knows and has worked with in the past. Naturally, it takes time to gain the trust of the landscape architect, so it's a good idea to start soon.

There's good reason to ally yourself with one or more landscape architects. First of all, they usually get top-end jobs, ones that are far better than those available to you as a small design/build contractor. Second, it's good for you to see how others design jobs and to install them according to their specifications. You'll learn a tremendous amount by doing this, even if the style of the job isn't your favorite. (*Tip:* Working with landscape architects can be rewarding or difficult, depending on the person involved. There's a tradition of mutual antagonism between landscape architects and contractors that's probably never going to go away. It can take some of the fun out of your work.)

How do you get on a bidders' list? First, contact the landscape architect—preferably by letter with a follow-up phone call. Ask to meet with them so you can show off your work. Bring in photos of your jobs, letters of recommendation, a job list so they can see your work in person, a list of references, and a list of your services. Put it all into a nice attractive portfolio. Give them a fistful of your business cards. Tell them you'd like to bid on some of their smaller jobs, and ask if they have anything right now that you could take home. If you conduct yourself well, you may walk away with a set of plans. If not, try them again in a few months when you have more finished work to show. Persistence pays.

Building Architects

Architects usually work with one or more landscape architects and will probably refer you to them. Still, it never hurts to let people know you're there.

General Contractors

General contractors (also known as generals, G.C.s, or simply builders) usually operate by subcontracting most of the work on a project. Sometimes, though not always, this includes landscaping. Your chances are better on big multi-unit residential or commercial jobs where the landscaping is part of the prime contract and not left up to individual owners.

The process of bidding these jobs is complex. Often the general will call for sub-bids and use them when he submits his own bid to the owner or developer. When you bid a job for a general, you need to survive two tests: Your bid has to be the low one for the general to accept you, and the general's bid has to be low for him (and therefore you) to get the job. Because it can take a tremendous amount of time to bid a big job, a strategy has been developed in the industry that allows everybody the best possible chance. Each sub finds out which generals are bidding the job and submits the same bid to all of them. Often generals will call you and ask if you're bidding on the Such-and-Such job on Tuesday. It's a good idea to contact all the generals you might want to work for and ask to be put on their bidders' lists. It'll help if you do the same song and dance as you would for landscape architects.

Another approach is to use the *Green Sheet* or something similar to find out what jobs are bidding in your area. These newspapers are just for contractors and have classified ads that list jobs, describe the kind of work involved, give other pertinent information. There may also be a plan room in your community that coordinates bids and sub-bids and has plans available for big jobs in the area.

Other Contractors

Get to know people in the other trades—plumbers, electricians, concrete people, etc. They're on the job before you are and often get asked about landscapers. They can get you a lot of work.

Believe it or not, other landscape contractors can also get you work, especially when you're starting out. Many larger contractors don't want to deal with small jobs or maintenance. They may not even do residential work, so they need somebody to refer people to. Sometimes contractors just get too busy to handle all the jobs. If they feel they can trust you, they might just send a lot of work your way. So don't be afraid of talking to the competition. Attend association meetings and barbecues; get to know these people. They can help you get going. (*Tip:* Offer to do the ninety-day maintenance on completed projects for large, busy contractors.)

Retail Nurseries

Get to know the managers of the local nurseries. They often get asked to recommend landscapers and gardeners.

Realtors

Real estate people know who's buying and selling. They're often asked to recommend tradespeople. If you can get their attention, you may get some referrals. Stay in touch with these folks, because they'll quickly forget about you. They tend to hang out at chamber of commerce mixers, Lion's Club meetings, and similar events.

Commercial Property Managers

Large commercial properties such as shopping centers or industrial parks usually have a staff person who handles the grounds and buildings. Call and ask for the name of the facilities manager. Smaller properties are often managed by a property management company that takes care of the properties of many owners for a fee. Look in the Yellow Pages under "Real Estate Management."

Public Agencies

Check the Green Sheet, or contact the city manager or other responsible person.

Developers

Are you *sure* you want to do this? OK, look up "Real Estate Developers," "Land Developers," or "Land Companies" in the Yellow Pages, for starters. Or ask around.

Landlords

Owners of rental property can often be located by doing a search at the county hall of records or by contacting a local apartment owners' association.

Garden Clubs

Garden clubs are usually populated by affluent, older garden enthusiasts who can't do all the work themselves anymore. Go to the meetings, get to know them, offer to give a lecture on your favorite topic.

Social Contacts

Don't forget the value of general schmoozing. Be sure your friends and acquaintances are a part of your sales force. Let them know about interesting projects you're doing, give them a few business cards, ask them to tell their friends.

Advertising

Since we've already agreed that traditional advertising often doesn't work too well, let's broaden the use of the word to include both traditional and nontraditional forms of making the public aware of you. Here's a rundown of the different approaches and a little about how and when to use them effectively.

(*Tip:* After a few years, possibly sooner, you'll begin to avoid advertising, because your reputation alone will bring in more work than you can handle. This is true. In fact, if this doesn't happen to you, ask what's wrong with your service, not with your advertising.)

Important: Whenever a client calls you, be sure to ask where they heard about you; that way you can measure the effects of your various advertising programs.

Traditional Advertising

Yellow Pages

Established companies often have very small Yellow Pages ads or none at all. You, on the other hand, should buy the biggest ad you can afford, at least for the first couple of years. Medium-sized ads are a waste of time; they just make you look second-rate; potential clients will ignore them. Have the ad layout done professionally, because the directory company doesn't usually have very talented graphics people. Include a lot of information in your ad; as the phone company says, "Listing only half of what you do is like closing your doors at noon." As with any advertising, list the reasons the shopper should call you, why you're better. Use color if the directory offers it.

Yellow Pages ads are astonishingly expensive. Rates depend on the size of the community, the size of your ad, and how many ads you buy. Rates for a quarter-page ad can run anywhere from $200 per month to much more. One of the problems with the Yellow Pages is that you have to make a one-year commitment that you can't back out of. Still, the Yellow Pages is a good place for a young company to advertise.

Newspapers

There are two kinds of newspaper advertising: classified ("want ads") and display. Perhaps your paper has a special "Services Offered" classified section where tradespeople advertise; the cost can be reasonable and results can be good. Display ads are outrageously expensive and generally not cost-effective. Remember, it doesn't matter what an ad costs, it only matters how much profit it brings in.

Try a classified ad for starters; they're especially good if you're looking for maintenance work. Make your heading bold or use all-capital letters, and include enough text to tell what you do. If you decide to use display advertising, have the graphics professionally done; don't rely on the hacks at the paper.

Don't run an ad for a week or two and decide that it doesn't work. Successful media advertising depends on *consistency*. Make a commitment to a strategy and stick with it for at least six months; if it's still not working, change your strategy. You can vary your ad during this time, especially the text, to see what works best. Use coupons or special offers to help measure the effectiveness of your ads.

Many papers have a garden section one day a week; it can be a good spot for your ad. Saturdays and Sundays are good, too. Get to know the paper's garden writer. They're always looking for stories and may feature your work—great *free* advertising!

Radio and Television

Forget television; it's just too expensive and the results aren't good. Radio can be helpful and is surprisingly cheap—a thirty-second spot can cost as little as a few dollars if you run it consistently. (*Tip:* The rates radio stations quote you are fictitious; dicker with them for a better deal.) One problem with radio is that it's hard to tell if your ads are doing you any good.

Choose a station that's listened to by affluent homeowners. Your favorite rock station is probably not the one. News stations and talk radio are especially good because people are really paying attention. As with other media, don't let the station produce your ad; invest in professional help. Use music if possible.

Direct Mail

This is anything you send through the mail to potential clients— brochures, newsletters, special offers. Direct mail is a great way to build your business; it's also a way to stay in touch with your regular clients. Though response to direct mail is usually only 2 to 3 percent, the profit per dollar invested is often excellent. You can vary your mailings with the season to highlight services that may be appropriate at certain times of the year. By generating your own mailing list or using the services of a list broker, you can target a select group, such as new homeowners, high-income families, or people in a certain neighborhood. Response to a direct-mail campaign is quick and easy to measure. (*Tip:* If you buy a list from a broker, be sure it doesn't include names of renters.)

The first job of a direct-mail piece is to get the recipient's attention; it's not easy when everyone's mailbox is full of junk mail every day. Use a "teaser"—a line of copy on the outside that creates interest. Classic teasers are "FREE!" or "Increase the Value of Your Property!" Inside, you need to make an offer, such as a week's free mowing with a three-month contract, a free half-hour consultation, or a free plant with every estimate. You need to describe all your services, even if it takes quite a bit of room. Use personal, direct language, as if you were talking to the person face-to-face. Then, tell them what action to take: "Call me today" or "Return the postcard for more information" or whatever. Repeating the offer never hurts. Be sure to appeal to the reader's needs and desires. They want to hear about greener lawns, less yard work, and more beauty; they don't want to hear about you. They *do* want to hear why you're the one to do the job. Finally, give them reasons to respond. Use professionally designed graphics to support your message. Have a professional lay out the ad for you; a hokey mailer is worse than none at all.

Door-to-Door Canvassing

Going door-to-door is a lot of work, but it can really bring in the business. It's especially good when you're just starting out. Dress up in your good clothes, and hit the streets. Choose affluent neighborhoods, either new ones where everybody needs landscaping or older ones where a lot of houses could use a face-lift. You could send out a mailer first or just show up unannounced. (*Tip:* Consider giving out a free gift, perhaps a small plant, to each person you contact. If no one's home, leave it on the doorstep along with a flyer and a business card; then come back the next day.)

There are four steps to canvassing.

1. *Making contact with the person, making a good first impression.* That's where clothing and demeanor count. You've got about five seconds to do this well. Be friendly, positive, outgoing. Be yourself, but be on your best behavior, as if you were meeting your fiancee's parents for the first time.

2. *Qualifying the person.* Some of this you do simply by avoiding unlikely homes: those that show no pride of ownership, have no landscaping, or are probably occupied by renters, for example. After you've talked with a homeowner for a while, you'll be able to tell whether they're interested in your services.

3. *The presentation.* This is your opportunity to describe your services, to tell why you're better than the competition and, specifically, what you can do for the person you're talking to. This is where you have it all over other door-to-door salespeople, because you've checked out the owner's front yard on the way up the walk and developed a mental list of things you could do to make the place better. If they show any interest, take them out and show them.

   The presentation could take a while, especially if the owner is really interested. Don't be in a hurry to go. If they walk you around their yard, you know you've got a serious potential client. However, don't waste your time with someone who just wants to chat; remember, you're there to get work, not to pass the time of day.

It helps to ask questions: "Who does your yard work now?" "Is there anything you've been wanting to do to improve your landscaping?" Listening is important; it helps you get to know the person a bit so you can customize your presentation for them. If you've done any work in the neighborhood, mention it. Be professional and be proud of what you're offering. (*Tip:* You have to give away some of your knowledge to prove you know what you're doing. But don't tell them so much that you come back later and find they've ripped off your ideas. See the section on design/build in chapter 8 for more information on this touchy subject.)

4. *The close.* This describes the way you complete the sale. If you don't close the sale right then, you'll probably never hear from the person again. See chapter 7 for tips on closing a sale.

Flyers

Printing an 8.5-x-11, one-page flyer, and handing it out to a specific audience or putting it under windshields at the mall is a simple, inexpensive way to get attention. It's especially good for seasonal or introductory offers. You can also post flyers at retail nurseries or on supermarket bulletin boards. A flyer can double as a direct mail piece.

Jobsite Signs

Have some signs made that you can put in the front yard on jobs you're doing, and leave them there for a couple of weeks after you've finished. They attract a lot of attention and are a way to show off your work. Custom-made metal or masonite signs, mounted on a steel stake, will cost $75 to $150 apiece, and they're well worth it. Make them easy to read, with large letters. Use color tastefully to attract the eye.

Truck Signs

People look at your trucks and will pay close attention to any signs you place on them. Use magnetic door signs, or mount signs on the sideboards. Put a sign on the back of your truck, too; it'll get read more often than the traditional ones on the side. Make signs easy to read. They may not generate any jobs, but they will reinforce other advertising and help build your name recognition. Just be sure to keep your trucks clean and in good condition.

Welcome Wagon

This group meets with new residents and tells them about services available in the community. Contact the local office, and find out how they can help you.

Home Shows and County Fairs

Renting a booth at one of these events can cost you several hundred dollars, and decorating it can run much more than that. Getting ready for the show and taking things down afterward can consume a lot of time. Still, a couple of good contacts can make it all worthwhile. Just be sure to avoid sleazy shows that will make you look bad.

Alternative Forms of Marketing

Some of the best advertising doesn't cost anything. You may find the following ideas very helpful.

Teaching and Lecturing

Teaching a class or giving a lecture establishes you as an expert and puts you in touch with people doing landscaping. Organizations that may be able to sponsor and advertise a class or lecture for you include adult education, botanic gardens, garden clubs, service clubs (like the Lions Club), and private learning centers. You might also be able to speak at a special event such as an Arbor Day tree planting. Take advantage of occasions such as water awareness month or a special community gathering. Become the local expert on something—water-conserving landscaping, organic pest control, whatever. Just be sure you know your stuff; b.s. won't do.

Public Service

You should do some public service just because it's good to give something back to the community that supports you. But there's no denying that public service has its marketing advantages, too. It's a great source of leads. Possibilities include environmental workdays for groups like The Nature Conservancy or the Sierra Club, community tree plantings, and urban creek cleanups. Your expertise will be welcome, and you'll make friends with a lot of good people who will recommend you to others. You can even think up your own cause. Is there a problem in your community that you could solve?

You can help these causes by donating materials, equipment, labor, and most of all, your expertise as a professional.

Political Activity

Also consider political activity, especially environmental issues, but be aware that taking a visible stand on a controversial issue can alienate a lot of potential clients.

Donations

Donate something to the local public radio or TV station; your name will get out to a large portion of your community. Do the same for local charities such as the boy's or girl's club, preschools, church benefits, etc. These are just a few suggestions; look around your community for other possibilities.

Press Releases

It's been said that 80 percent of the "news" in the paper and on TV is generated by press releases sent in by publicity agents. That seems high to me, but it is true that many people and companies promote themselves very successfully by using press releases. Whenever you win an award, donate your services to a worthy cause, or give a talk, send a press release to the local newspapers and other media. Be sure to use the standard format for the release, which can be found in many books on publicity.

Keeping Track of Potential Clients: Contact Report

This form holds the basic information about a potential client. There are two parts to a good contact report. The first part contains basic data about the client (name, address, etc.). If you plan on running a credit check on the client, find out what your local credit bureau requires and include that. Include a place to indicate how the client found you—Yellow Pages, referral, newspaper ad, etc. This will be important in evaluating the effectiveness of your marketing and advertising.

The second part includes information about the project (address, type of project, work to be done, schedule, etc.). If you're bidding plans drawn by a landscape architect, include the name, address, and phone number of the firm, the person in charge, drawing numbers, dates and revisions, specification section numbers, and dates. If you will be subbing out part of the work, have a space to list the various trades and the names of potential subs. If you'll be working as a subcontractor, provide a place for the name, address, and phone number of the general contractor. Also have a place for the job phone number and the name of the superintendent or contact person. On the following page you'll see a sample contact report form.

Contact Report

Date _____ By _____

PROJECT

Name _____ Address _____

City/State/Zip _____ Phone _____

Contact _____ Fax _____

Type: Residential _____ Commercial _____ Other _____

OWNER

Name _____ Address _____

City/State/Zip _____ Home phone _____

Work phone _____

LANDSCAPE ARCHITECT

Name _____ Address _____

City/State/Zip _____ Phone _____

Contact _____ Fax _____

GENERAL CONTRACTOR

Name _____ Address _____

City/State/Zip _____ Phone _____

Contact _____ Fax _____

DETAILS OF PROJECT

Drawing Nos./Dates/Revisions _____

Specification Section No./Date _____

Submit proposal to: Owner _____   L.A. _____   G.C. _____   Other _____

Bid date/time _____   Date work to start _____

Budget _____   Getting other bids?   Y _____   N _____

Description of work:

_____

_____

_____

Subcontractor bids required:

_____

_____

Notes:

_____

_____

Referred by _____

7

Bidding

Seldom will anyone offer you a job without wanting to know what it will cost. It's your responsibility to provide them with a price before you actually do the work, and that's what the science of bidding is all about. Your price has to be both attractive to the client and profitable to you. Accurate bidding is one of the keys to your success. Bid too high, and you won't get any work; bid too low, and you'll go broke.

The Main Elements of a Bid

Boiled all the way down, a bid consists of *costs* and *profit*. First you figure what the job is going to cost you, then you add on a fair profit, and you've got yourself a bid. See the outline on the next page for the way it looks in detail.

Note: Contingency is an allowance for things you can't foresee (delays caused by others, price increases, etc.). Some people call it "fudge factor." Contingency can also be used to include what I call "courtesy padding"—a little extra money in the bid so you

---

COSTS (money you have to put out to do the job)

Direct (things that go into the actual job)
    labor
    materials
    subcontractor costs
    equipment costs (both owned and rented)
    fees (dump fees, permits, etc.)
    contingency
Indirect
    general conditions (job costs not part of the actual job)
    overhead (what it costs to run your business)

PROFIT (money you earn for doing the job)

---

won't have to nickel-and-dime the client every time some little change comes up on the job.

Remember that you have to recover all your costs before you can make a profit. Most important, *the business never pays for anything; it's always the client who pays.* They pay for your labor and materials, your overhead, your truck and tools, and (if you make that profit) your house and groceries as well.

How a Bid Differs from an Estimate

A bid is a commitment. When you submit a bid, you are agreeing to do the job for the bid price; if you back out you can be sued. An estimate is a way to let the client know approximately how much a job will cost. Be clear with clients about whether the figures you submit are an estimate or a bid.

Time-and-Materials Jobs

Sometimes a firm bid isn't appropriate. Some things, such as cleanups, are difficult to bid fairly. Others, such as small repair jobs, are so trivial that a bid isn't necessary. That's when you'll work on a time-and-materials basis, also known as T&M. You do the job, then bill for the labor (at a profitable rate) and materials (marked up from wholesale to retail or at least to a profitable price). A common variation is called "T&M not to exceed," in which you place an upper limit on what you'll charge for the job; this is used when the client doesn't want to write you a blank check.

There are good and bad things about doing business this way. It's great to know that you'll get paid for everything you do (unlike a bid, which may not be high enough to cover costs and profit). When you've built up a relationship of mutual trust, both you and your client know that everyone will be treated fairly. Still, some clients will look over your shoulder all day, and when you present your bill, they'll whine because someone showed up at 8:33 instead of 8:30.

To be successful with the T&M approach, you have to make your billing policies clear. Let the client know that you'll charge for time spent off the site (going to the dump, picking up materials, etc.), and tell them what prices you'll be charging for labor and materials. Give them an estimate of the total costs, and let them know about anything that might increase those costs. That way there won't be any nasty surprises for either of you at the end of the job.

Unit Price Bidding

Suppose you install a lot of sod lawns. There's no point in going through the whole complicated routine each time you bid a job. Instead, you do it once to set a fair unit price, say $1.05 per square foot, then you use that price every time you bid a lawn. If conditions are unusual (a long carry into the backyard, extra weed control, difficult soil), you adjust accordingly. If you're smart, you'll still cost out every job (see Job Costing on page 183) to be sure you did OK. If you're consistently making less than you should at a given unit price, adjust it. Every few months you should check your unit prices to be sure you're still making money.

(*Tips:* A badly figured unit price will lose you money every time you use it, so do your homework. Don't just imitate somebody else's prices; their costs may be different than yours; they may even be losing money. Base your unit prices on your own situation. Don't use unit prices for everything, just for things like plants, lawns, and other routine tasks. Never unit-price bid a large or complex job; go through the regular bidding process.)

Bidding Maintenance Jobs

Maintenance is mostly labor, so bidding can be somewhat simpler. Otherwise there's no difference. But remember that you have to live with your bid not just once but every month for at least a year or until you can justify a price increase.

When to Charge for Bids

In most circumstances, charging for estimates or bids shows no class at all. Insurance estimates are an exception. Many times, when landscaping is damaged, the owner will use your free estimate to get money out of the insurance company and then spend it on something else. You'll probably never get the work, so you can justify charging a modest fee up front for the estimate; you might make it refundable if you get the job.

The same goes for design work. A common con, often tried on inexperienced landscapers, is for the owner to pick your brains for *exactly* what you'd do to the backyard, then use your ideas to do the work themselves. That hurts enough that you'll soon start charging for design work, as you should. Estimates and general ideas are free; specifics should not be. (You could offer to refund part or all of this charge if you get the work.)

The Bidding Process, Step-by-Step

Step One: *Do You* Really *Want This Job?*

Some jobs are best left to your competitors. To be successful you need to be selective; don't try for every job that comes along. Here are some of the questions you'll learn to ask.

Will it make me money? Did you hear about the landscaper who won $1 million in the lottery? When they asked him what he was going to do, he said he'd probably just keep on doing landscaping until the money was all gone. Well, there's no point in going to work unless you can make a profit, so you have to be sure you're not going up against all the low-ballers in town, or that the owner wants a Mercedes for a Yugo price.

Is this the kind of work I'm good at doing? If the project is beyond your abilities, let it go. To do otherwise is to ask for trouble.

Is it the right size? Big jobs aren't for beginners. You won't be able to bid it right, do it right, or finance it right. Evaluate your available manpower, equipment, subcontractors, and financial capabilities before you get involved.

Is it in the right location? Don't take work that's 200 miles away. You'll go crazy commuting. When the job's done and the client wants you to come out every three days to see if the plants are doing OK, you'll realize you should have stuck closer to home.

Do I have time for it? It seems like there's always too much work or too little work. Overextending is a major cause of failure. Learn how much work you can handle at one time, and take on only what you can do thoroughly and completely. Although you want to provide service as promptly as possible, clients will wait for you if you have a good reputation. In fact, knowing you're busy seems to make people feel better. (I have a message on my answering machine that includes a comment about my three-to-four-week backlog; it makes people more eager to get in line to have me do their landscaping. Strange but true.)

Is the client a turkey? Sometimes you look at a job and something just doesn't feel right, something about the way the guy looks at you or whatever. Maybe you can't put your finger on it, but after a few bad experiences you learn that the little voice inside that was telling you to flee was right. Sometimes you'll take on a job with a potential turkey because things are slow (we've all done this), then, sure enough, a week into it you'll wish you'd never seen the place.

Evaluate potential clients for sincerity (weed out tire-kickers), integrity (don't fall for that stuff about "give me a good deal on this job, and I can get you lots of work"), ability to pay (the bank does credit checks; why not you?), agreeability (when someone complains about every other contractor or gardener they've ever had, you know they'll be talking about *you* the same way soon enough), and sanity (some people are just too loony to do business with). Apply the same tests to the project landscape architect, general contractor, or anyone else who may have power over you.

Is the project a turkey? Is this a hideous job that you'll be ashamed to be associated with? Are there unreasonable risks involved (erosion, soil problems, safety hazards)? If a landscape architect designed it, is it a dreadful design? Are there unreasonable restrictions (too little time to bid it or to complete it, outrageous guarantees, etc.)?

How do I get rid of a funky job? If you don't want it, say so. True, some people will bid it sky-high, but that can give you a reputation you don't want. Others just don't call the client back, but that looks bad, too. No, just tell them it's not your kind of project or (if you must lie) that you're too busy to take it on. Thank them for their interest, and move along.

Step Two: *The Plans and Specifications*

Study the plans and specifications with utmost care, because they describe the job and set the standards to which you'll work. Be sure you have the latest version of the plans plus all addenda and revisions. Ask the landscape architect specifically if this is the case. If you're doing design/build, you'll be setting your own standards, which makes things a lot easier.

Many people have gone broke because they missed some little note or detail that cost them everything. For instance, what if you misread the scale of the plans and bid on 4,000 square feet of lawn instead of 16,000? What if you missed the part that said, "Contractor shall obtain and pay for all building permits"? Plans often include lists of plants and other materials; check the quantities shown on the drawings against the materials lists for discrepancies. (Often the specifications state whether the drawings or the lists take precedence in the event of an error.) Read the specifications several times; do the same with detail drawings and any other attachments.

Step Three: *The Site Inspection*

Anyone who bids a job without doing a *thorough* inspection of the site is plain crazy. Site conditions can make a big difference in the cost of the job. Some of the things to look for are soil conditions (Is digging easy or difficult? Are there rocks?), terrain, and existing features (structures, trees and shrubs, weed growth, underground utilities that affect digging, overhead wires that affect equipment operation, accessibility for equipment and materials delivery). Compare the actual dimensions of the site to what's shown on the plans, because plans are often horribly inaccurate. Look at the finish grade: Is it high or low, indicating potentially expensive earth-moving work? Think about where you'll park trucks, where the staging area will be, where people will go to the bathroom. Think the job completely through from beginning to end. The Site Inspection Report (Landscaping) on page 182 will help you with this process. For maintenance work, use the Site Inspection and Bid Worksheet (Maintenance) on pages 184–185.

Step Four: *The Takeoffs*

A takeoff is a list of all the direct costs (materials, labor, equipment, and subcontractors) required to do the job. The takeoff will follow you through the job, serving first as a basis for your bid, later as a shopping list, and finally as a way to do your job costing. Have a look at the Bid Takeoff Worksheet on pages 186–187 to see how to organize the information in a usable form. (This process will get easier as you gain more experience. For starters, stick to small, simple jobs.)

Materials

List your materials first. As you go along, mark the plans with a highlighter to make sure you counted everything. Be methodical and careful to get everything. Remember that the plans may show certain items like plants, but not others like staking materials or soil amendments. You need to allow for shrinkage, too; for example, compacted soil can shrink up to 30 percent. There's wastage in almost all materials, so include more of everything. Don't forget supportive materials like concrete forms that might not be reused. Finally, be sure to include sales tax, on a separate line. (*Important Tip:* The key to successful bidding is building the job in your mind. You've got to visualize every act from start to finish: spraying the weeds, digging the holes, hauling the mulch up the hill. That way, you'll get a good idea of the materials, labor, and equipment required, not just a wild guess.) Remember, when you get to doing the actual job, you'll need what you need, and it'll cost what it costs. Now's the time to face it.

Labor

The materials takeoff was the easy part: just counting. Now you've got to figure your labor. Labor is usually what makes or breaks you. It's also a lot harder to estimate than materials because you're dealing with people.

There's nothing on the plans that you can count to get your labor costs, so how do you do it? One way is to get a book of time-and-motion studies, often available through trade associations. You'll find information on how many one-gallon plants a laborer can plant per hour in different soils, how much area a mower can mow per hour, and so forth. Of course, these figures don't have much to do with *your* people on *this* particular job, do they? So use them only as a guide, adjusting for the particular circumstances you face. A better way is to base your labor on what you and your people have done in the past. As you do more jobs, you'll be able to develop your own time studies as well as adjustment factors for different soil conditions and so forth. Include plenty of fudge factor in your labor takeoffs, because you'll need it.

What about your own salary? Well, if you'll be working on the job, pay yourself an hourly wage. But even if you never leave the office, you need to apportion an appropriate amount of your salary to the job, based on the amount of time you'll spend on it. Don't assume you'll just take your living expenses out of the profit; profit is another matter entirely.

Equipment

Next, list the equipment you'll need. If you're going to rent a tractor, figuring the cost is easy: how many days (or hours) and how much per day or hour? But you need to recover costs on your own equipment, too. One way is to charge what the rental yards would charge you if you had to rent the item. Their business is making money on equipment, so if they don't know costs, who would? Just remember to deduct the profit they include, since you don't want to add profit on twice. The other way is to figure actual costs of ownership: Purchase price plus maintenance, less salvage value, divided by the estimated hours of useful life will determine a rate per hour. Naturally, you do this only on trucks and mechanized equipment, not rakes and shovels.

Subcontractors

Include the cost of any subcontracted work. To do this, you need to get bids from your subs. Allow plenty of time for this; don't wait until the last minute and expect them to come up with a price. After all, they've got to go through the same routine you do. Get them involved right at the start. It's up to you whether to get more than one sub-bid for each trade. Do it if you need to be low bidder; otherwise, stick with your regular subs and don't pit them against each other.

General Conditions

Finally, you've got to deal with a category called "General Conditions." These are costs that don't become a part of the finished job but have to be paid for anyway. Examples are time spent every day to clean up the site, loading and unloading, travel time, port-a-potties, dumpsters, moving equipment on and off the job (called mobilization), record drawings, and photos. And what about time spent looking for plants, replacement of plants that die and other warranty work, and dump fees? There are lots of general conditions and they vary from job to job.

Total Direct Costs

Now add all this up to get your Total Direct Cost.

Step Five: *Figuring Overhead Recovery*

Remember overhead? It's the cost of running your business, and it gets paid only if you charge it to the jobs you do. Where else would it come from—the overhead fairy?

You know from your business plan what your overhead should be in the first few years. You also know that your overhead will be low as long as you work out of your home and do things yourself. When you've planned in advance for overhead recovery, you'll know that overhead won't have to come out of profits because you failed to account for it in your bids. (*Tip:* You need to recover most of your overhead from your labor, because labor causes more of it in the first place. After all, if you were just selling materials, you wouldn't need trucks and equipment and tools, you wouldn't have to pay worker's compensation insurance, and so forth. So, a job that's labor-intensive needs to have more overhead charged to it than one that's materials-intensive.)

Now, divide your projected annual overhead into daily chunks. When you bid a job, figure out how many days it will take and add the overhead amount to the bid price.

Another approach is to precalculate your overhead as a percentage of direct costs. This works better after you've been in business a year or two and will then be more accurate than the previous method. Let's say your overhead is 15 percent of your direct costs; you mark up the direct costs of the job you're bidding by 15 percent. (*Crucial Warning: Adding on* 15 percent doesn't *recover* 15 percent!! If you have a "markup/markdown" key on your calculator, use it to get the true markup. If you don't, or if you're setting up a bid form on a computer spreadsheet, *divide* your direct costs by the *reciprocal* of your overhead—85 percent—to arrive at the 15 percent. Or add on 17 $2/3$ percent to arrive at the same figure. Play around with this on your calculator until you get the idea. This same principle is true of any markups or markdowns.)

Step Six: *Adding On Your Profit*

Now you know what this job is going to cost you, but you haven't yet figured out what you're going to make on it. (If you're feeling guilty about the prospect of making a profit, go back to chapter 3 and read the section on Net Profit/Loss.) Remember that it doesn't make sense to earn less profit than the interest the bank will pay you on your money. Remember, too, that profit is your reward for investing in your business and for taking the risks involved in the jobs you do. In fact, the riskier the job, the more profit you should add on.

So, the least profit you should accept is equal to the interest rate at the bank plus maybe 2 percent to cover your risk. The highest acceptable profit is what will still get you the job and not make you feel like a gouger. When you've got twenty years of high-quality work behind you and people are beating down your door, you can probably ask whatever you want for your services. But that doesn't mean you need to be a low-baller now, just because you're the new guy. Setting prices too low gives people the idea that you must do lousy work.

Remember that you can't charge the same profit on a commercial or competitively bid job as you can on a residential job. Smaller jobs should earn more profit than big ones. You may have to lower your profit margin when times are lean and money is tight. Going against low-ballers may make it impossible to do the job at any profit. (Here are a few reasons low-ballers can bid jobs so low: They aren't licensed and don't pay worker's comp or other insurance. They do all the work themselves, dig smaller holes and shallower trenches, use cheaper materials or use less than what's called for, and do sloppy work. They use money from the next job to pay for the last job, don't pay their suppliers, and don't pay their taxes. Some have rich parents that support their little hobby of landscaping. Then too, many low-ballers are in the process of going broke.)

No one can help you any more than that; your profit margin is your decision.

Step Seven: *Checking Your Bid*

Double-check everything—your takeoffs, your assumptions, your arithmetic. If you have a partner or someone else who can go over it too, so much the better. Remember, your livelihood is riding on every bid. Who needs Las Vegas?

Look at the Bid Summary Sheet on pages 188–189 to see how to organize your final bid information.

Alternates

Many times the client will ask for other, possibly cheaper, ways of doing the job. They're called *alternates,* and you need to provide a separate bid for each alternate. Many people hate having to bid alternates, but they're really one of your best selling tools. By getting the client involved in whether to use brick or gravel for the walks, you make it easier for him to say yes to the job. Use alternates even when people don't ask for them—everybody appreciates a choice rather than a take-it-or-leave-it approach. It shows that you're thinking. Besides, you can make the same profit on the alternate simply by marking it up higher.

Conditions, Exclusions, and Qualifications

Most bids include a section where the contractor clarifies the work beyond what's on the plans and specifications. Often it's used to tell what you won't do. For instance: "Painting not included," or "110-volt supply to clock to be installed by others," or "Not responsible for survival of transplanted trees." Often there's a rock clause, limiting your liability for unobservable soil conditions and establishing a billing procedure for extra labor required to deal with the problems that might arise from boulders and other junk buried underground.

Bidding Secrets

Here are some things it takes the average person years to learn (if they ever do):

Front Loading (for jobs where you receive progress payments): Get your profits out of the job early on by putting a higher markup on the things you'll be doing first: demolition, earthwork, etc. To do this, you need to do a separate bid sheet for each segment of the job and submit a price for each segment. Prices for early stages of the work will include more of the overhead and profit than later stages. You also need to base your progress payments on completion of specific segments.

Loading "Sure Thing" Items: Sometimes the owner will get your bid and start eliminating frills like lighting or water features. By putting most of your profit into the basic portions of the work, you're sure to make your money. Since they can't cut out weed control or grading, put more of your profit there.

Rounding Off: I have a sub who always turns in bids that look like this: $43,167.16. That's absurd. Round everything up to cover some of your contingency. Turn in round-number bids. (*Tip:* Use a printing calculator to run a tape so you can double check your addition; save the tape with the bid sheets for later reference.)

The Bid Package

On a private residential job, you'll usually submit your bid directly to the homeowner, or in some cases to the landscape architect. Be sure it's neatly typed on your letterhead and that you've included all details, exclusions, and other necessary information. The bid package is your showroom, so make it professional and attractive. Include the contract (where applicable), a list of jobs you've done that the client can drive by and look at, a list of references, your brochure or other sales literature, a credit application if you wish, and a cover letter. Put all this in a nice folder with your business card stuck to the outside where people can see it.

There are a lot of approaches to the format of the bid presentation. The example on pages 190–191 shows some of the information you should include; this is a format that works well for me. Remember that your presentation will vary depending on the circumstances.

Submitting the Bid

On a residential job, it's traditional to meet with the client and go over the bid. On a big, competitively bid job, there's often a formal bid opening that all bidders attend. Whatever the circumstances, this is your moment of truth. Here are a couple of things that can happen at this stage.

So You're the Low Bidder?

One of the scariest things is to be low bidder on a competitively bid job, especially if you're a *lot* lower than the other bidders. What did you forget? How much is it going to cost you? Is this the end of your career?

Generally speaking, once your bid has been accepted, you're obligated to do the work. Still, there are certain circumstances under which you can back out or adjust your bid. For example, courts have found that if an error is so obvious that even the client can see that something's wrong, the bidder can withdraw or rebid. If this ever happens to you, see an attorney at once. (*Tip:* Always get the bid results of every job you bid so you can see what the other contractors are bidding.)

What If You're Over Budget?

Usually the client has a number in the back of their mind, the price they think you ought to do the job for. Or the landscape architect has provided them with a cost estimate. Naturally, they won't tell you what that number is until you've submitted your bid. If your number is a lot bigger, you've got problems. The client may be shocked. The landscape architect may be embarrassed. They may want to throw you bodily into the street. What do you do?

Let's say they really want you to do the work, but the price is just too high. You have an opportunity to salvage the situation by telling them what you can do for *their* price. What can you change or delete? Naturally they won't get as much work as the original project (*Never* lower your bid price to get a job. *Never.*) but surely you can change *something*. Start stripping the bid of nonessentials (those low-profit frills like lighting and ponds). Show them on paper how the price drops every time you take something out. Downsizing plants—fifteen gallon to five gallon, fives down to ones—can cut costs in a hurry without changing the quality of the project much. If this doesn't get you to their price range, suggest doing the work in stages, half now and half in fall, for example. Go as far as you can without cutting quality or profit. Usually this works as long as people's expectations aren't wildly off the mark.

Sample Bidding Forms

When you look at the sample forms in this chapter, remember that there's no one right way to do bidding; you'll surely develop your own approach over time. The examples on pages 182 and 184–191 will help you understand the basics. *Note:* These forms are provided for illustration only. All figures are fictitious and should not be used in your own bids. (*Tip:* You may want to provide a place on each page of any legal documents for the client to put their initials. That's a standard way to protect yourself against later claims that they "never saw that page.")

The Contract

The contract is one of the key documents in your business. Required by law, the contents of the contract will vary, depending on the regulations in your state. You must not get creative with these requirements or you risk losing money or even your contractor's license. Check with your attorney or the contractor's

Site Inspection Report *(Landscaping)*

JOB NAME: _____

JOB LOCATION: _____

CLIENT'S NAME & ADDRESS: _____

_____

CLIENT'S PHONE: _____

LANDSCAPE ARCHITECT: _____

GENERAL CONTRACTOR: _____

DATE BID DUE: _____

START DATE: _____ COMPLETION DATE: _____

ACCESS: _____

DISTANCE/DRIVING TIME: _____

VEHICLE PARKING: _____

SUPPLIERS NEARBY: _____

WATER/POWER/TEMPORARY IMPROVEMENTS: _____

BATHROOM FACILITIES: _____

STAGING AREA: _____

SOIL CONDITIONS: _____

DIGGING CONDITIONS: _____

EXISTING GRADE: _____

WEED GROWTH: _____

VERTEBRATE/OTHER PESTS: _____

EXISTING PLANTS: _____

EXISTING STRUCTURES: _____

OTHER CONSIDERATIONS: _____

license board to find out what you need. Preprinted forms are sold at contractor's bookstores and office supply places. Be sure to use forms that comply with local laws. Another good source is your state landscape contractor's association. *Warning:* Sometimes the standard forms are out of date, since laws change so often. Compare the form to the law before you use it.

If you're submitting a bid to a general contractor, developer, or landscape architect, they will probably give *you* a contract rather than the other way around. Many times these contracts are heavily weighted against you. Read them carefully, and negotiate changes in any clauses that are unfair to you.

Some people turn in the contract along with the bid, which makes it easy for the client to say yes just by signing on the dotted line. Other times, you turn in the bid and wait for the client to say yes before you send or bring a contract. It's best to meet with the client to sign the contract. For one thing, they may have questions. More important, people often get cold feet at the last moment, so you want to be there to help them make the final decision in your favor.

Job Costing

Logically, this topic belongs at the end of the chapter on project management since it's done at the end of the job, but job costing is so closely allied to bidding that we need to discuss it right now.

Job costing is the flip side of bidding. It's adding up your actual costs at the end of the job to see whether you made any money. To do it, simply take the bid form and enter actual costs (taken from invoices for materials and equipment, payroll records, and subcontractor billings) where before you entered projected costs. It's a simple and absolutely necessary procedure. After all, how else would you know if you made any money? Force yourself if you need to, but do job costing on all your jobs.

Site Inspection and Bid Worksheet (Maintenance)

JOB NAME: _____   JOB LOCATION: _____

CLIENT'S NAME & ADDRESS: _____

_____   CLIENT'S PHONE: _____

WORK AREA: _____

DURATION OF WORK: _____   VISITS PER MONTH: _____

LAWN: MOW (sq. ft.) _____   EDGE (lin. ft.) _____ TIMES PER WEEK: _____

AREA: (sq. ft.) FRONT _____ REAR _____ TOTAL _____

TYPE: EQUIPMENT: ROTARY _____ REEL _____ OTHER _____

MOWING HEIGHT: _____   REMOVE CLIPPINGS? _____

EDGING: MECHANICAL _____ CHEMICAL _____

FERTILIZATION: FREQUENCY _____   FERTILIZER TYPE _____

WEED CONTROL: _____   PEST CONTROL: _____

DISEASE CONTROL: _____

WATERING: _____ TIMES PER WEEK

OVERSEEDING: _____   AERIFICATION: _____   DETHATCHING: _____

RESEDDING: _____   RESODDING: _____   TOPDRESSING: _____

WEED CONTROL: BEDS   SLOPES   OTHER

PEST CONTROL: TREES/SHRUBS   BEDS   OTHER

FERTILIZATION: TREES/SHRUBS   BEDS   OTHER

PRUNING: TREES/SHRUBS   BEDS   OTHER

WATERING: TREES/SHRUBS   BEDS   OTHER

IRRIGATION SYSTEM: SPRINKLERS   DRIP   VALVES
                     BACKFLOW   REPROGRAM CLOCK

SPECIAL: _____ WATER FEATURES   _____ DRAINS/GUTTERS
           _____ SNOW REMOVAL   _____ COMPOSTING   _____ OTHER

OTHER:

LABOR HRS.   PER VISIT: PER MONTH: RATE:

MATERIALS   PER VISIT: PER MONTH: TOTAL:

DUMP FEES   PER VISIT: PER MONTH: TOTAL:

DRIVING HRS. PER VISIT: PER MONTH: RATE: TOTAL:

                                                          TOTAL:

TOTAL BID:

COMMENTS:

Bid Takeoff Worksheet (Landscaping)

Qty./Unit	Bid Item	Unit Cost	Materials	Labor	Equipment & Other	Total
	Grow & Kill (3,000 SQ. FT.)					
1 Pt.	Roundup	22.00	22.00			
1 Hr.	Labor	9.50		9.50		
	SUBTOTAL		22.00	9.50		31.50
	Demolition					
30 Hr.	Weeds on slope	9.50		285.00		
6 Hr.	Remove shrubs	9.50		57.00		
	SUBTOTAL			342.00		342.00
	Lawn					
3000 SF.	Fescue sod	.27	810.00			
1 L.S.	Sod delivery		40.00			
10 C.Y.	Compost	30.00	300.00			
50 Lb.	16-6-8	1.50	75.00			
30 Hrs.	Till & F.G.	9.50		285.00		
20 Hrs.	Lay Sod	9.50		190.00		
1 Day	Tiller rental				100.00	
	SUBTOTAL		1225.00	475.00	100.00	1800.00
	Planting					
2 15g.	Ulmus parvifolia	40.00	80.00			
14 5 g.	Ligustrum Texanum	9.00	126.00			
72 1 g	Assored (See list)	3.50	255.50			

Qty/Unit	Description	Unit Price				Total
450 Ea.	Fertilizer tabs	.09	40.50			
26 Hrs.	Planting	9.50		247.00		
	SUBTOTAL		697.00	247.00		944.00
18 C.Y.	**Mulching** Walk-on Bark	32.00	576.00			
20 Hrs.	Apply mulch	9.50		190.00		
	SUBTOTAL		576.00	190.00		766.00
	General Conditions					
4 Hrs.	Mobilization	9.50		38.00		
3 Hrs.	Cleanup	9.50		28.50		
2 Hrs.	Hauling	9.50		19.50		
1 L.S.	Dump Fees				22.00	
1 Day	Truck use				200.00	
	SUBTOTAL			86.00	222.00	308.00
	Subcontractor					
1 L.S.	Electrician				125.00	
	SUBTOTAL				125.00	125.00
52 Hrs.	**Maintenance** (90 days) 4 Hrs/Wk x 13 wks	8.00		416.00		
1 L.S.	Fertilizer		10.00			
1 L.S.	Herbicide		5.00			
1 L.S.	Pesticide		5.00			
	SUBTOTAL		20.00	416.00		436.00

Bid Summary Sheet (Landscaping, Lump-Sum Bid)

Qty./Unit	Bid Item	Materials	Labor	Equipment & Other	Subcontractors
3000 S.F.	Grow & Kill	22.00	9.50		
1 L.S.	Demolition		342.00		
3000 S.F.	Lawn	1225.00	475.00	100.00	
1 L.S.	Planting	697.00	247.00		
18 CY	Mulching	576.00	190.00		
	SUBTOTALS	2520.00	1264.00	100.00	
	General Conditions		86.00	222.00	
	Subcontractors				125.00
	Maintenance	20.00	416.00		
	ADJUSTED SUBTOTALS	2540.00	1766.00	322.00	125.00
	Labor Burden (30%)		996.00		
	Sales Tax (7.5%)	190.50			
	TOTAL DIRECT COSTS	2730.50	2762.00	322.00	125.00

Contingency (10%)		274.00	276.00	32.00	13.00
Overhead	(15%) 482.00	(30%) 1184.00	(10%) 36.00	(10%) 14.00
TOTALS	3487.00	4222.00	390.00	152.00

SUMMARY:

Total Materials	$3487.00
Total Labor	4222.00
Total Equipment	390.00
Total Subcontractors	152.00
Total Direct Cost	8251.00
Profit (17%)	1690.00
Grand Total	9941.00
Bid Price	$9975.00

Bid Presentation *(Landscaping)*

GREEN WITH ENVY LANDSCAPING CO.
221 S. Marchant Rd., Turfburg, PA. 07468
(555) 771–2239

PROJECT: Petersen Residence, 701 E. 4th St., Turfburg
INFORMATION: Bid on Proposed Landscaping Work
DATE: July 12, 1994

LOCATION OF WORK: Front yard only, at the above address.

GENERAL DESCRIPTION OF WORK:
Kill existing weeds in turf area. Remove weeds and shrubs. Trim and prune shrubs and perennials in beds around lawn. Install new automatic sprinkler system to irrigate lawn and surrounding beds and bed along driveway. Install hybrid fescue lawn to replace existing. Install plants per list below. Mulch all beds.

DETAILS OF WORK:

1. GROW and KILL: Spray weeds with Roundup herbicide (two sprayings max.) Owner to water area three days prior to each spraying.

2. DEMOLITION: Remove weeds (including roots, as practical) on west slope above lawn. Remove shrubs along driveway from sidewalk to mailbox. Trim hedge behind east flower bed. Prune foundation plantings.

3. IRRIGATION: Install 1 Hardie RD600-EXT controller, wiring, and 5 WeatherMatic 11024F electric valves in valve boxes. Install 32 Toro 570P heads in lawn and adjacent borders, including pipe and fittings.

4. LAWN: Prepare soil per sod grower's specifications and install 3,000 sq. ft. of "ToughGreen" hybrid fescue sod.

5. PLANTING: Plant 2 15-gal. *Ulmus parvifolia,* 14 5-gal. *Ligustrum texanum,* 73 1-gal. assorted plants per sketch approved by owner.

6. MULCHING: Apply 2-inch-thick mulch of walk-on bark to all planted beds in front yard.

CONDITIONS, LIMITATIONS, and EXCLUSIONS:
1. Owner must locate and flag buried water main and sewer.
2. Extra work due to large rocks or other buried obstructions to digging will be billed at regular rates.

3. Small flower bed under dining room window is not included in irrigation work.
4. Work includes ninety days maintenance on all newly installed landscaping, including mowing and edging, weed and pest control, cleanup.

GUARANTEES:
All work is guaranteed against defects in materials and workmanship for ninety days from date of installation, except irrigation system, which is guaranteed for one year.

PRICE OF WORK:
$ 11,930.00

PAYMENT SCHEDULE:
Ten percent deposit on acceptance, balance due on completion of work.

SCHEDULE:
We can begin work the second week in August, except for grow and kill, which will be done immediately on acceptance of the proposal and after watering by owner.

CONTRACT:
A written contract will be prepared for all work.

LICENSES:
State Contractor's License No. 77462. City of Turfburg License No. 1773.

REFERENCES:
References and a job list are enclosed.

CONTACT:
For more information, please contact Andy Tomlinson, owner. (555) 771-2239 (office) or (555) 771-9903 (beeper).

Thank you for allowing us to provide you with a proposal. Please get in touch if you have any questions. We're looking forward to working with you!

Respectfully submitted,

Andy Tomlinson, owner

Salesmanship 101

To get the job, you have to do more than provide a good price. In fact, price is often of less concern to potential clients than other things. To get the job, you have to give people what they want, whatever it is. Some want the beauty of a new garden; others want the convenience of low-maintenance plantings or an automatic sprinkler system. Some are looking for improved resale value or status or better relations with their spouse. To get a potential client to do business with you, you have to figure out what they want, then prove you can give it to them. Do that, and you've got a job; fail, and you're down the road, no matter how low your price is.

The idea of "selling" is disagreeable to many people, but we actually sell ourselves every day. Selling your services is nothing more than the following perfectly honorable set of actions:

1. Find out what the client wants.

2. Figure out how to provide it.

3. Tell (and show) the client what you propose.

4. Answer any questions they have.

5. Answer any objections they have.

6. Share your enthusiasm for the project.

7. Close the sale.

Selling isn't about bullying people into buying something; it's about educating them. Remember, every good business deal is a win-win situation. The client gets a garden (or care of a garden); you get a job.

Closing the Sale

Whole books are written on how to close a sale. There are dozens of manipulative closing techniques, most of which you won't need if you've done a good job so far. To me, the only dignified close is to simply say something like, "So, shall we go to work, then?" Just give them the opportunity to say yes to your wonderful proposal. You don't have to act like a car salesman.

After They Say Yes

Try something like this: "Great! Well, I'll order the plants in the morning so they'll be here on time. Listen, I'm really excited about this job. It's going to be beautiful! Thanks for letting me go to work for you. Here's my beeper number in case you can't get me in the office; call me any time you need anything. I'll call you Friday to let you know what day next week we'll start." (*Tip:* In some cases, you have to offer the client a "Three Day Right of Rescission," giving them three days after they've signed the contract to back out of the deal.)

What If They Say They Want to Think About It?

There are numerous variations on this: "I'll have to talk it over with the wife." "I've got to ask my partner." "We're still waiting to hear from one other bidder." Salesmanship books will tell you that you're losing the sale at this point, and it's time to dig in your heels, ask what you could do to sign them up right now, offer them extras, do any desperate and ungentlemanly thing to close the sale on the spot. I've never been able to make myself do this. I suggest you remind them of a few of the benefits you've mentioned and throw in a couple of new ones for good measure. Don't give them a long spiel, just make one more try, then thank them, ask them when they'll be making a decision (so you can call them for an answer), and leave.

Call back in a few days to see whether they've made up their minds. If you thought up something else you could offer to help close the sale, offer it. And accept the fact that you're not going to get all the jobs you bid. In my experience, a capture ratio of 50 percent is decent, though you can do better under some circumstances.

Good luck!

Tips on Making the Selling Process Pleasant and Effective

Never mail a bid. Nine times out of ten, when you mail somebody a bid rather than meeting with them, you never hear from them again. Always set up a meeting so you can go through the seven steps of selling.

Relax. Your life doesn't depend on this job. Take it easy, be yourself, and let the process happen naturally.

Talk People's Language. If the client is an artist, talk about how beautiful the garden will be when you're done with it. If the client is an accountant, talk about the cost effectiveness of your proposal. Be more formal with formal people and more casual with casual people. *But:* Never lose your professionalism. Don't swear just because the client does, for example.

Dress well. Set your appointments for the morning, before you've had a chance to get dirty, or at the end of the day when you can go home and clean up first. Nobody expects you to arrive in a suit, but they'd just as soon you didn't track mud from your last job all over their carpet either.

Don't bad-mouth the competition. It's tempting to tell stories about how lousy your competitors are. Don't do it. It makes you look bad, and besides, you might get sued for slander. If you know the client is looking for other bids, give them the names of a couple of the best (and hopefully most expensive) competitors. That way you'll be bidding against qualified people, not hacks. You might even tell these competitors you've given out their names and ask them to do the same for you in the future. It sure is nice to be able to choose who you're bidding against.

Listen. You can learn so much by paying attention to what the client says. Don't just walk in and do your song-and-dance. By being attentive, you make the client confident that you care about them.

Show. Bring photos of your other jobs. Walk them through the yard and paint a word picture of what it will look like when you're done. Make them see the hammock under the trees, next to the new lawn, and them lying there with a cold drink and nothing to do all afternoon.

Never say no. No is the worst word in the English language when you're trying to sell someone something. When they ask, "Does this plant flower all year?" say "It flowers from March through October" not "Well, no, actually it doesn't." Who wants to hear no?

Be flexible. Remember, you're there to meet the needs of the client. If they want something, figure out how you can get it to them.

Watch for closing signals. People act differently as soon as they've made up their minds. Here are examples of signs that you should stop talking and close the sale:

Kinds of Questions They'll Ask

1. How long would the job take?
2. When could you start?
3. Would you be supervising the work yourself?
4. Does the flagstone come in any other colors?

Body Language

1. Relaxes, settles back, unfolds arms
2. Studies plans or proposal in detail
3. Any sudden change in attitude

8

Finally You Get to Do Some Real Work

Designing the Project

Doing installations based on your own designs is called design/build. In California it's legal for a licensed landscape contractor to design private residential projects, as long as she or he also intends to build them (you have to be a licensed landscape architect to do just design). Regulations vary from state to state, so check with your contractor's license board.

Before you get into design/build, be sure you're qualified. Many landscape contractors do a really bad job of designing. Just because you can build things doesn't mean you can also design them. There are lots of great books on landscape design and plenty of other opportunities to educate yourself. As with any aspect of landscaping, start with small, simple projects.

Homeowners are the best source of design/build projects. The best ones will come as referrals, people who have seen or heard about your work from their friends or neighbors. You can also solicit design/build projects through advertising or by going door-to-door.

The design process usually goes something like this:

1. *The Initial Meeting.* The purpose of your first meeting with the client is to evaluate the project, to learn the client's needs, and to define the basic elements of the design. Usually the client will have a list of problems and questions for you. The first step is to have them show you around, while you listen and take mental notes. Then it's your turn. Walk around again, this time asking questions and proposing solutions. By the end of this one-to-two-hour meeting, you should have established a general approach to the design and an overall budget (be prepared to provide per-unit prices for the installation and give a rough idea of what the entire project will cost). At the end of this meeting, you should measure the property so you can prepare drawings. (*Tip:* Ask the client if they have a set of house plans that you can make a tracing from; this might save you much of the measuring.) You won't need to do a set of plans for a very simple project, but the ability to prepare an attractive quick sketch helps the client to visualize your proposal.

2. *The Preliminary Design.* Design is the process of going from the general to the specific. The preliminary design is a scale drawing that shows the general outlines of proposed improvements (where the patio's going to be, the location of shade trees, the shape of the lawn) but not every last detail (an exposed aggregate patio, six 24-inch boxed *Ulmus parvifolia,* such-and-such variety of hybrid tall fescue). At this stage you also prepare a preliminary list of plants, with several options for each area (two or three varieties of shade trees, several kinds of hedge plants, etc.) and some alternatives for the hardscape features (tile versus stamped concrete for the walks). Preparing the preliminary plan and plant list could take four to ten hours. (*Tip:* It's helpful if you can color in your sketch with

marking pens or colored pencils; it makes the plans more readable, and clients really like the way it looks.)

3. *The Second Meeting.* When you present your preliminary sketch, bring along photos of the plants on your list (use your own and/or bring some picture books) and also photos of some of your projects that might be similar to this one. Also bring a more detailed cost estimate. At this meeting you'll make decisions on the specifics of the design. The second meeting should last one to three hours. In some cases, you won't need to do any more designing than this. If the client understands and likes your approach, you can provide a final bid and get on with the installation.

4. *The Final Design.* Where the complexity of the project warrants it, you'll prepare a final drawing that shows specific locations, varieties and quantities of plants, and exact dimensions and construction details for all hardscape features. If the irrigation system is complex, you may want to do an irrigation plan on a separate sheet. The final plans should take six to twenty hours to prepare. (*Tip:* Take a class in landscape drafting. The drafting skills of most contractors need major improvement. It helps if you're artistically inclined, but anyone can learn to produce a professional-looking set of plans.) Naturally, you'll have another meeting to go over the final plans and the final bid.

Specifications

Whatever the complexity of your design, you should provide the client with a set of written specifications for the work. Specifications detail exactly what you'll be doing and how you'll be doing it. Here's an example of a specification for soil preparation:

> Soil shall be rototilled to a depth of 5 inches. Any rubbish and loose stones larger than 2 inches shall be removed and disposed of off site. Soil shall be amended with nitrolized fir bark compost at the rate of 4 cubic yards per 1,000 square feet; compost shall be spread evenly over the surface and fully

blended with the tilled soil by tilling a second time. Area shall then be finish graded to plus-or-minus 1 inch.

Specifications protect the client, but they can also protect you by defining the limits of your responsibilities. Here's an example:

Owner will be responsible for all care and maintenance of plantings after completion of the work, following instructions of contractor.

There are other protective clauses that you should always include in any set of specifications. A rock clause limits your liability for buried obstructions that were not reasonably foreseeable. A "Site Conditions" clause defines what you expect the condition of the site to be when you show up—cleanliness, finish grading, access, etc. A detailed guarantee explains what is and is not covered and for how long. You should state that guarantees are valid only if the client has complied with payments and other terms of the contract.

There are many other protective clauses. Check with your trade association and possibly your attorney for specific information. Also, if you do jobs designed by landscape architects, you'll get to see the specs they use. (*Tip:* If you have a computer, you can easily print out a customized set of specifications for each job.)

How to Charge for Design Services

Some contractors do designs for free, in the hopes of getting the installation. This is foolish because it makes you look desperate and unprofessional. It also exposes you to the danger of getting your design ripped off. Besides, why should *anyone* work for free? If you feel you must offer an incentive, refund part of the design fees on completion of the installation work. Once you've built a good reputation, you should charge full price for designing.

You can work by the hour or do the design for a set price. Charging less than $30 to $40 per hour for designing makes you look like a beginner, since landscape architects usually charge from $50 to $150 per hour or more for the same work. Charge what you think you're worth, but never undervalue yourself. As you get better, gradually raise your prices.

Many people find it difficult to do installation work all day, manage the business, and have energy left to do design work at night and on weekends. At first, avoid complex projects that require a lot of designing; this will make it easier for you to get things done right and on time.

Project Management

As you become more successful, you'll need to keep track of more and more details. That means developing project management skills. The following techniques and methods will help you.

Scheduling

The day will come when you find yourself overbooked—too many projects and not enough time, personnel, and equipment to do them all on schedule. Even if you're working by yourself or with one or two helpers, scheduling projects is a challenge. As the complexity of your services grows and you add more people, scheduling becomes a big and important part of your job. One of the commonest complaints about service businesses is the broken promise: You said you'd be there Tuesday, and you still haven't shown up a week later. Whether you'll be doing maintenance, landscaping, or both, your approach to scheduling is the same. Get a large desk calendar that you can use to make your schedule. Every time you get a job, put the job name on the calendar on the days you promised you'd do the work.

Here are the main factors that will govern your scheduling of work:

1. Size of jobs (number of man-hours required)

2. Number of jobs awaiting completion

3. Available manpower

4. Available equipment

5. Urgency of each job
6. Availability of materials
7. Weather conditions
8. Season of the year
9. Needs of the clients

Let's go over these. Getting a big job means tying up your crew, making it necessary to delay other work. Getting a lot of small jobs means you'll spend a lot of time running around setting up and closing out jobs. Consider the efficiency of your routing when you schedule jobs, so you don't have people driving from one end of town to the other unnecessarily. This is especially important for maintenance routes. Use a map to route jobs by area and by day.

Every time you add a project to your list, you need to calculate the number of days it will take and mark it on your work schedule. If you have a lot of jobs stacked up, it means clients are waiting; this is a possible source of dissatisfaction. But if you're honest about your backlog, most clients will understand and wait for you. On the other hand, if you constantly make promises you can't keep, you'll make people unhappy.

If you get more work, you have to decide whether to add more employees or create a longer backlog. If you don't have the equipment you need, should you rent it or buy it? How urgent is each job? Will you have to interrupt the job because some of the plants are on backorder? This can cause inconvenience because you have to move your equipment to another job and then back again when the plants come in, and it can also make the client unhappy. Bad weather can throw your schedule off; you need to let clients know if there's a possibility of delay due to weather. Remember that it often takes a few days for the soil to dry out after a rain. You can go back to work in sandy soils sooner than you can in clay soils, and this may affect which jobs you do first after a rain.

Naturally, some work is done in specific seasons, such as tree pruning, fertilizing, planting, and lawn installation. Other jobs like cleanups, hardscape construction, and irrigation aren't as dependent on the season. Finally and most important, what's your client expecting from you? If they feel they're not getting it, your scheduling has failed. (*Note:* Sometimes there's a starting date and completion date that aren't negotiable, especially on commercial projects. You do the job on that schedule, or you don't get to do it.)

Getting to Work

Finally you've got all the nit-picking little details out of the way and you're ready to begin to do the actual work. But wait, there's one more thing you need to do before this little miracle can take place. You need to define the exact details of the work. This is especially important if you'll be sending someone else out to the job without you. If things aren't written down, how will they know what to do?

Fortunately, there's a form that can help you. It's called a Job Work Order, and there's an example on pages 204–205. This form is often used as the starting point for small jobs. It can serve as instructions for your crew (where to go and what to do), a final invoice for the client, and on the back, a record of materials and labor used and a quick job-costing form, all in one. It's one of the cleverest forms around.

The Prejob Walk-Through

Before you start any job, spend some time inspecting the site. If you have employees, bring them along, especially if someone other than you will be in charge of the work. A walk-through shouldn't take much longer than an hour even on a fairly large job. It's time well spent, because it can make the work go more smoothly and prevent problems. The client should accompany you on at least part of the walk-through so you can agree one more time on the details of the work and answer any questions they might have. You might want to reserve some time for meeting with just your crew so you can discuss the sequencing of the work, the equipment that will be needed, and who will take responsibility for which parts of the job.

Job Work Order

Wilson Landscaping & Design
6602 12th Street • Greenville, OK 00020
(405) 222–8888

DATE
7/14/94

JOB NAME	SEND BILL TO
Bundy Residence	(Same)

JOB LOCATION	ADDRESS
93 Oak St.	

CITY	CITY
Lawndale, IL.	

PHONE	STATE	ZIP CODE
222–1121		

DESCRIPTION OF WORK:	STARTING DATE
1. Remove weeds in parkway	7/15/94
2. Prep soil in parkway	DAY OF WEEK
3. Plant 2 flats ivy in parkway	Monday
4. Trim shrubs in front of house	8:00 ☑ A.M. P.M.
5. Check sprinklers. May be a leak in back	FOREMAN
lawn near veg. garden. Repair as	LR
necessary.	LABORER TS, ML

☐ TOTAL AMOUNT DUE FOR ABOVE WORK: OR
☑ BILLING TO BE MAILED AFTER COMPLETION OF WORK

I hereby acknowledge the satisfactory completion of the above-described work:

_____
CUSTOMER'S SIGNATURE

WORK ORDERED BY	ORDER TAKEN BY
Mrs. B.	T.W.

MATERIAL AND LABOR RECORD

Quantity	Material Used	Price	Amount
1 L.S.	Roundup		9.00
1 C.Y.	Soil Amendment		28.00
2 Flat	Ivy	12.00	24.00
1 ea.	½ ST ELL, PVC		.29
	TOTAL		61.29

Job Completed?	Less Returned Materials		
☑ Yes ☐ No			
Date Billed 7-19-94	Net Cost of Materials		61.29

Date	Employee	Work Done	Hrs.	Rate	Amount
7/15	L. Rodrigues	Parkway	3	7.	21.00
7/15	T. Sanders	Parkway	3	7.	21.00
7/15	M. Lewis	Shrubs/	3	12.	36.00
		Sprinklers			
		TOTAL LABOR COST			78.00

TOTAL MATERIAL COST	61.29	TOTAL SELLING PRICE		200.00
TOTAL LABOR COST	78.00	LESS TOTAL COST		148.29
SUBCONTRACT COSTS		GROSS PROFIT (29 %)		51.71
OTHER DIRECT COSTS *	9.00	LESS OVERHEAD (14 %)		28.00
TOTAL COST	148.29	NET PROFIT (15 %)		23.71

* DUMP FEES

Keep your eyes open for potential problems that you hadn't noticed before. Also make written notes (preferably with the client present) of any existing damage, so you don't get blamed for it later. Be sure the client gets a copy.

Locating Buried Utilities

Before doing any digging, be sure to locate buried utilities. First, call the underground locating service in your area; they will contact all the utility companies that serve the property (gas, electric, telephone, cable, water, sewer, etc.) and send them out to mark the location of their pipes and wires where they enter the property. Generally the call and the service are free. Using them is not optional; it's required by law. If you damage something and you haven't called, you can be liable for *very* expensive repairs and possibly legal action against you. Next, you have to ask the client about any water mains or other utilities within the property lines. You can also hire a locating service to find the utilities before you dig. Mark everything with flags or chalk before you do any digging.

Building Permits and Other Nuisances

In most communities, most of the work you do won't require a permit. Some things, like backflow prevention devices, decks, fences, and retaining walls may require permits. Before you do your first job, visit the city and county zoning and building departments to find out all of the many requirements you'll have to adhere to. Tree removal may be prohibited or controlled. Structures will have to be built within the setbacks on the property. Etcetera, etcetera. Do your homework, or you'll end up in a lot of trouble.

Getting through the permit process can be lengthy and trying, so allow something extra in your bids to cover the permit fees, at least one visit to city hall, and numerous inspections. Building officials can be arbitrary and obnoxious. Force yourself to be nice to them even if they're jerks, because they have total power over you and can make your life miserable. It's an unpleasant reality that'll never change. Don't get a reputation as a troublemaker with the folks downtown.

On-the-Job Management Techniques

Loading the Truck

It's 7:30 in the morning, and you're wide awake and going full steam ahead, bursting with enthusiasm for this bright new day and the start of yet another fun, profitable job. Then again, maybe you're just a bit groggy from a long weekend and not thinking too clearly yet. Your helpers are waiting for leadership, and you're waiting for the caffeine to kick in. You know there's a lot to think about, but you can't seem to remember what it is.

Fortunately, you took the time yesterday to plan ahead a bit. You filled out your Job Work Order and made lists of the materials and equipment you'd need. Now you can pull this all out and look like the true captain of industry that you are. In no time, you and your team will be on the road.

It helps if you have a preprinted form or two to help you. Loading lists for equipment and materials can be very handy. See the examples on pages 208 and 210–211.

Keeping Track of Daily Activities

Once you're out on the job, you still need to keep track of many things. You'll be buying materials, taking deliveries at the jobsite, subs will be coming and going, the landscape architect might stop by for an inspection, and the owner may request changes in the work. You may pick up, use, and return rental equipment.

You'll also need to keep a record of the work you've completed today and any problems that came up. Finally, you have to plan for tomorrow—what equipment, materials, and labor will be needed and the goals for the workday. If you don't keep after this, you'll lose control of the job in no time. Believe me, it's worth the trouble. Besides, if there's a dispute or (God forbid) a lawsuit, you'll need lots of documentation to protect your interests.

Guess what? There's yet another handy form that prompts you for this information. It's called a Daily Job Report. Fill one out every day, or have your lead person do it. See the example on pages 212–215.

Equipment Loading List

In addition to the regular tools and equipment, take/rent the following special items for this job.

Power Equipment
__1__ Rototiller
____ Lawn renovator
____ Aerator
____ Reel mower
__1__ Sod cutter
____ Hedge trimmer
____ String trimmer
____ Spray rig
____ Vibratory plate compactor
____ Jackhammer, electric
____ Jackhammer, pneumatic
____ Tamper
____ Power auger
____ Chainsaw
____ Circular saw
__1__ Tractor w/box scraper
____ Tractor w/backhoe
____ Tractor w/bucket
____ Skid steer loader
____ Flatbed truck
____ Dump truck
____
____

Layout Equipment
__30__ Flags (10-yellow, 20-blue)
____ Flagging tape
____ Mason's twine
____ 2x12 stakes
____ 2x2 stakes
__1__ 100 ft. tape
____
____

General Equipment
__2__ Tarps
__2__ Planks
__6__ Tie-downs
____
____

Nonpower Equipment
__1__ Fertilizer spreader
__1__ Lawn roller
__2__ Wheelbarrow
____ Hand truck
____ Tree dolly
____ Backpack sprayer
____ Hoses
____

Hand Tools
____ Tripod ladder
____ Extension ladder
____ Climbing gear
____ Posthole digger
__1__ Hand tamper
____ Stake driver
____ Sighting level
____ Measuring wheel
____ Chalk box
____ Sledgehammer
__2__ Hand pruning saws
__1__ Loppers
__1__ Pole pruners
____ Brush hooks
____ Ax
__2__ Grading rakes
____ Come-along
____ Rebar cutter
____ Bolt cutters
____ Plumber's torch
____ Carpentry tools
____
____

Other
__1__ Water meter key
____
____

Keeping Track of Materials and Labor

One of the worst and most common experiences is to get to the end of the job and realize that you haven't kept good records of materials and labor. If it's a time-and-materials job, you can't get paid without providing this information on your invoice. If it's a bid job, you'll have no way of knowing how you did. Sometimes the information can be laboriously reconstructed from crumpled invoices you discovered under the seat of the truck and from people's best guesses about who worked when, but sometimes it's just not possible to go back and sort it all out.

Like everything else about business, developing good habits early on will help you eliminate this problem. Keep a daily record of the materials and equipment you use and of everyone's labor. You may even want to keep track of the hours of use on each piece of major equipment and on vehicles.

The best way to do this is to start a record at the beginning of each job and add to it every day. Then at the end of the job, you're ready for billing and/or job costing. The standard approach is to use a Material and Labor Report. An example of one that works pretty well is on pages 216–217. You may want to customize it for the peculiarities of your own operation.

Site Management

Train yourself and your employees to keep the jobsite clean and safe. Let everyone know they have to clean up at the end of every day. Make site safety everyone's responsibility—everyone has to watch for, report, and immediately eliminate hazards. These include unmarked open trenches, tools left in walkways, unsecured chemicals, vehicles with the keys left in, and so forth. Safety also has to do with behavior: Never assume the client (or the client's children) are smart enough to watch out for you. Keep the public away from all activities, especially things like power equipment, tree trimming, and laborers swinging picks. Remember that regular safety training for all your employees is not only a good idea, it's also required by law.

Materials Loading List

Job Name: Francis Residence
Job Address: 1117 Marsh Rd.
Date: 9/17/94   Prepared by: Joe

LOADED	QTY.	MATERIAL	SIZE	PRICE	TOTAL	YARD	VENDOR	SUPPLIER
		IRRIGATION:						
	200'	CLS 200 PVC Pipe	3/4			X		
	600'	CLS 315 PVC Pipe	1/2				X	Irrig. Supply
	42	Toro 570 P Heads					X	✓
	1	Blue Glue	PT				X	✓
		Fittings Boxes				X		
		SOD LAWN:						
	6	ORGO-Mulch	C.Y.	30	180		X	Turf Supply
	50	16-5-5	LBS.	11	11		X	✓
	1100	Bluegrass Sod	SQ.FT.	.25	275		X	Green-sod

PLANTS:					
17	Raph. 'Ballerina'	1		X	Tim's Nursery ✓
7	Ilex cornuta	5		X	
2	Strawberry	Flat		X	Cal. Growers
1	Planter Mix	Scoop	X		

Daily Job Report

JOB NAME Eastside Shopping Center

JOB NO 94-112

JOB ADDRESS 414 E. 37th St.

JOB PHONE 717-2207

SUPERVISOR John Peters

DATE 7/7/94 **TEMPERATURE** 94 HIGH / 78 LOW

WEATHER

(Clear) Snow Windy Rain Overcast

INVOICE #	VENDOR NAME	MATERIALS
70724	Irrigation Central	Pipe & Ftgs.
A4717	Landscape Depot	Mulch
2376-22	Statewide Nursery	Trees

INVOICE #	VENDOR NAME	MATERIALS
9171	Henry's Equip. Rentals	Tractor

SUBCONT

NAME	WORK PERFORMED	START/STOP/HRS.
Electricians 'R' Us	Install J Box for controller	10:30–3:00/4½
We Are Boring Co.	Bore concrete curb for drain	8–10 / 2

C H G S				
08	Add weeding on slope	125.	(Spot trees in parking lot)	
09	Deduct 3 flats ivy	<-140.>	Earl Yamamoto—Bldg. Dept.	
			(Inspect backflow device)	

EMPLOYEE NAME	JOB FUNCTIONS/HRS.							TOTALS
	PLANT	FINISH GRADE	MULCH	IRRIG.	CLEANUP			
Janice Cartwright	8							8
Ernesto Munoz		2		6				8
Robert Dowd	4	2	1					7
Lupe Rodriguez	8							8
Sonny Kline					8			8
Totals	20	4	1	6	8			39

EQUIPMENT								
Dump Truck					4			4
Kubota		3			5			8
Totals		3			9			12

Work Completed Today

WORK	LOCATION
1. Planted 24" trees	Entry
2. Finish graded	Front of main bldg.
3. Mulched	Entry
4. Sprinklers	Entry
5. Cleanup	Behind bldg. 2

Work Scheduled for Tomorrow

WORK	LOCATION
1. Finish planting 24" trees	Entry
2. Finish mulching	Entry
3. Test & adjust sprinklers	Entry
4. Start planting	Main bldg.
5. Hook up controller #2	

Need for Tomorrow

TOOLS & EQUIPMENT: Kubota

Small trencher

SUBCONTRACTORS: Electrician (box for controller #2)

MATERIALS: 12 24" Elms

3 C.Y. Planter mix

14 C.Y. Mulch

FOLLOWUP NEEDED:

1. Find out why no power to controller

2. Re-stake 1 tree at entry

PREPARED BY: _John Peters_   **TIME:** 4:40 p.m.

NOTE: This form appears on the reverse side of the Daily Job Report

Material and Labor Report

DATE 7/9/94

JOB NAME Frances Residence

ADDRESS 1717 Marsh Rd.

EXPLANATION OF WORK Sprinklers & lawn

PHONE 707-1103

JOB NUMBER 94-1104

DESCRIPTION	QTY	COST	TOTAL AMOUNT
1/2 CLS 315 PVC Pipe	200'	.12	24.00
3/4 CLS 200 PVC Pipe	100'	.20	20.00
1/2 SS ELL PVC	12	.25	3.00
3/4 SS ELL PVC	6	.32	1.92
1/2 SSS TEE PVC	3	.32	.96
3/4×1/2×1/2 SSS TEE PVC	2	.47	.94
1/2 ST ELL PVC	12	.29	3.48
1/2 Poly cutoff risers	12	.38	4.56
TORO 570P Heads	12	4.55	54.60
Champion 3/4 ASV	1	9.40	9.40
3/4×18 Galv. nipple	1	4.90	4.90
3/4 TEE Galv	1	1.27	1.27

DESCRIPTION	QTY	COST	TOTAL AMOUNT
EQUIPMENT			
Small trencher, hours	4	20.00	80.00
Total Equipment			80.00
VEHICLES			

					Total Vehicle
Teflon tape roll	1	1.40	1.40		120.00
Subtotal Irrigation			139.83		
Sod, bluegrass, S.F.	1100	.25	275.00		
Amendment, C.Y.	6	30.00	180.00	MISCELLANEOUS EXPENSES	
Fertilizer, sacks	1	17.00	17.00	Delivery—sod	50.00
Subtotal, Lawn			472.00		
Total Materials			611.83		

	Amount
MISCELLANEOUS TOTAL	50.00
EQUIP. TOTAL	80.00
VEHICLE TOTAL	120.00
MATERIAL TOTAL	611.83
SALES TAX	42.83
LABOR TOTAL	268.00
TOTAL	1172.66

TIME AND LABOR

EMPLOYEE	IN	OUT	HOURS	RATE	TOTAL AMT.
J. Martin	7:30	3:00	7	8	56.00
T. Orlando	7:30	3:00	7	7	49.00
W. Hadley	8:00	4:00	7½	10	75.00
M. Fisk	8:00	4:30	8	11	88.00
TOTAL					268.00

SIGNATURE *Anna Johnson*

Jobsite security is another concern. Thefts of equipment and materials are common and you need to keep all valuables guarded by day and locked up at night. Leaving that chainsaw on the sidewalk while you're around back looking at the flower beds is asking for trouble. Things will disappear from the backs of trucks, side yards, and garages. Getting insurance to cover theft from vehicles and jobsites can be next to impossible, and even when available, it will cost you plenty.

Finally, you've got to think about courtesy to the client. To you it's just a jobsite, but to them it's home. Prohibit radios, dogs, and alcohol. (A radio tuned to a loud rock station and left playing all day long is a sure way to lose a client.) Train people to behave themselves—no shouting, swearing (in any language), peering in windows, or behaving in a rowdy manner. Provide uniforms for employees or enforce dress codes banning really shabby clothing, T-shirts with vulgar sayings printed on them, or anything else that might be offensive to your most conservative clients. Get rid of anybody who won't comply. One of the most awkward issues is where employees go to the bathroom. Often the client will have a bathroom people can use; it's a good idea to verify this before you start the work. On a large property, people often just go in the bushes, but you risk problems if they're caught. If there's any doubt and the job is big enough, rent a port-a-potty.

Purchasing

Where You Buy Things

If you're a gardener, you may have to buy your supplies from retailers, which cuts you out of a lot of profit. If you're a licensed contractor, you can buy directly from growers and wholesalers, at about half the retail prices in many cases.

Nurseries. The retail nursery is a source of small quantities of plants and supplies. Retailers usually offer a modest discount (10 to 20 percent) to professionals and are happy to cultivate your business. They will usually be willing to order plants in for you, which wholesalers often are not.

The wholesale nursery grows plants and sells them to retail

nurseries and to landscaping professionals, usually at about half the retail price. Many wholesalers also offer a cash-and-carry discount, usually an additional 10 to 20 percent. Wholesalers prefer to deal with large orders, but will sell any quantity to regular customers. Some wholesalers also carry soil amendments and other planting supplies. Many specialize in certain kinds of plants. Some wholesalers also act as brokers, ordering plants from other growers and assembling a complete shipment for your larger jobs. There are also independent plant brokers who do the same thing.

Other Suppliers. You'll need things other than plants: irrigation materials, fertilizers, lumber, rock and gravel, other building materials, lighting and electrical supplies. There are places in your town where professionals buy these things, probably not at the Home Warehouse. Visit suppliers; get to know them. They're an important part of your team.

Discounts aren't as good on most building materials as they are on plants. For example, the typical discount to contractors at a lumberyard is 10 to 20 percent. Take that into consideration when pricing your jobs. Sprinkler materials, on the other hand, are usually heavily discounted to contractors. (*Tip:* You have to ask for these discounts; no one's going to give them to you automatically.)

Picking Things Up Versus Having Them Delivered

You can spend all day running around from supplier to supplier, picking up materials and delivering them to the job. Sometimes it makes sense to pick things up, especially small orders; but delivery is often a better option, even if there's a delivery charge. After all, your time's worth something, not to mention the wear and tear on your truck.

Vendor Credit

Many vendors will be happy to establish a line of credit for you, even though you're just starting up, as long as your personal credit rating is good. Try this with businesses you already have a relationship with, then after a few months of paying your bills on time, use them as a credit reference to open accounts with other vendors. Then, whether you need a few sacks of fertilizer for spring feeding or $1,000 worth of materials for a patio installation, you can charge it and pay the bill in thirty days, hopefully long after the client has paid you.

Neat, huh? That's the standard way of doing business—letting your suppliers carry your materials purchases so you can get through the job on their cash instead of yours. Just remember to pay them off on time every month or you'll lose this most important of privileges.

Until you establish credit everywhere, you may have an alternative: Some vendors will accept VISA or MasterCard. A few years ago, I got a credit card that offers frequent flyer miles with every purchase. I charge tens of thousands of dollars worth of business expenses every year and get to fly places for free. Think about it. Be sure to pay credit card bills on time, because the interest rate can exceed your profit margin on the job.

The Purchase Order

When you have open accounts at vendors, you're vulnerable to a stranger (or a competitor) walking in and charging materials to your account just by telling the clerk he's a new employee. Send all vendors a certified letter telling them not to charge anything without a signed purchase order from you. Then use the purchase order to document and clear your purchases with the vendor. The purchase order also helps you keep track of your purchases, making job costing easier. Match the purchase order to the invoices when you receive them, to verify purchases and prices. Look at the standard purchase order on page 221, it's filled out so you can see how it works.

Changes on the Job

The morning you finally start a job, you're certain that everything's perfectly organized. Everyone knows what to do; you've talked it over a million times. The only thing left is to do it. There can't possibly be any changes after all this planning.

Wrong. Every job has changes, often lots of them. There's the

Wilson Landscaping & Design
6602 12TH STREET
GREENVILLE, OK 00020
(405) 222–8888

Purchase Order

NO. 2329

Show this Purchase Order Number on all
correspondence, invoices, shipping papers
and packages.

TO

Green Gulch Sod Farm

1717 Benson Road

Greenville

DATE OF ORDER 7-25-94	JOB NO. 94-712
JOB NAME Dennison	
JOB ADDRESS 201 25th St.	
	JOB PHONE 700–1121

WHEN SHIP	F.O.B. POINT	SHIP VIA	TERMS
7-27	Job site	Vendor	Charge

QTY. ORDERED	QTY. RECEIVED	ITEM/DESCRIPTION	UNIT PRICE	TOTAL
1500 sq. ft.		"Tall Green" Hybrid Fescue Sod	.22	330.00
		Delivery		50.00
		Sales Tax		19.00
		Total		399.00

Kim Wilson

AUTHORIZED BY

ORIGINAL

"While-You're-Here-Syndrome": The client wants something pulled out or put in or trimmed. There's the "Oops Syndrome": You can't get one-gallon junipers, only fives; or the family dog ate the hollyhocks in the middle of the night. Soon your perfect little plan is a mess of additions, deletions, and alterations, and your head is swimming with details. It's easy at this point to lose control of the project, especially where costs are concerned.

The solution to this problem is a form called a Change Order. (See the example on page 223.) If you don't document changes, the client may not realize there are additional charges and might refuse to pay you. Change orders also force you to keep track of the billing as the job progresses, which is a lot easier than sorting it all out at the end. Most contractors are terrible about using change orders. They're afraid to tell the client the price of that birdbath that he asked for at the last minute, or they're too busy to figure out how much the additional planting will be. Ignore change orders at your peril.

Change orders should also indicate any additional time required to do the extra work. Use a change order even if there's no price change; it's important to document any and all alterations to the scope of the work. If you do something extra at no charge, put it on a change order so the client knows what a generous, peachy person you are.

Getting Along with Others

Business is about people: liking them, making them feel good, bringing out the best in them. Every interested party on a job has his or her own agenda, and it helps if you understand what it is and how to deal with it. Communication is vital to your success; keep everyone supplied with all the information they need to stay aware of what's going on.

Studies show that people hear only a third of what you say. That means you've got to say things three times to be understood! That's why writing things down is such a good idea. Whenever something occurs on a project that might affect your interests,

Wilson Landscaping & Design

6602 12TH STREET
GREENVILLE, OK 00020
(405) 222-8888

Change Order

TO Mr. and Mrs. T. W. Francis	CHANGE ORDER NO. 01
ADDRESS 1717 Marsh Rd.	DATE 7/9/94
Ashton, OH	PHONE 707-1103
JOB NAME AND LOCATION Same	JOB NUMBER 94-1104
	DATE OF EXISTING CONTRACT 6/25/94

1. ADD: Prune shrubs by front door	75.00
2. ADD: Plant 2 flats annuals (including soil prep)	67.00

WE AGREE hereby to make changes as specified above, at this price ➡ **142.00**

DATE 7/9/94

Kim Wilson

AUTHORIZED SIGNATURE

PREVIOUS CONTRACT AMOUNT	$	2714.00
REVISED CONTRACT TOTAL	$	2856.00

ACCEPTED: The above prices and specifications of this Change Order are satisfactory and are hereby accepted. All work to be performed under same terms and conditions as specified in original contract unless otherwise stipulated. This revision becomes part of the existing contract.

DATE 7/9/94   SIGNATURE   *Tom Francis*

send a letter to the parties involved to advise them of where you stand. Keep a copy permanently in your job file; it could prevent big problems later on.

Keep people (especially the client) *delighted*, not just satisfied. Remember that a small problem can become a big annoyance to your client, and it can spoil the whole experience for them, no matter how good everything else was. (Think about the last time you went to a restaurant where the food was great, the atmosphere was wonderful and the service was OK except that you never got your coffee. What did you walk away thinking about? Did you go back?)

Make common courtesy part of your every interaction with people. Use these phrases regularly: "Please," "Thank you," "Excuse me," and "I'm Sorry." When you're wrong, admit it. What's the big deal?

Working with Your Employees

This is simple: Develop a team spirit in all your employees. Help them to work together. Explain the job to them before they start doing it. Share your enthusiasm. Encourage people to come up with good ideas, and reward them when they do. Work hard and have fun.

At the same time, watch how your employees relate to the client and others on the job. They may not be as sensitive and personable as you are. Because they don't know all the details of the work, they may also make statements that are well intentioned but end up being detrimental to your interests. Train everyone to treat others with respect and courtesy and to defer to you or your supervisor when a client asks a question they can't answer. Also make sure your employees don't do work that's not part of the contract, only work they're assigned to do.

Working with Landscape Architects

If you work from plans prepared by landscape architects, your activities will be partially under the control of the landscape architect. Depending on the arrangement he or she has with the client, the landscape architect may inspect the project at various stages. For example, you may need to call for an inspection after the main irrigation lines are installed and pressurized but before the trenches have been backfilled. Many times the landscape architect will place the plants before you plant them. Often, you have to submit copies of your invoices for materials (to prove you purchased the right kind and quantity) and provide extra plants that can be torn apart to inspect them for root growth and condition. It's your responsibility to give the landscape architect advance notice of inspections and to be prepared for them.

Working with a landscape architect can be a delicate balancing act. You're in the middle, trying to satisfy both the client and the landscape architect. Sometimes you'll find a problem with the plans—a shade plant that's being planted in the sun, for instance—and then you have to decide how to proceed. If you keep your mouth shut, then when the plant fails, they can hold you responsible: You were the *proximate cause* because you knew there was a problem and didn't say anything. On the other hand, if you tell the client (who pays you), then you're finking on the landscape architect and you may never get another job from them. *But* if you tell the landscape architect, *they* may get haughty about a mere contractor telling them what to do (landscape architects can be that way). The best approach is to tell the landscape architect first, using your most diplomatic walk-on-eggs behavior. If they refuse to do anything about it, and you're sure you're right, give a written notice to all parties that you aren't going to take responsibility for that portion of the work.

Include some extra fudge factor in your bids when there's a landscape architect involved. You'll have to spend time dealing with them and may get sucked into doing extra work because of some capricious decision they make halfway through the job. Some landscape architects can be a pleasure to work with; others can be an absolute pain.

Working with General Contractors

If you're working as a subcontractor under a general contractor, you'll have little or no contact with the client, especially on commercial jobs. You'll have to be a team player and do things the way the general wants. You'll also have to get along with the other subs on the job, often under difficult conditions. Fortunately, the landscaper is the last person on the job, after many of the other subs are out from under foot.

Some generals can be pretty hard-boiled. Many of them eat landscapers for their midmorning snack, so be prepared to deal with someone who's way ahead of you in the construction game and isn't afraid to make you dance. It's a great learning experience but not one for the fainthearted.

Working with Your Subcontractors

Subs know more than you do about their specialties. Once you know they're capable, stand back and let them do their thing. To meet your obligations to the client, you need to coordinate the work of subcontractors and keep things moving. You also need to monitor the quality of the work and make sure it complies with the specs and with standard good practice. To meet your obligations to the sub, you need to provide firm dates for the work and be sure you're ready for the sub when he or she shows up. You also need to pay your subs in accordance with the terms of their contract with you.

Backcharges

Sometimes a subcontractor will create a problem for you. Let's say the concrete guy leaves a big mess that you have to clean up. Since you owe him money, you can deduct the cost of the cleanup from his bill. This is called "backcharging." You might even backcharge one sub to pay for work done by another. Backcharges are an effective way to make subs really angry at you and should only be used after discussing the matter and trying to reach an agreement on what's to be done.

Other Outside Services

There are other resources you may want to tap at times. Your county or state may employ pathologists who diagnose pest and disease problems. Check with the County Agricultural Commissioner or similar agency. The farm adviser (also known as extension agent, farm and home adviser, or cooperative extension specialist) can also help you with horticultural problems and often has publications available on a wide range of subjects.

Consulting Engineers and Laboratories

Overlooked by many beginners, these folks can keep you out of trouble. Say you have an area that just won't grow anything, and you can't figure out why. Send a sample of the soil to the lab, and have them run a series of tests to determine the nutrient levels, salinity, pH, and whatnot and make recommendations for correcting whatever problems they find. Or maybe a client has asked you to plant a slope that you think may be geologically unstable. Call in a consulting geologist. Can't figure out how to build a retaining wall? Call a structural engineer.

In certain situations, the city or county may require that you hire a consultant to make certain that a complex project is done right. Certain things will always be beyond your abilities. Don't try to do it all. Whenever somebody knows more about something than you do, hire them. Be sure the cost of their services is reimbursable under the terms of your contract, or have the consultant bill the owner directly.

Getting Paid

Maintenance work is billed at the end of the month. Small landscaping jobs are billed when you're finished. For larger landscaping jobs (those lasting more than a week) you should arrange for progress payments to be made as sections of the work are completed.

Progress Payments

You specify in your contract when progress payments are due. In many cases you can ask for a deposit upon acceptance of the contract. The amount of this deposit is often limited by law. You can require that the balance is to be paid in weekly payments or on demand. You'll base the amount of the payment either on completion of specific work items (such as demolition, sprinkler system, lawn, etc.) or on the percentage of all work that has been completed at the end of the week. To receive a progress payment, present the client with an itemized list of completed work showing the contract amount and any change orders, all payments made to date, the amount of the current payment you're requesting, and the balance due on the contract. (*Tip:* It's a good idea to state in your contract that failure to make a progress payment within three days of the due date is a material breach of contract. That gives you the right to stop work until you get paid.)

Final Payments

On a landscaping job, you collect the final payment when all the work is completed to the client's satisfaction. The first step in getting a final payment is to do an end-of-the-job walk-through with the client to see if there's anything that's been left undone. During this walk-through you make a list that's called (for some reason I never understood) a "punch list." On it you write things like, "Nozzle missing on sprinkler head in east lawn," and "Need to stake peach tree." You give the client a copy and agree on when the work will be corrected. (*Tip:* An even better idea is to do this walk-through on the last day of the job and have one or two of your workers follow you around actually taking care of the punch list items as you identify them. Now that's service!)

When you go to get your final payment, be sure you present a complete itemization of all billings, change orders, and payments to date and a final invoice.

If you're working for a general contractor, through a landscape architect or on a public or commercial job, you may have to wait for thirty days or longer to get the final payment because of a requirement called "retention." Retention is a way to protect the client by holding on to some of your money until the lien period runs out (see explanation following on pages 235–236) and until you complete the work satisfactorily. It's also a way to be sure you honor your guarantees and, not incidentally, a way for the client to earn a bit of extra interest on your money.

Invoices

These can vary a lot in style. A time-and-materials job is billed differently from a lump-sum job; maintenance might be billed differently from a landscaping job. If you're using handwritten invoices, it's easy to use any format that works for the occasion. With a computer, I've found it impossible to avoid setting up several kinds of invoice templates, since computers lock you into rigid formats for everything.

Always present a neat, complete invoice so the client understands what he's being billed for. Make your terms of payment as short as possible—no longer than ten days. After all, you're not in the loan business.

(*Reminder:* Remember that if you're charging for materials, you need to show sales tax as a separate line item.)

As with all forms, consistency is important, but it seems to be more elusive with invoices because of the varied nature of the work. Whatever system you use, try to do the same thing every time if possible, because this will make it easier for the client (and you) to understand. Sample invoices are shown on pages 230–232.

Credit Card Billing

If you accept VISA or MasterCard charges (not a bad strategy, even though you do have to pay a 2 to 3 percent service charge), you'll have to use the bank's system for recording a sale. You still have to fill out one of your own regular invoices, though, or you'll end up with no way to track those jobs through the bookkeeping system. Keep the fees in mind when you bid a job that you know will be paid by a credit card. Some banks have stopped issuing these credit card merchant accounts to home-based businesses. If you want one, select a bank that will work with you.

Maintenance Invoice

INVOICE

INVOICE NO.
6751

Joe's Gardening Service
601 CARTER BLVD.
WEST PLAINS, NJ
717–2271

CLIENT NAME				JOB NAME		
Pete & Brenda Thomas				Thomas Residence		

STREET & NO.				STREET & NO.		
1045 N. Locklin St.				Same		

CITY	STATE	ZIP	CITY	STATE	ZIP
West Plains	NJ				

WORK PERFORMED/DATE	TERMS	DATE
MAINTENANCE / JUNE	Payable on receipt	7-10-94

1 BAG	16-6-8 Fertilizer	$17.50
1 PT.	Roundup	19.00
	Subtotal	36.50
	Sales tax	2.19
	Total materials	38.69
1 LOAD	Dump fees	12.00
	Monthly maintenance	120.00
	Total	$170.69

Time and Materials Invoice

INVOICE

INVOICE NO.
6751

HARRIET'S SPRINKLER REPAIR
101 TEANECK BLVD.
SAWTOOTH, VT 00310
224-2424

CLIENT NAME				JOB NAME		
Ted Meyers				Meyers Residence		

STREET & NO.				STREET & NO.		
22 Barton Lane				Same		

CITY	STATE	ZIP	CITY	STATE	ZIP
Sawtooth	VT	03310			

WORK PERFORMED/DATE	DATE
Sprinkler Repair, Back lawn — 7/13/94	7/17/94

Qty	Description	Rate	Amount
1 PC.	½ Slip-Fix		$2.79
3 PC.	Rain Bird nozzles	.54	1.62
2 PC.	Cutoff risers	.35	.70
	Subtotal		5.11
	Sales tax		.31
	Total materials		5.42
2 HRS.	Service call	23.00	46.00
	Total		$51.42

Lump-Sum Invoice

INVOICE

INVOICE NO.
6753

GARDENSMITH LANDSCAPES
29357 45TH ST.
PEACH GROVE, GA 17462
947–2212

CLIENT NAME				JOB NAME		
Mrs C.W. Rubenstein				Rubenstein Residence		

STREET & NO.				STREET & NO.		
93 Tipton Terrace				Same		

CITY	STATE	ZIP		CITY	STATE	ZIP
Peach Grove						

WORK DONE/DATE	DATE
Backyard Landscaping (per contract of 5/20/94)	7/9/94

1 L.S.	Landscaping - Per Contract	$7,490.00
	Add: Change Order #1 - Additional irrigation work	315.00
	Add: Change Order #2 - Extra trees/mulch	270.00
	Deduct: Change Order #3 - Downsize privets	-105.00
	Adjusted Total	7,970.00
	Less: deposit Rec'd 5-22-94	-749.00
	Less: progress payment Rec'd 6-14-94	-2,200.00
	Balance due	$5,021.00

Handling Credits and Refunds

Sometimes you have to give money back for some reason. It doesn't happen often, but if you don't document it right, a credit or a refund can throw your bookkeeping off.

The standard approach is to use a Credit Memo. This is just like an invoice but is used for refunds or credits to clients. The easiest way to handle this is to use a regular invoice, clearly marked CREDIT MEMO at the top and CREDIT at the total line. This indicates to the client and you that this time the money went to the client or was credited to their account.

Sending Out Statements

If you have credit sales (you shouldn't, but still . . .) or someone wants to pay you off in installments or if you've sent out a slew of invoices to one client and haven't gotten paid for all of them, you need to send out a statement. It's a listing of what's been paid and not paid, in chronological order. Notice how the arithmetic works on the sample on page 234; it's a standard presentation.

Slow Pays

Sadly, not everyone will pay you on time. The best ways to avoid this are to do good work and to make sure the client is so happy that they can't wait to reward you for your great service with a nice fat check. You should also come calling with your invoice at the end of the job, making sure your body language says (in a nice way), "Yes, as a matter of fact, I *do* want to get paid right now, thank you."

Getting Your Money When They Won't Give It to You

Stage One: The Polite Phone Call

You know how it is. Sometimes we all forget to pay a bill or lose it or just need a little more time. Clients are no different. If you've waited a little too long to get your money from someone, start by

STATEMENT

Wilson Landscaping & Design
6602 12TH ST.
GREENVILLE, OK 00020
(405) 222–8888

Peter Wilson & Brenda Ryan
217 Elm Rd.
Greenville, OK 20021

AMOUNT PAID_____

6-30-94	Balance Forward		70.50
7-3-94	Maintenance -June	221.00	291.50
7-11-94	Payment-Thank You	<-70.50>	221.00
7-17-94	Sprinkler repairs	107.20	328.20
7-26-94	Potted plants	157.00	485.20

WILSON LANDSCAPING & DESIGN

giving them a friendly phone call. Diplomacy is important, because you don't want to sound like you're dunning the person, even though you are. Sometimes the conversation will actually go like this: YOU (nervously): "Hi, Mr. Jensen, this is Mary of Mary's Lawn Care." THEM (even more nervously): "Oh, hi Mary. Say, I'm going to send you that payment tomorrow morning." If you're not that lucky, try starting the conversation by asking how their garden's doing or talking about anything *except* the late payment. Then, casually mention that, by the way, you haven't received a check for last month's bill yet, and ask them if they could send it in the next day or two. That works about 80 percent of the time. Also be sure to find out if there's some reason they haven't paid you—a problem with the work or other dissatisfaction that you can correct.

Stage Two: Collection Notices

When payment is more than ninety days past due and you've called several times to no avail, you may have to goad people into action with a written notice. Forms printers sell a set of forms that you can use; there are usually three or four, each one more strongly worded than the last. Start with the mildest one, wait thirty days and graduate to the next and so on. It's best to avoid written collection notices until things look really hopeless. They offend a lot of people and you could lose a good client with this approach.

You could also take the bill to a collection agency at this point. Getting a call from a collection agency can be more motivating than getting a call from little ol' Tom the gardener, and you might get your money sooner, though not all of it. If the agency collects anything, they'll keep anywhere from 10 to 50 percent for their troubles and give you the rest.

Stage Three: The Lien Laws

Anyone who performs work or supplies materials on private property is entitled to be paid. The mechanic's lien is a special statutory protection that permits you to attach the client's property if they don't pay you. By attaching the property, it could be sold and the proceeds used to pay you. Naturally, this hardly ever actually happens, but it certainly is motivating, and the person usually finds some money to pay you real fast. The lien laws are particularly helpful if you're working as a sub having little contact with the owner of the project. In order to preserve your lien rights, you need to follow certain specific procedures during and after the job. Requirements vary from state to state.

Discussion of the lien laws is much too complicated to get into here, but you must learn about them and how they work. If you've gotten your contractor's license, you've already been exposed to this information. If you haven't, call the contractor's license board, your trade association, or your attorney for help with this. It's important, so do it.

Stage Four: Legal Action

Litigation is costly, time-consuming, and often nonproductive. The only time I got into a lawsuit, I won, but my attorney's fees (which I had to pay) exceeded the amount of the judgment. Sometimes it's better to just drop the matter. Other than doing that, you have three alternatives: small claims court, municipal court, and arbitration.

Small claims court only deals with small monetary judgments, usually limited to around $1,500. This approach is fast, inexpensive, and often effective. Neither party can be represented by an attorney. The atmosphere is informal, and all proceedings are conducted in plain English. The defendant can appeal, but you can't. Unfortunately the court doesn't collect the money for you or even guarantee that you'll get it. But once you win a judgment, you have other methods for getting the money. The court will explain those to you.

Municipal court is for larger claims and is more cumbersome and expensive. You will probably need to hire an attorney to handle the case. Think three times before you get into a lawsuit in municipal court.

Arbitration is an informal alternative to going to court. Cases are often heard in a conference setting by attorneys and experts in your business. You can use an attorney or represent yourself. The results of an arbitration hearing are often not appealable. Some contracts include a provision for mandatory arbitration; decide if this is agreeable to you before you sign it.

Following Up on Your Jobs

Site Visits

One day you'll drive by a job you did a couple of years before, and it'll be a horrifying mess—dead plants, weeds, bad pruning, trash everywhere. It beats me why anybody would pay thousands of dollars for landscaping and then let it run down like that, but some people do. Naturally it's bad advertising for you. Besides, maybe they didn't know how to take care of it (*you* were supposed to have *told* them) and just gave up.

It's your job to make sure this doesn't happen. Schedule regular visits over the first year. I suggest you come back two weeks after the job is finished, then a month after that, then every two to three months. Naturally you don't charge for this. You can either arrange these visits with the client or do them as a surprise, as we discussed in chapter 6. Regular follow-up of this kind helps the client learn to deal with their new landscaping and to keep things in good condition. It gives you an opportunity to prevent dissatisfaction and to sell the client more work, including perhaps maintenance.

Another approach is to include ninety days of maintenance in all landscaping proposals. The cost to the client is minimal, the landscaping will perform much better than if the client struggles with care during this critical period, and you may get hired on permanently at the end of the ninety days. It's such a good idea that many landscape architects specify a ninety-day maintenance period on all their jobs.

It's also a good idea to provide written information on care of the landscaping, especially for the plants. This could be a printed brochure or specific information for the plants you used on that job, or both.

The other document you should provide the client with is a record drawing of the irrigation system, showing the location and size of pipes, valves, wires, and anything else that might be hard to find without a diagram. It'll help you, too, if you get called back five years later and need to find something.

Quality Audit

It pays to find out if clients are satisfied with your performance. It gives you an opportunity to correct any problems, and it also alerts you to changes you need to make in your operation. It's a great goodwill builder.

Include a questionnaire with your final bill (or annually for maintenance clients) that gives the client an opportunity to comment on the quality of the work, the service, the employees and other reactions to your company. Allow people to answer anonymously if they wish. If they do include their name, respond personally to any complaint as soon as you receive the questionnaire back from them.

Thank-You Card

How many people take the time to do this? Imagine failing to thank someone who just paid you thousands of dollars! Also send thank-you cards to people who refer you to others.

Business Nightmares: Keeping Your Nose Clean

Used to be, business people were free to do just about whatever they wanted. Unfortunately, over the centuries ne'er-do-wells took advantage of this freedom one way and another, and eventually laws and regulations were put into effect to protect the public. Most of these laws are well intentioned, and some of them even work the way they're supposed to. Today, there are hundreds of them, and if you run afoul of even one, you can be in a world of trouble, especially since the courts usually assume that because you're in business you must be the one who's wrong. Never mind that most business people are decent and struggle day and night to keep their customers happy, never mind the 95 percent failure rate of business start-ups in this country, and never mind that the average self-employed person earns slightly less than he or she would in a "real" job doing the same tasks for someone else. Everyone just assumes you're rich, corrupt, and not to be trusted. The business person is often presumed guilty even after being found innocent.

Worse than this is the proliferation of lawsuits that has affected nearly everyone in business. Even if you haven't been sued, every action has to be considered from a liability standpoint. What if the client steps on my rake while I'm mowing the lawn? What if the dog dies the day after I sprayed the fruit trees? What if a valve sticks open and saturates the hillside with water, causing a landslide? The attention given to legal liability probably now exceeds that given to tax liability, and the fear of a lawsuit is right up there with the fear of being audited for most business people. Heck, even if you don't do *anything* wrong you may still have to defend yourself against a shotgun lawsuit where the attorneys go after everybody they can, in the hopes of finding some deep pockets somewhere. They'll even sue people they know didn't have a thing to do with the problem and then extort money from them on the grounds that a settlement will cost less than defending oneself. It's a yucky, nasty mess.

So, what do you do? First, you make sure everything you do is completely legal. That way nobody can attack your integrity. Next, you keep impeccable records of everything you do, say, and think: contracts and change orders, meeting notes, daily job sheets, letters and memos, and more. You do the best quality work you possibly can and know in intimate detail all the laws, building codes, and regulations applying to that work. You check your jobs constantly to be sure no one has left an open trench, forgotten to do a part of the job, or made an irresponsible statement to anyone. You keep your clients happy so they'll work with you if a problem comes up, not just sic their lawyers on you right off the bat. You go over your situation periodically with your attorney to see if you're sticking your neck out somewhere. Finally, you buy lots of insurance.

This takes a lot of the spontaneity out of being in business, but it's a whole lot better than ending up in court, because whenever you go to court, you lose, even if you win. Ask anyone who's been there.

Here are a few examples of the pitfalls that await you: (*Warning:* These are only examples and are not all-inclusive or complete, nor are they intended to inform you of all possible legal liabilities or obligations that may affect you or your business under various conditions and circumstances. These examples are fictitious and do not in any way depict actual legal cases or real people, living or dead. The author hereby assumes no responsibility of any kind whatsoever for the consequences of the use of the information hereunder by the reader or anyone else.)

The Oral Contract

Lacking a detailed written contract, the client may claim that you did less than you said you would or that you somehow violated an oral understanding, justifying nonpayment of the whole amount due. This isn't at all far-fetched or unusual; it happens every day. As the old saying goes, an oral contract isn't worth the paper it's written on.

The Oral Change Order

During the job, the owner makes a number of requests for additional work. Naturally, you take care of these, and since the owner's a real good guy, you don't take the time to let him know how much these changes are going to cost, much less get written approval. At the end of the job, you total everything up and present your bill, being careful to itemize the changes. He's outraged at the additional charges and refuses to pay you. You lose the money and the client, with no recourse from the courts. Maybe you even have your contractor's license suspended for a while. Again, happens every day. Get written change orders.

Omission of Information on Contract

The law has a lot to say about how home improvement contracts are worded. You need to include things like a "Notice to Owner" explaining the lien laws, a "Three-Day Notice of Cancellation" giving the owner time to back out of a contract, a place for your license number, the address of the state contractor's board, and a lot more. Your state will have its own unique set of requirements. If you omit even one, or word it wrong or use the wrong size type, you risk voiding the entire contract and losing the money for the work you did. Remember that the law is logical but crazy and will deny you payment even if everyone agrees the work is fine and by any reasonable reckoning you should be paid. It's not fair but it's the way it is. That's why it's so important to follow the rules down to the last little nit-picking detail.

Work Not Done to Specifications

You complete a beautiful flagstone walkway, done just like you told the owner you'd do it. You bring the owner out and proudly show off your creation. She sniffs and hunches up her shoulders and says, "Well, this is not what I expected. Take it apart and do it over." Yikes! Not only is your ego heavily abraded, you've got a lot of work to do. Sometimes this occurs because the owner really did have a different expectation of the work. Other times, the owner is trying to jack you around, to delay paying you for some reason—lack of funds, personal problems, or just plain orneriness. There are a lot of real vicious people out there. Either way, you failed to clearly specify, through written specifications and detail drawings, exactly how this walk was going to be constructed, and like it or not, you'll have to redo it. If you had something on paper, you could just point to it and say, "See? Just like I said it would be."

This problem can even come up in garden maintenance. I once had a persnickety client accuse me of cutting his hedge too far back, even though many of the stubs from the previous trimming were still present underneath the foliage. I spent more time settling him down than I spent trimming the hedge. (*Tip:* Talk to your clients a lot during the job. Get their approval on something every day. Explain what you're doing and why you're doing it. Come back after they're home from work if need be. Keep them informed and happy. It's worth the effort.)

Work Fails After Completion

You install a retaining wall; two years later it falls down. You're liable for replacement of the wall and for any consequential damages. Build things right the first time. If you don't know how to do something right, find out or hire a subcontractor who does or just pass up the job.

Proximate Cause

You do a job that was designed by a landscape architect. It's obvious to you right from the first time you look at the plans that there are serious problems with the design. But, of course, you don't want to step on the architect's toes, so you keep quiet and install the job as it was designed. Later it fails, just like you thought it would. The owner comes after *you*. They win. Not fair? Well, the law says you should have said something, and by not doing so, you became the "proximate cause": the last professional to work on the project and therefore at least partially responsible for the problem.

The Faked Back Injury

One Friday afternoon, a new employee hobbles in to the office in apparent pain. Off you go on a possibly phony injury claim that will cost you big bucks in worker's compensation insurance premiums. Typically, the insurance company will charge a couple hundred thousand dollars to your worker's compensation account to cover possible costs of an extended disability. There are attorneys out there that specialize in counseling employees in how to turn a little muscle cramp into a permanent vacation with generous pay, compliments of you-know-who. It's a national scandal, and it doesn't look like it'll get better any time soon.

Hold regular safety meetings, provide training for all new employees, and most important of all, screen new employees carefully for a history of injuries or claims. Then hope for the best. In fairness, legitimate injuries, especially back injuries, are common in this business, what with all the lifting and bending we do. Teach your people how to stay healthy, for their benefit and yours.

La Migra

That's what the Immigration and Naturalization Service (INS) is unaffectionately called by the millions of undocumented aliens who live and work in the United States. More and more landscaping businesses are hiring people from south of the border, because they're usually far superior to our own workforce—hard working, honest, faithful, decent, and willing to work for less. However you feel about this controversial issue, you need to be aware of your risks as an employer of undocumented workers. The INS regularly follows landscapers' trucks in Southern California and asks for employees' green cards. Roundups and deportations are common, and by law, the employer can be subject to stiff fines for hiring illegals. Plus, it's no fun to find that your entire crew is on a bus back to Mexico instead of on the job.

Well, I don't mean to scare you to death. Most of the time things go just the way you planned. Still, knowing that these things can happen is important. Now that you're aware of some of the problems, it'll be easier to avoid them.

9

The Long Haul

After the Work Is Done

Your work isn't over when you load the last tool on the truck at the end of the job. Remember that you've set up a living ecosystem for your client, and your ongoing expertise is needed to make it work properly. That means you have to follow up on your jobs and be available for questions, even if you aren't doing the maintenance on the job. A little of your attention now and then can prevent major problems that lead to dissatisfaction, failure of the work, and possible legal action against you.

I always offer free follow-up on all my jobs. Forever. I urge clients to call me any time they have a problem or a question, no matter how dumb it might seem. I ask that they call me within twenty-four hours if they notice a problem with a plant, so I can try to save it. If a leaf falls off, I'll try to tell them *why* it fell off. People do call, especially during the first few weeks after the job is done, and I'll go out anytime and look at things if I can't help them over the phone. I also drop by recently completed jobs now and then, because I can usually see developing problems before the owners or their gardeners can.

Liability for Your Work

These days it seems as though every little thing that happens triggers a lawsuit. If your work is deficient in some way that causes a problem, you may be held responsible. Obvious failures like retaining walls falling down or plants dying aren't the only problems you face. Suppose someone trips over a sprinkler head that you installed too high and too close to the corner of a walkway. Suppose you build a set of steps that's uneven and causes someone to fall. Suppose a client's neighbor is allergic to one of the pesticides you use on their lawn. Suppose the tree you planted grows too big and cracks the foundation of the house. All these things happen all the time. Even if your liability insurance covers your losses (which it may not), you still have to spend hundreds of hours in court defending yourself.

Guarantees

To what degree you must stand behind your work is defined in a number of ways. The first is statutory—in some states the law defines the guarantee period for home improvement work. Next, a more detailed guarantee will be included in your agreement with the owner. Often the landscape architect will specify the terms of the guarantee. If you're working under a contract prepared by a general contractor or developer there will certainly be guarantee requirements. (*Tip:* Watch for unreasonable requirements in other people's contracts. If you can't live with it, negotiate to change it.) If you're doing design/build, it's your responsibility to develop a guarantee that will satisfy both you and the client.

Each kind of work is guaranteed in a different way and for different periods of time. It would be ludicrous to guarantee a planting of annual flowers for three years, but it's equally ludicrous to guarantee a deck for ninety days. Here's my standard boilerplate guarantee, just to give you an idea of the details:

GUARANTEE

GENERAL: Landscape contractor guarantees all work to be free from defects in materials and workmanship. The duration of the guarantee is one year for sprinkler systems, hardscape construction, and low-voltage lighting systems and ninety days in the case of all other work, except as noted. CONDITIONS, LIMITATIONS, AND EXCLUSIONS: In the case of weed control, no guarantees of effectiveness of treatment or duration of treatment are made and treatments are made with the express understanding that such work is done entirely at risk of owner with regards to the effectiveness of treatment. The same limitation of effectiveness shall apply to renovation, fertilization, pest control, and other similar procedures. In the case of irrigation, landscape contractor shall guarantee adequate coverage for the purposes intended with a minimum of overspray or dry spots. In the case of lawns, plants, and other living things, no guarantee of survival, vigor, ultimate size or appearance, or suitability to site conditions is made. Plants that die will be replaced one time at no expense to owner, provided owner's responsibilities for care and notification are fully met. Seeded lawns are not guaranteed to germinate and grow, as success of a seeded lawn is chiefly determined by the watering and care given by owner and is beyond the control of the contractor. Sod lawns are guaranteed for fourteen days against infestation of pests and diseases, otherwise no guarantee is made, because watering and care are beyond the control of the landscape contractor. Guarantee period for boxed trees is one year. In all cases with living things, owner must notify landscape contractor within twenty-four hours of noticing a problem. Allowing plants, lawns, etc. to die or reach an advanced state of decline before notifying landscape contractor automatically and without recourse voids all guarantees on that portion of the project. In no case shall landscape contractor honor any guarantee when evidence of abuse, gopher, insect or other damage, misuse, improper care, or any other condition beyond the control of the contractor is found. Guarantees shall be effective only if the owner has complied with all the terms and conditions, payments, and other provisions of the contract.

Notice that this guarantee does four things: It says what will be guaranteed, it establishes the guarantee period, it defines limitations on the guarantee, and it establishes responsibility (including responsibilities of the client).

Guarantees boil down to this: You're responsible for defects in the materials and workmanship that you provide and, if you designed the project, for defects in your design. If elephants stampede through the garden, that's not your fault. Also, because you're dealing with nature, you can't guarantee that plants will thrive or that weeds will die. After all, the surgeon doesn't guarantee that his patients will live, only that he won't commit malpractice.

Still, when a plant dies within the first ninety days, it's good public relations to replace it, no questions asked. Maybe the client forgot to water or watered too much or the dog peed on it, but why make them feel bad by arguing about who screwed up? Just put a smile on your face and a fresh plant in the ground. You see, the client paid you a lot of money to build them a nice garden, and they don't want to hear about your problems. Nobody likes a whiner. (Besides, you did include something in your bid for warranty replacements, didn't you??)

By the way, if you're doing the maintenance on a job you installed, there's no question about replacements. If a plant dies or is looking bad during the maintenance period, you just replace it. On the other hand, if you're doing maintenance on an *existing* garden, you're not responsible for plants dying unless you killed them.

Naturally, you have to budget something into your bids to cover the replacement of a reasonable number of plants. This doesn't show up as a line item on your bid, but you've got to allow for it in your planting price, because no matter how careful you are, plants *do* die and you *will* be out there replacing them. Depending on the plant (some are harder to establish than others), you might allow 2 to 10 percent in your bid for replacement. The loss rate for small plants is higher than for larger plants, so if you're planting a lot of ground cover from flats, plan on coming back for sure. Specimen trees are a special case: Sometimes they're planted at a low mark-up with no guarantee, and other times they're guaranteed for a year, but at a much higher price. After all, replacing a $1,000 tree is not trivial. Transplants are normally not guaranteed at all. (*Tip:* You normally replace plants only once, because repeated failure is probably caused by a soil pathogen or other problem beyond your control. With subsequent replacements it's a good idea to bill the client at your cost. They'll appreciate it.)

Long-Term Management

Managing Cash Flow

Your goal in managing cash flow is to always have just the right amount of money on hand—never too much or too little. To do this, you need to keep good records, know the cash-flow pattern of your company, and project cash flow.

Reread "The Cash Forecast" in chapter 3 to remind yourself how easy it is to get into financial trouble by neglecting your cash flow and how easy it is to prevent this deadly problem by doing a Cash Forecast regularly—at least every month, especially if you're getting bigger jobs and more work than you've been accustomed to.

There are some classic cash-flow pitfalls. Getting a big job means you'll have to invest a lot of money up front in labor and materials, administrative expense, and possibly even capital investments in new equipment to do the job. If you can't cover those costs by getting payments from your client, you'll have to dip into your reserves. If the reserves aren't enough to cover it, you have a cash-flow crisis. This means you'll be delinquent in paying your bills, a red flag for your creditors, who may put you on C.O.D.—no more charges. This is often the start of a tailspin that the small operator may never recover from. After all, if you can't charge things, you can't buy the materials you need to do the job, let alone start the next job.

A short-term but deadly solution is to pay for the last job out of money you collect in advance from the next job. In addition to digging you even deeper into the hole, such behavior may be illegal. Once you're in this deep, you may be beyond saving. You might be able to limp along for a while, but unless something unusually wonderful happens, you'll eventually succumb to your financial weakness.

Even a steady-state business like maintenance can run into cash-flow problems if unusual expenses aren't anticipated or if clients quit paying you promptly. Let's say your faithful old truck finally breaks down. Do you have the money for a new one? Even a down payment? If not, what are you going to do? So, you have to plan ahead for future expenditures. (*Tip:* Set up an equipment replacement fund and pay into it every month. That way when you need something, you pay cash for it, saving thousands of dollars in interest.)

Other sources of cash-flow problems include failure to anticipate upcoming tax liabilities, ignoring the cost of monthly loan payments, buying equipment you don't need and can't generate the income to pay for, having too much money tied up in inventory of materials that aren't allocated to any upcoming jobs, failing to anticipate seasonal slowdowns in business, and taking too large a draw for yourself (you fool).

How do you avoid these problems? One answer is to always run your business lean. Don't spend any more than you have to, don't fall for fancy geegaws, don't overinvest in fixed assets, don't let salespeople talk you into unnecessary purchases. On the income side, make sure you bill people on time and in full and make sure they pay you, on time and in full. Your first responsibility is to be sure you provide the resources your business needs to run smoothly. Your second responsibility is to be sure the business lives within those resources. In business, there's a lot to be said for being a tightwad.

Seasonal Cash-Flow Management

Remember that even though business will be slow during part of the year, your fixed expenses go on. If you spend all the money you make during the busy periods, you won't have any money to pay the bills during the slow times. A year's cash forecasts will tell you how much you'll need to set aside in the bank to cover yourself during your slow time. Remember, you might feel pretty cocky if you have $15,000 at the end of the busy season, but if you need $25,000 to carry you through the slow times, you'll be in for a shock. *Rule: Cash in the bank is not necessarily profit.* Part of it may be profit, but much of it is the reserves you need for future expenses.

Estimate seasonal sales and expenses based on past experience (yours or other people's), modified by projected changes. My sales doubled every year for the first few years, then leveled off. Sales volume can vary with the state of the economy, price changes, your own marketing efforts, local business conditions, the weather, and other factors. A realistic sales projection takes these into account.

Some people work night and day during the summer, then kick back in the off season, happy to have enough money in the bank to get them through until spring. Others turn to other kinds of work in winter, snow plowing is popular, but there may be other opportunities in your community. Naturally, you could get an entirely different kind of job in winter, but why not use your entreprenurial talents to do something more interesting, such as, selling Christmas trees, repairing people's lawnmowers, or putting up gutters.

Accounts Payable Management

Pay bills marked "2 percent 10 days" by the tenth of the month to get your discount. Pay bills on time to avoid late charges and interest (not to mention damage to your credit rating). Anticipate large or out-of-the-ordinary payments. Keep a running total of your payables: one total for everything in the Invoices Unpaid file and another for the Accounts Payable files. Always know how much you owe.

Accounts Receivable Management

The most important strategy is to pick credit-worthy clients, but there are other strategies. On big jobs, structure your progress payments so they cover anticipated expenses. Provide the client with a written schedule of progress payments along with the contract. Have a clause in your contract that makes failure to pay progress payments within three days of the due date a material breach of contract. Stipulate in writing that the final payment is due on completion of the work. Reinforce all this verbally when you present the contract to the client.

Get signed change orders for all changes, whether they increase or decrease the contract price or even if there's no price change. Keep track of all changes and payments on a job ledger so you can bill promptly for progress payments and at the end of the job. Present clients with understandable invoices and progress billings so they won't have reason to delay payment because of questions. Bill immediately on the schedule you agreed on when you signed the contract and at completion of the job. Hand deliver bills on big jobs, and try to get payment on the spot. For all bills, provide a return envelope, addressed and stamped, for clients to send in payments.

Track the aging of all receivables and send notices to anyone who is thirty days past due. Better yet, give them a friendly reminder call on the phone. Comply with all requirements for protecting your lien rights, and file liens within the allotted time limits. Stop working for clients who are more than sixty days past due. Take seriously delinquent clients to small claims court. Keep a running total of current and past-due receivables; update it every week.

Cash Budgeting

In chapter 3 you learned how to do a cash forecast. Have another look at it. The cash forecast isn't just for the business plan; it's something you do regularly as part of your cash management. (*Tip:* A neat trick is to go back and compare your forecast with reality. To do this, just add another column for each month. One column is for projected figures, which you fill in before the fact, and the other is for actual figures, which you fill in from what really happened. If you're too far off, you know you need to adjust future forecasts.)

Tax Planning

In addition to taking care of employee's taxes, sales taxes, and other business taxes, you've got to deal with your own taxes. This is no place for an exhaustive treatise on income taxes, but a few tips are in order.

First, your tax situation will be very different when you're in business for yourself than when you were an employee. Before, the government (using your employer as an accomplice) just picked your pocket every week, and you got what was left over. At the end of the year, you probably filed a short-form tax return, maybe got a small refund, and that was that. Now, you'll be faced with a lengthy and complicated tax return, quarterly estimated tax payments, and tax liabilities that may shock you if you don't anticipate them.

When you're in business, everything you do has tax consequences, and the prudent business owner thinks about taxes every time there's a decision to be made, no matter how small. He or she also visits the accountant toward the end of the year to estimate the taxes that will be due for the year. I go see my accountant in October or November, when there's still time to change my strategy if necessary.

Getting a Handle on Taxes

The IRS puts out a great, free book, revised annually, called "Tax Guide for Small Business" (Publication #334) that gives you all the basics of income taxes for business people. Get one and read it all the way through.

Who Has to File a Tax Return

If your net earnings from self-employment exceed $400 in one year, you have to file a return, even if no taxes are due.

What Kinds of Taxes Do You Have to Pay?

Federal (and possibly state) income taxes and federal Self-Employment Tax (the equivalent of social security tax, only you have to pay a much larger percentage than employees do).

Making Estimated Tax Payments

If you estimate that your combined federal taxes will exceed $500 in the current year, you have to pay estimated taxes every quarter. The payments are due April 15, June 15, September 15, and January 15. Estimates are based on the previous year's taxes. If your actual income is different from your estimated income, you have to adjust your payments accordingly. There are penalties for failing to pay estimated taxes and for underestimating them. Get IRS Publication #505, "Tax Withholding and Declaration of Estimated Tax," or talk with your accountant. Your state may also require estimated tax payments.

Planning for Growth

So many people who go into business fall for the notion that the only successful business is the one that gets big. Don't even *think* about getting big for at least three to four years. You'll learn a lot during that time and maybe your ideas about growth will change. If you still want to get big, come back and reread the following information.

The One-Big-Job Syndrome

Many's the contractor who was cruising along just fine when he decided to take on a Really Big Job. Maybe a good residential client offered him a chance to bid on a shopping center development. Perhaps an opportunity came up to bid on a big commercial maintenance job. Whatever the source, big jobs are different critters than small ones, and they can be a death trap for the naive. Suddenly this happy person is transformed into a panic-stricken basket case, unable to cope with his new responsibilities, to han-

---

Tax Forms and Returns You Must Fill Out

You have to file the long Form 1040, U.S. Individual Income Tax Return, with some or all of these supporting schedules and forms. You may need others as well; check with your accountant.

- Schedule A: Itemized Deductions
- Schedule C: Profit or Loss from Business
- Form 4797: Sales of Business Property
- Form 8829: Expenses for Business Use of Your Home
- Form 4562: Depreciation and Amortization

Your state may require a separate set of tax returns, so check with them or your accountant.

---

dle lots of employees, to control the quality of the work, to manage cash flow, or to complete jobs. Maybe he grossly underbid the job and is stuck with the consequences. Maybe something goes wrong—a serious accident, an unintentional legal transgression, or a major flaw in the work. Within days or weeks, the doors are closed, the business is bankrupt, and the entrepreneur is facing the loss of everything. It happens all the time, and it's not funny.

Evaluating Your Ability to Get Big

Why do you want to get big? If it's to make a lot of money, be aware that it usually doesn't happen. If it's because you want to be a big shot, that's OK, but you've got to walk the walk, not just talk the talk.

To get big, you've got to develop technical and management skills far beyond the basic ones you've learned from this book. Believe me, you just have no idea how complex this business can be. Be prepared to go to school or spend a lot of time studying before you go beyond the cozy world of your little home-based cottage-industry business.

You've also got to have plenty of money to get big, because you'll have to invest in equipment, increase your overhead, and finance those big jobs.

Finally, to make money on a big job, you've got to develop new efficient methods for getting the work done in the least possible time. On a big job, there's no slack and no room for error. There's also no kindly, forgiving homeowner who'll let you slide when you screw up. If you swim with the sharks, you'd better have a good set of teeth.

Planning for Retirement

To be honest, I haven't given much thought to retirement. For one thing, I'm not sure I could afford it! Besides, I love this business. It's more fun than anything I've ever done, and I just can't imagine quitting. I look forward to every new day, just to see what crazy thing is going to happen next. How do you beat that? Certainly not by sitting on the porch or watching soap operas! Then, too, I figure that by the time I'm sixty-five I'll just be getting good at this.

Still, you do need to set aside some money for when you don't want to work any more, or can't. (*Tip:* You're not protected by disability insurance the way employees are, so get yourself a good disability policy, just in case something awful happens.) Talk to your accountant about setting up an IRA, Keogh Plan, or SEP, which are pension plans for the self-employed. Remember, too, that you're investing much of your money (maybe most of it) in a business that you can eventually sell.

In Conclusion

I'm sorry the book is finished, because there's so much more I want to tell you. I know that if you've read this far, you really want to succeed, and I believe you will. I wish I could be there to help you on your great adventure and to share the excitement with you, because I remember the feeling, and it's the greatest thing in the world. I think it's best to conclude with a true story, one that happened to me just yesterday. Maybe you'll enjoy it.

It was late Friday afternoon, and I had dragged myself out to a meeting with one of my best clients. It had been a pretty grueling week—a family medical emergency, the end of one job and the start of two others, car problems, a huge backlog of work, and no time for rest. I was exhausted and thought about canceling the meeting, but I went anyway.

These clients, both teachers, are some of the nicest people you'll find anywhere, and we had worked hard over a fifteen-year period to transform their property into a real showplace. Now, the flowers were blooming, the cats were running back and forth across the new footbridge, and the shade from the oak trees danced across the lawn. We were really enjoying our walk around the garden.

We paused down by the hammock, and Dennis said, "You know, recently Carolyn and I were both asked, independently of each other, where our favorite place was, and we both answered, without hesitation, 'Our garden!' " I remembered how their place looked the first time I saw it in 1978, and I knew why they appreciated it so much now.

I get that kind of feedback from people all the time, and it's always an emotional experience. You'll get it, too, and I can't think of a better payoff for all your hard work. Learn your profession well, work hard, and have a great life. I'll be with you in spirit all the way. Good luck.

Appendix

The following resources are limited to business management. It's impossible to list all the books, magazines, videos, and other information on the technical aspects of landscaping.

Trade and Professional Associations

The suppliers out my way have a saying: "When a landscape contractor gets elected president of his trade association chapter, put him on C.O.D." That's a way of recognizing that people can get too wrapped up in their trade association, to the detriment of their business. Still, trade and professional associations offer you a lot, and you should join them and become involved. The following organizations offer technical and management assistance, training, and certification programs; they conduct and promote research, publish magazines, print forms and contracts, promote the industry to the public and government, lobby to support favorable legislation, sponsor awards programs, and put on trade shows.

National

American Association of Landscape Contractors, 155 Throop Street, North Babylon, NY 11704, (516) 661-1966

American Association of Nurserymen, 1250 I Street NW, Suite 500, Washington, DC 20005, (202) 789-2900

American Horticultural Society, 7931 East Boulevard Drive, Alexandria, VA 22308, (800) 777-7931

American Landscape Maintenance Association, P.O. Box 223218, Hollywood, FL 33022, (305) 925-7996

American Society of Consulting Arborists, 5130 West 101st Circle, Westminster, CO 80030, (303) 466-2722

Associated Landscape Contractors of America, 12200 Sunrise Valley Drive, Suite 150, Reston, VA 22046, (703) 620-6363

Eastern Regional Nurserymen's Association, 24 West Road, Suite 53, Vernon, CT 06066, (203) 872-2095

International Erosion Control Association, P.O. Box 4904, Steamboat Springs, CO 80477, (303) 879-3010

International Society of Arboriculture, P.O. Box 908, Urbana, IL 61801, (217) 328–2032

The Irrigation Association, 1911 North Fort Myer Drive, Suite 1009, Arlington, VA 22209, (703) 524–1200

Landscape Maintenance Association, Inc., P.O. Box 728, Largo, FL 34649, (813) 584–2312

National Landscape Association, 1250 I Street NW, Suite 500, Washington, DC 20005, (202) 789–2900

National Xeriscape Council, Inc., P.O. Box 767936, Roswell, GA 30076, (404) 998–5899

Professional Grounds Management Society, 10402 Ridgland, Suite 4, Hunt Valley, MD 21030, (410) 667–1833 410 589-9754

Professional Lawn Care Association of America, 1000 Johnson Ferry Road NE, Suite C–135, Marietta, GA 30068, (404) 977–5222

Professional Lawn Care Association of Mid-America, P.O. Box 35184, Kansas City, MO 64134, (816) 765–7616

State and Regional

Arizona Landscape Contractors Association, 2720 East Thomas Road, #A205, Phoenix, AZ 85016, (602) 956–4252

Associated Landscape Contractors of Colorado, 5290 East Yale Circle, Suite 100, Denver, CO 80222, (303) 757–5611

Associated Landscape Contractors of Massachusetts, 200 Linden Street, Wellesley, MA 02181, (617) 431–1617

Bergen County Landscape Contractors Association, P.O. Box 117, Closter, NJ 07624

California Landscape Contractors Association, 2021 N Street, Suite 300, Sacramento, CA 95814, (916) 448–2522

Carolina Grounds Management Association, P.O. Box 220942, Charlotte, NC 28222, (704) 577–5933

Colorado Association of Lawn Care Professionals, 309 South Summitview Drive, Fort Collins, CO 80524, (303) 224–2293

Connecticut Groundskeepers Association, Inc., P.O. Box 876, Bethel, CT 06801, (203) 791–8615

Georgia Green Industry Association, P.O. Box 369, Epworth, GA 30541, (706) 492–4664

Grounds Management Association of Wisconsin, Inc., 6515 Seybold Road, Madison, WI 53719, (608) 274–6311

Illinois Arborist Association, 33 North Waukegan Road, Suite 1, Lake Bluff, IL 60044, (708) 234–7226

Indiana State Lawn Care Association, 375 Ridge Point Drive, Carmel, IN 46032, (317) 575–9010

Landscape Contractors Association MD-DC-VA, 9053 Shady Grove Court, Gaithersburg, MD 20877, (301) 948–0810

Nassau Suffolk Landscape Gardeners Association, P.O. Box 489, Brightwaters, NY 11718, (516) 665–2250

New York State Arborists Association, ISA Chapter, P.O. Box 58, Latham, NY 12110, (518) 783–1322

North Carolina Irrigation Society, Inc., North Carolina State University, P.O. Box 7625, Raleigh, NC 27695, (919) 515–6792

North Carolina Landscape Contractors Association, P.O. Box 400, Knightdale, NC 27545, (919) 266–1777

Ohio Chapter of the International Society of Arboriculture, P.O. Box 967, Hilliard, OH 43026, (614) 876–3694

Pennsylvania Horticultural Society, 325 Walnut Street, Philadelphia, PA 19106, (215) 625–8250

Virginia Horticultural Council, Inc., 383 Coal Hollow Road, Christiansburg, VA 24073, (703) 382–0943

Wisconsin Landscape Federation, 9910 West Layton Avenue, Greenfield, WI 53228, (414) 529–4705

Schools

Many community colleges offer programs in landscape horticulture (also called ornamental horticulture or environmental horticulture) that will give you the basic skills you'll need to get started. More advanced programs are available at some state colleges and universities.

Trade Shows

Contact your trade association for information about trade shows. They're a great way to learn about new products, schmooze with sales people and other contractors, pick everybody's brains, and have a good time. Anybody who doesn't go to trade shows is nuts.

Magazines and Periodicals

Trade publications: Many trade and professional magazines are sent free to qualified companies in the hope that you'll buy lots of stuff from their advertisers. Others charge like regular magazines do. In addition to the magazines listed, most trade and professional associations publish their own magazines; many of them are excellent.

American Lawn Applicator, 4012 Bridge Avenue, Cleveland, OH 44113 (Free)

American Nurseryman, 77 West Washington Street, #2100, Chicago, IL 60602

Grounds Maintenance, P.O. Box 12901, Overland Park, KS 66212 (Free)

Interior Landscape Industry, 111 North Canal Street, Chicago, IL 60606 (Free)

Journal of Arboriculture, International Society of Arboriculture, P.O. Box GG, Savoy, IL 61874

Landscape Design, Gold Trade Publications, Inc., 6913 Valjean, Van Nuys, CA 91406

Landscape & Irrigation, 6913 Valjean, Van Nuys, CA 91406

Landscape Management, 7500 Old Oak Boulevard, Cleveland, OH 44130 (Free)

Lawn & Landscape Maintenance, 4012 Bridge Avenue, Cleveland, OH 44113 (Free)

Lawn Care Report, 13555 Bishop's Court, Brookfield, WI 53003

Southwest Lawn & Landscaping, 1445 East Tropicana Avenue, Las Vegas, NV 89119 (Free)

Books
Horticultural Subjects

Note: This is a selected list of some of my favorite books on horticulture.

Bailey, L.H. and others. *Hortus Third.* New York: Macmillan Publishing Co., 1976.

Booth, Norman K. and James E. Hiss. *Residential Landscape Design— Design Process for the Private Residence.* Englewood Cliffs, N.J.: Prentice Hall, 1991.

Brookes, John. *The Garden Book.* New York: Crown Publishers, 1984.

Clausen, Ruth Rogers and Nicolas H. Ekstrom. *Perennials for American Gardens.* New York: Random House, 1989. (Definitive)

Johnson, Hugh. *The Principles of Gardening.* New York: Simon & Schuster, 1979. (The best book on how to garden.)

Kourik, Robert. *Designing and Maintaining Your Edible Landscape Naturally.* Santa Rosa, Calif.: Metamorphic Press, 1986. (Much more than just edibles, this is a thorough treatment of good horticultural practices.)

Melby, Pete. *Simplified Irrigation Design.* New York: Van Nostrand Reinhold, 1988. (Everything you need to know about irrigation design and installation.)

Olkowski, William and others. *Common-Sense Pest Control.* Newtown, Conn.: The Taunton Press, 1991. (Best pest control book; covers nontoxic and least-toxic methods.)

Wyman, Donald. *Wyman's Gardening Encyclopedia.* New York: Macmillan Publishing Co., 1986. (Thorough, concise, easy to use.)

_____, Sunset Western Garden Book, Land Publishing Co, Menlo Park, CA, c. 1988 (the Bible of western gardeners, must have if you live in the west)

Landscaping Business Management

Associated Landscape Contractors of America. *Designing Your Accounting System.* Reston, Va.: Associated Landscape Contractors of America, 1990.

Associated Landscape Contractors of America. *Managing Information Systems: Making Data Work for You in Your Green Industry Business.* Reston, Va.: Associated Landscape Contractors of America, 1991.

Associated Landscape Contractors of America. *Process Management the Total Quality Landscape Contracting Company.* Reston, Va.: Associated Landscape Contractors of America, 1992.

Associated Landscape Contractors of America. *1991 ALCA Operating Cost Study.* Reston, Va.: Associated Landscape Contractors of America, 1992. (Financial data for typical landscape companies.)

California Landscape Contractors Association. *California Landscape Standards.* Sacramento, Calif.: CLCA, 1989. (Standard specifications for all phases of landscaping. Well done; a good way to learn how to do things right. There may be similar publications for other parts of the country but most of this book will apply anywhere.)

Dietrich, Norman. *Kerr's Cost Data for Landscape Construction.* 1992. (Unit prices for all facets of the business, based on annual cost data regionalized for entire U.S.)

Eckel, Howard, with Charles Vander Kooi. *Growing and Staffing Your Business.* Littleton, Colo.: Charles Vander Kooi, 1990. (How to increase sales, keep employees happy, and improve service to clients. Amusingly written.)

Griffin, James M. *Landscape Data Manual.* Sacramento, Calif.: California Landscape Contractors Association, 1972. (Excellent set of all kinds of tables you'll use every day—soil volumes for different sized holes, coverage for plants, mulches, and so forth, time studies, capacities of equipment, lots more. Must have.)

Griffin, James M. *Landscape Management.* Sacramento, Calif.: California Landscape Contractors Association, 1970, rev. 1978. (Packed with information but badly written.)

Vander Kooi, Charles. *Estimating and Management Principles for Landscape Contractors.* Littleton, Colo.: Charles Vander Kooi, 1989. (Excellent, readable introduction to bidding, with a little bit on other aspects of project management.)

Vander Kooi, Charles. *The Employee Packet Sample.* Littleton, Colo.: Charles Vander Kooi, 1988. (Great set of forms for the employer, including a personnel manual, job descriptions, safety handouts. Nothing else like it.)

Vander Kooi, Charles. *Labor and Equipment Production Times for Landscape Construction.* Littleton, Colo.: Charles Vander Kooi. (Based on a survey of landscape contractors. Includes cost data, wages, handy tables.)

General Business and Construction Industry Management

Brock, Susan L. and Sally R. Cabbell. *Writing a Human Resources Manual: A Reference Guide for Managers.* Los Altos, Calif.: Crisp Publications, 1989. (How to write an employee manual, step-by-step.)

Dungan, Christopher and Donald Ridings. *Business Law.* New York: Barron's, 1990. (Readable and thorough.)

Fritz, Roger. *Nobody Gets Rich Working for Somebody Else, An Entrepreneur's Guide.* New York: Dodd, Mead & Co., 1987.

Harris, Godfrey, with Gregrey J. Harris. *Talk is Cheap: Promoting Your Business through Word-of-Mouth Advertising,* 1991.

Kamoroff, Bernard. *Small Time Operator.* Laytonville, Calif.: Bell Springs Publishing. (Classic book on starting a small business. Must have.)

Levinson, Jay Conrad. *Guerrilla Marketing: Secrets for Making Big Profits from Your Small Business.* Boston: Houghton Mifflin, 1984.

Phillips, Michael and Salli Rasberry. *Marketing Without Advertising.* Berkeley, Calif.: Nolo Press, 1988.

Prentice Hall Editorial Staff. *The Prentice Hall Small Business Survival Guide.* Englewood Cliffs, N.J.: Prentice Hall, 1993. (Focuses on sales, employee management, and cost accounting.)

Steingold, Fred S. *The Legal Guide for Starting & Running a Small Business.* Berkeley, Calif.: Nolo Press, 1992.

Thomsett, Michael C. *Builder's Guide to Accounting Revised.* Carlsbad, Calif.: Craftsman Book Co., 1979.

Walker, Nathan and Edward North Walker and Theodor K. Rohdenburg. *Legal Pitfalls in Architecture, Engineering and Building Construction.* New York: McGraw-Hill Book Co., 1979.

Whitmyer, Claude and Salli Rasberry and Michael Phillips. *Running a One-Person Business.* Berkeley, Calif.: Ten Speed Press, 1989.

Whitten, Bobby R. *How to Hire and Supervise Subcontractors.* Washington, D.C.: Home Builder Press, 1991.

Sources of Business Forms and Office Supplies

New England Business Service, Inc. (NEBS), 500 Main Street, Groton, MA 01471, (800) 225–6380. Has special catalog of business forms for contractors.

Paper Direct, 205 Chubb Avenue, Lyndhurst, NJ 07071, (800) A–PAPERS. Special and preprinted papers for custom stationery and brochures.

Earth Care Paper Inc., P.O. Box 7070, Madison, WI 53707, (608) 277–2900. Recycled and special papers.

Reliable Home Office, P.O. Box 1501, Ottawa, IL 61350, (800) 869–6000. Furniture and accessories for the home office.

Streamliners, P.O. Box 480, Mechanicsburg, PA 17055, (800) 544–5779. Preprinted business forms.

Fidelity Products Co., P.O. Box 155, Minneapolis, MN 55440, (800) 328–3034. General office supplies; drafting supplies.

Quill Corp., P.O. Box 50–050, Ontario, CA 91761, (909) 988–3200. General office supplies. Excellent service and prices.

Index

About the Author

OWEN E. DELL is a licensed landscape architect and landscape contractor who has been beautifying yards for twenty years. He teaches classes in horticulture at the Santa Barbara Botanic Garden and the California Landscape Contractors Association and has been a guest lecturer at many conferences and symposiums. His articles have appeared in *Southern California Gardener, National Gardening,* and *California Landscape Magazine,* as well as in other horticultural publications. An award-winning garden designer, his gardens have been featured in *Sunset* magazine, *Landscape Architecture, California Landscape,* the *Los Angeles Times,* and other publications.